TO INDIAN CHILDREN, PARENTS, TEACHERS, MINISTERS, SCHOOLS, AND OTHERS CONCERNED

by the Author

Read how to prevent an on-going tragedy. Replace the cause with hope and joy. Learn the truth and the good news. The highest suicide rate in America is among Indian children roughly ages ten to twenty. Recent news reported eight cases in seven days. This need not be. Learn what the Indian race, your people, has given to civilization and the world.

It is your heritage and should cause you to stand tall and straight. Be proud and enthralled, no need to live in despair.

Remember your heritage and what you have going for you. Prize it, rejoice and build your life on its principles.

Teach it to your youth, boost their morale and hope. Be honest and truthful.

Information in this book can help you. Especially read Chapter II.

August Nylander

SURVIVAL
OF A
NOBLE RACE

by
August Nylander

Dedicated with love
TO MY WIFE ANN

for her understanding, help and support during those conspiratory days.
Also for the proofreading and supervision of the typing of the manuscript.

AND

to the many Indian men and women for their warm and loyal friendship and support.

ISBN 1-877976-11-3

ACKNOWLEDGMENTS

Much of what I have written is based on information and experience that I gained in my forty-five years of continuous close association with Indians, including twenty-six years as a Civil Service employee of the Bureau of Indian Affairs.

I have had access to many reports and records including Task Force reports, Auditors and Inspectors reports, the media, personnel files, the USDI's authorized *History of Indian Policy and Indian Treaties*. And, to mention a few others, personal visitation at the National Archives, Chicago's Field Museum of National History, the annual Pipe Stone outdoors pageant, at colleges and universities, also use of their research.

Also, information and confirmation or collaboration of ideas obtained from the Bureau of Indian Affairs, United States Department of Argriculture, United States Department of Interior, and the Personnel Management Office, Indian schools, Indian colleges, conferences, other writers and authors, and the Farmington, New Mexico, Chamber of Commerce.

Much of the information and opinions are based upon the teaching of the Bible.

We appreciate the assistance received from Senator Abdnor and staff, other members of Congress, Betty Krsnak, Glenn and Marguerite Jespersen, Doug Bertsch, Rosie Koupal, Dr. Herbert Hoover of the History Department at the University of South Dakota, Kendall Rehwaldt, the Wagner Rotary Club, Andrew Virgilio, New York State Assemblyman and staff and others.

St. Joseph's Indian School acknowledges the kindness of Anastasia Nylander, widow of the late August Nylander, for her gift of exclusive copyrights to her husband's book "Survival Of A Noble Race."

ABOUT THE AUTHOR

August Nylander was born and raised in Wyoming. He received his B.S. degree from the University of Wyoming in Laramie and began his career with the Bureau of Indian Affairs in New Mexico with the United Pueblo tribes in the mid 1930s. In 1938 he transferred to South Dakota to the Yankton and Rosebud Sioux Reservations until 1962 when he retired. He has put together this, his first full-length publication, largely from knowledge and experience obtained during this long-time employment. He had written an editorial column for a South Dakota weekly for many years and has been married for twenty six years to the former Anastasia (Ann) Reinhart. After retirement from the B.I.A. they traveled extensively over the United States, in Canada and Mexico, visiting and researching many Indian reservations and the Archives in Washington, DC. They have continued to live at Wagner, South Dakota, and maintain contact with the Great Plains Indians.

They started a new Agri-business in town involving them in purebred livestock, feeds, seeds, equipment, doing State Dairy testing and statistical surveys for the U.S. Department of Agriculture with on-the-farm interviewing in much of south central South Dakota. His wife was founder and former publisher of the *Wagner Announcer* and worked many years for the Opinion Research Ass'n. of Princeton, New Jersey. Mr. Nylander helped improve crop varieties and livestock breeds. He created the County Mid-Winter Fair and was honored as founder on its 25th anniversary in 1982. He raised purebred hogs and was a director on State and National Swine Breed Associations.

He won trophies and ribbons at State Fairs, etc., including Grand Championships. He had been a member and on the board of directors of the South Dakota Water Development Association working for irrigation in the state many years. He was made a lifetime Honorary Director — only two ever received this honor. In 1980 he was given an engraved gold plaque and a lifetime Honorary membership by the Wagner Chamber of Commerce due to many years of dedicated service. He still serves on the Irrigation Committee, also on the farm and Irrigation committees for Rotary International of which he has been an active member for thirty years. He helped organize the Community Council (Wagner and eleven townships) and served as president and in other offices. He has been active in soil conservation in this state since his work in that line with the B.I.A.

His favorite hobbies are reading and collecting good literature and books dealing with the cultures of the world, habits, religion, art, etc., and working with plants and livestock.

CONTENTS

August Nylander

PROLOGUE

The first thing this writer does—upon picking up a book he might be interested in—is to learn something about the author. Who is he? What is he? What are his qualifications and background for his subject? What is his motive?

Therefore, likewise, I like my readers to know something about me. Any author, with his personality, his character, his ability to observe, research, and analyze his subject material, and his ability to write about it, all become a vital and important part of his product.

I was born, raised and educated through the university in the wonderful state of Wyoming. My background is in argriculture. I had very little experience with Indians in my youth. But, I was fascinated with what I had read about them and the Indian agencies, especially the Carson Indian Agency in Nevada. I have lived with and among Indians for forty-five years, including twenty-six years as a Civil Service employee of the Bureau of Indian Affairs (BIA)—the greater part in South Dakota. My job dealt chiefly with general agriculture, credit, rehabilitation, soil and moisture conservation, resources development and conservation, irrigation, large-scale gardening using relief labor, and management of co-operatives. But the duties covered other phases of the Indian's welfare and life, as well.

Since my retirement from official duties, I have traveled, visited reservations, studied and researched the history of the government's Indian policies and affairs and the progress of Indians, principally those of the continental United States and some in Canada. I have visited almost all of the states and parts of Mexico.

The principal purpose of writing this book, besides my love for learning, writing and researching, is to get the true picture and understanding of the Indian race and its culture, to be able to transcribe it into terms and language that will best convey the same to the non-Indians. It is appalling to realize how ignorant most of us are on this subject—how lacking we are of understanding and appreciating them and their contributions to the world and its impact on our present civilization. Their God-endowed talents and culture surpasses many others.

The gift is rich to the entire world and civilization. Let us discover it and enrich our knowledge by doing so. The extent to which we in the United States have ignored it and buried it is unbelievable. The Indians' wisdom has advised us "To walk a mile in his moccasins before criticizing him."

The writer has attempted to get into the inner-being of this race of human beings and thereby enrich his own life, understanding and knowledge of God and His universe and be able to pass it on to others. Our next life promises to be something for us to behold.

Let us remember that in many respects the Indian race is homogeneous, but in other respects there are definite differences between tribes of various areas of the country. What we find in one area of our country does not necessarily apply to those of another one. The influence of the different peoples from Europe varied. Also the different native environments have affected the Indian's character and culture. The writer's experience has been mostly with the Great Plains Tribes and the United Pueblos of New Mexico. In certain respects, what we find in one tribe does not necessarily apply to another tribe in some other area.

The Indians did have some universal means of communication with other tribes, especially by the sign language, even though their language may have differed from band to band. There were hundreds of different languages and dialects among them.

While the Indians had a very rough time for nearly four-hundred years adjusting to the ways and civilization of the conquering white man, he has progressed to civilization much faster than many of the world's other races and groups of people such as the Arab, African and Asian peoples.

May we state over again that the many tribes of Indians had developed on this continent an ethos (a character or disposition) that was nearly universal among them and that makes them one in general character—though there are tribal variations, such as hundreds of different languages.

We should realize how the new Indian is emerging after two-hundred years of inhumane treatment and brainwashing by the government's Indian policies which for so long denied them civil rights and protection under the United States Constitution. This left them exposed to the depredation of the white settlers.

Their survival has been tenacious and long suffering. Half of the nation's Indian population still live on reservations and until recently they have accepted what government told them because they have had no advocates nor recourse to the Constitution of the United States.

What is the one final act that brought about the government's change in its Indian policy and the revival of a noble race? Read on and we will show the what and why.

I have not thoroughly nor completely covered any of the subjects in this book. The writer has tried to cite typical examples in each case where needed. Many more can be cited. Several books could be written for more comprehensive and complete coverage. Any one of these chapters could be extended into a complete book.

In the Department of Interior's book, *History of Indian Policy*, are many more facts and events of prime importance that could be incorporated into the chapters of this book. I have picked some of the highlights, the landmarks and the milestones as I saw them and then listed them in outline form for a better comprehensive picture. Then I followed the outline with a story and details of each adopted policy. I have tried to show the reasons for the purposes of each change made in the government's Indian policy and to show the progress made all the way along the line from the beginning to the present time.

This writer hopes that his efforts will help to bring out the true facts and correct any myths that may persist.

How could the history books that are used in our schools almost completely ignore the Indians and their rich heritage, talents and enormous contributions to our country? This is a national disgrace for the United States. The peoples of other nations understand this fact far more than do our own people. Indeed, we have many myths and derogatory attitudes about our Indian citizens that need to be dispelled.

SURVIVAL OF A NOBLE RACE

CHAPTER 1: A NOBLE RACE

George Catlin's Classical Creed About American Indians—Inscription On A Stone Tablet in the Chapel at Bacone College—Chief Joseph, Nez Perce—A Great American—A Narrative by John Collier—Abraham Lincoln's Noble Words—Indian Bureau Agent's Report-Nature of Indians—Santo Domingo—A Unique Example—

A noble race! What is a noble race? What constitutes nobleness? What are its qualities and characteristics?

In what way is the Indian race a noble race? Has the Indian race lost any of its nobleness since its encounter with the European peoples during the last four-hundred years since they invaded his domain and forcefully pushed him from his country—since they submitted him to defeat after defeat and indignities galore?

The *American College Dictionary* defines nobleness as "of an exalted moral character of excellence: noble thought; 5. admirable in dignity of conception, or in manner of expression, execution or composition. 6. imposing in appearance, stately. 7. calm dignity."

Indian nobleness is not the type bestowed upon certain individual people by Europeans as a titled honor, distinguished by birth, rank or title, possessing a hereditary social or political preeminence. It is that of a race accomplished by adhering to a moral code, established and ingrained by a long and consistent disciplined education, preserved and kept pure by legacy.

We need to go back to the genesis of the Indian and examine him in his native state to find his God-endowed and inherent qualities which prove him to be a noble person. We then follow through to see how these noble qualities have remained an integral part of his character and soul.

Let us examine the record and see that he was endowed with true nobleness. Columbus described them as gentle beings, souls of hospitality, serious and happy, faithful and trustful, walking in beauty, and in possession of a spiritual religion.

George Catlin that great and renowned portrait painter of Indians, stated that "I look upon the Indian in his native state the most honorable that I have ever lived amongst—and that have fully corroborated my fixed belief that the North American Indian in his primitive state is a high-minded, hospitable and honorable being."

One of America's leading military men, General Nelson A. Miles, who directed wars against the Indians for fifteen years, appraised them in his memoirs as follows: "History can show no parallel to the heroism and fortitude of the American Indians in the 200 years fight during which they contested inch by inch the possession of their country against a foe infinitely better equipped, with inexhaustible resources and in overwhelming numbers. Had they been equal in numbers, history would have had a very different story to tell." Chief Red Fox has said that the Indian, developed through centuries by the adamant forces of nature, is a subdued, stoical figure.

It was traditional among most of the tribes but particularly among the Plains Indians, that no one in the village ever went hungry as long as anyone in the camp had food. They fed others, who happened along, regardless how little they may have had for themselves. They shared to the last bite.

In 1832, Lewis and Clark described the Indian people in the Arikara village as extremely hospitable, but their experiences with the white traders had already changed that attitude.

George Catlin said "without ever hearing the Bible or the Ten Commandments they lived it. They never used lock and key. They never stole a thing."

Black Hawk said that the Indian does not tell lies, nor do they steal. No tribe of Indians has a word with which to take the name of the Great Spirit in vain, nor do they have curse words, such as the white man has.

Chief Red Fox said that the North American Indian is the noblest type of a heathen man on the earth. He recognizes a Great Spirit; he believes in immortality; he has a quick intellect; he is a clear thinker; he is brave and fearless; and until betrayed, he is true to his plighted faith. He has a passionate love for his children and counts it a joy to die for his people. (The writer does not agree with the term heathen as used here, i.e., the Indian recognizes the one universal God, creator of all things, which he calls the Great Spirit, Great Mystery, or some similar name.)

The Indian possesses and expresses a great sense of humor. A proper sense of humor denotes intelligence. It reveals the background of his mental thinking, his analytical mind and sense of values.

Mace's school History of the United States records, "An interesting event (Indian War 1790-1794) common at the close of great Indian Wars, was the giving up of all the men, women, and children that had been captured by the Indians.

The Indian was resourceful, inventive, and a great contributor to our present civilization. Mr. George Dorsey, the historian and philosopher, has said that the American Indian has contributed far more to our present civilization than the Romans have. I shall have much more to say about the Indians' contributions in another chapter of this book.

We must also recognize the Indians' great oratory and literary contributions to our nation's enrichment, even though our historians and schools have grossly by-passed them. There is none superior in the annals of our history.

George Catlin's Classical Creed About American Indians:

I love a people who have always made me welcome to the best they had.

I love a people who are honest without laws, who have no jails and no poorhouses.

I love a people who keep the commandments without ever having read them or heard them preached from the pulpit.

I love a people who never swear, who never take the Name of God in vain.

I love a people who love their neighbors as they love themselves.

I love a people who worship God without a Bible, for I believe that God loves them also.

I love a people whose religion is all the same, and who are free from religious animosities.

I love a people who have never raised a hand against me or stolen my property where there was no law to punish for either.

I love a people who have never fought a battle with white men, except on their own ground.

I love and don't fear mankind where God has made and left them, for there they are children.

I love a people who live and keep what is their own without locks and keys.

I love all people who do the best they can. And oh, how
I love a people who don't live for the love of money!

George Catlin was a renowned portrait painter of Indians. He
lived with them while doing the painting and researching for his
picture and narrative portrayal of the American Indians. He entered their lives when most of them had never seen a white man
before. They knew only a few fur traders at that time.

It was 1830 to 1836. He knew them in the raw.

The following is inscribed on a stone tablet in the Chapel at
Bacone College, Muskogee, Okla.

We have been broken up and moved six times. We have
been despoiled of our property. We thought when we moved
across the Missouri River and had paid for our homes in
Kansas that we were safe, but in a few years the white man
wanted our country. We had good farms, built comfortable
houses and big barns. We had schools for our children and
churches where we listened to the same gospel the white
man listens to. The white man came into our country from
Missouri and drove our cattle and horses away, and if our
people followed them, they were killed. *We try to forget these
things, but we would not forget that the white man brought
us the blessed gospel of Christ, the Christian hope. This more
than pays for all we have suffered.*

The nobleness of character and spirit exemplified by the American Indian is the highest type of Christian love one can find in
any people. Their love for Christ was great enough to forgive their
enemies who treated them so inhumanely, even as Christ on the
Cross forgave His torturers, and Pope John Paul II forgave his
attempted assassin. This spirit of forgiveness has been exemplified by Indians, as recorded by history, as far back as the colonial
days when the missionaries tried to convert the Indians, but their
gospel was rejected by the Indians because they felt the white
man was a hypocrite in respect to living his embraced religion.
They agreed fully with the tenets of the gospel and many of them
could have otherwise accepted Christ.

Some accepted Christ anyway. It was a sort of combination of
Christianity and their own religion. They practiced it their own
way. But it was a wedge into Christianity which grew and grew
and became more acceptable to them down through the decades
until now, for many of them, their Christian faith is exemplary

18

and exalted. More will be said about their Christ-like forgiveness of those who used them so inhumanely in the chapter on religion.

The writer values as one of his life's precious possessions the loyal and warm friendship of the Indians whom he came to know. I remember those impressive, beautiful, young Navaho ladies at the Inter Mountain Agency in Utah and the young Taos ladies and the young men with their poise, grace, kindness, dignity, intelligence, and their figures, standing straight as arrows, with composure and unperturbed exaltation.

Chief Joseph, the Nez Perce, one of the greatest Americans of our entire history, was one of the last of the Indians to surrender to the U.S. Army (10-5-1877). His nobleness was well exemplified as he handed over his rifle to General Miles with that calm dignity which marks the Indian. He spoke the utterance of a noble man:

I am tired of fighting. Our chiefs are killed. Looking Glass is dead. Toohullulsote is dead. The old men are dead. It is the young men who say yes or no. He who led the young men is dead. (Joseph's brother Alocut.) It is cold and we have no blankets. The little children are freezing to death, my people, some of them, have run away to the hills and have no blankets, no food. No one knows where they are. Perhaps they are freezing to death. I want to have time to look for my children and see how many of them I can find. Maybe I shall find them among the dead. Hear me, my chiefs, I am tired; my heart is sick and sad. From where the sun now stands, I will fight no more forever.

After his retirement from the army, General Miles became the Indian's champion and struggled valiantly to safeguard their rights and to protect them from wars and persecution.

It is recorded that when Columbus' ship reached these shores the Indians greeted them with friendship, provided them with fresh food, showered them with gifts, and in return the captain and crew of the *Santa Maria* kidnapped several of the men, women, and children and took them back to Spain where they were probably exhibited as wild beasts. That was the first act of barbarity against the Native Americans, and as time passed others took possession of the homes and the land of the people, degraded them with whiskey, raped their wives and daughters, and introduced contagious diseases among them.

We must remember that when the Indian massacres in retaliation it does not belie the claim of his loyalty to his friends. To the Indian it was not a sin to steal from his enemies or even to kill them. In fact, in his sight it was usually a virtue and an honor to him.

The Indian, by his native nature, was always loyal to his friends and true to his word. He hated hypocrisy, but when engaged in war he was a brutal and ruthless fighter, usually sparing no one; killing men, women and children. It is probably true that he never fought the white people, except in retaliation.

One of the most publicized acts of brutality against the Native Americans is in the book titled the *Trail of Tears*, by Gloria Jahoda when four thousand Cherokee Indians died and many others were forced from their native homes by that long and brutal march in the dead of winter to the new Indian country, hundreds of miles to the west.

As narrated by John Collier: As the final company of the Cherokees started on the long trail, their leaders held the last council they would ever hold on their home ground. They adopted a resolution which ought to be remembered forever. They did not ask pity for their people (what nobleness and Christian fortitude! because they knew there would be no pity (what a travesty of justice by the American white people!) and asking pity was never the Indian's way. They did not reproach or condemn Georgia or the U.S. government. They did not quote John Marshall's decision, since that decision, for them, had been written in water. To the violated and fraudulent treaties they made no reference, for they had now learned that which General France C. Walker was to phráse immortally when in 1871, writing as Commissioner of Indian Affairs, he described the white man's view concerning honor towards Indians as follows: "when dealing with savage men, as with savage beasts, no question of national honor can arise whether to fight, or run away, or to employ a ruse, is solely a question of expedience." Their treaties, the Cherokees had learned, had been "ruses" of the white man, so the resolution passed in what then seemed to be their final hour was addressed to no man and leaned on no consideration, except the principle of justice, which they believed was undying. That was all. Then these men of TRUE GREATNESS, through fraud and violence, stripped of every thing, set forth on the bitter trail to a place which was to be no lasting home. They were cohesive, resistant and recuperative. They accepted their fate like a noble people.

The Book of Life says that tragedy either makes a person better or bitter. Much of the Indians' history, since the coming of the white man, has been tragic for him. The overall reaction of the Indian has not been bitter, so it must have made him better. Of course, there always have been and still are those who became very bitter. In the long run, the bitter lose their cause. There were others who generally found peace and avoided or bridged the devastations of bitterness and have survived to remain noble. *Their capacity to forgive and forget is part of their nobleness and their capacity to survive.*

Abraham Lincoln's Noble Words

One of our historians and author of a United States history textbook has called the closing words of Lincoln's second inaugural address, "words belonging among the NOBLEST examples of American literature."

There are many examples by Indian leaders over the time of our nation's history equally as noble and of importance in the nation's history that get no recognition whatsoever. Why have we so totally educated our people to be so ignorant on this important part of our history and the making of this nation?

I would like to cite just a couple of examples for comparison. First, Lincoln's words: "With malice towards none, with charity for all, with firmness in the right as God gives us to see the right, let us strive on to finish the work we are in, to bind up the Nation's wounds, to care for him who shall have borne the battle, and for his widow and his orphan, to do all which may achieve and cherish a just and lasting peace among ourselves and with all nations." Second, the Indian's words (on the occasion of the last forcible stand of all Indian wars, Chief Joseph, leader of Nez Perce and the man of peace who had merely asked for justice, stood alone and spoke so eloquently): "It is cold, and we have no blankets. The little children are freezing to death. My people, some of them, have run away to the hills, and have no blankets, no food. No one knows where they are, perhaps freezing to death. I want to have time to look for my children, and see how many of them I can find. Maybe I shall find them among the dead. Hear me, my chiefs! I am tired. My heart is sick and sad. From where the sun now stands I will fight no more forever. I only ask to be treated as well as all other men are treated. If I cannot go to my own home in some country where my people will not die so fast. . . .

"Whenever the white man treats the Indian as they treat each other, then we shall have no more wars. We shall be all alike—brothers of one father and one mother with one sky above

21

us, one country around us, and one government for all. Then the Great Spirit Chief who rules above will smile upon this land and send rain to wash out the bloody spots made by brothers' hands upon the face of the earth. For this time the Indian race is waiting and praying."

After suffering the injustices and inhumane treatment for so long with no other recompense, many of the Indians were left without bitterness and revenge. They have said on more than one occasion that they were thankful for the white man bringing Christ to America. This, for them, more than offset the injustices and suffering brought upon them. They could forget and forgive. They would assume a new start, if given equal treatment, and strive for unity, peace, and harmony to build a united and stronger nation.

The words of the Indian leaders were as well spoken and noble as those of our great President, Abraham Lincoln. Why did not their words become immortal and recorded in history, as were those of Lincoln, Washington and others of our race? So eloquent was the oratory of the Indian that President Thomas Jefferson remarked that he wished that the men of Congress could orate half as well.

During the mid-1850s an Indian Bureau agent on the Upper Platte made the following report on the nature of the Indian and the resulting relations with the relentless white invaders of his territory:

There is not to be found among any people a more cheerful, contented and kindly disposed being than the Indian when he is treated with kindness and humanity. His friendships are strong and lasting and his love for and attachment to his children, kindred, and tribe have a depth and intensity which place him on an equality with the civilized race. His love and veneration for the whites amount to adoration which is only changed to hatred and revenge by oppression, cruelties and deep wrongs and injustice inflicted upon the poor Indian by the white man, without cause or reason. By his education on the war path, which leads to honor, fame and distinction, the Indian is a relentless, a terrible enemy, he spares neither age, sex, nor condition, but slaughters indiscriminately, everyone that falls in his path.

The Indian race has a strong sense of independence and self-dependence. To this day these qualities show through in many places. I found individuals in the eastern states who still resist accepting relief aid and programs from the federal government because of their general principles. It was frowned upon by them.

A good example is the Santo Domingo tribe in New Mexico. When the writer was working in that jurisdiction the only federal employees (or any whites) they allowed to reside in their village were the teachers and doctors or nurse. And when they held certain ceremonies they were required to leave also. John Bird, one of their members, because he hired out as a ditch rider on an irrigation canal that passed through their reservation had to move out of the village. He built himself another house out from the village alongside of the canal and continued with his job.

The small tracts of land that they farmed lay on the opposite side of the Rio Grande River. To get across with their teams and wagons carrying whatever equipment, seed, etc., they needed and the return trips with the produce raised, they swam the river with it. That probably went on since the advent of horses and wagons for them.

In the early or middle 1930s the federal government built a bridge across the river at this point. Some of the Indians refused to use the bridge and continued to swim their equipment and produce across the river alongside of the bridge, rather than cross over on the bridge. This was their reaction towards accepting any assistance from the federal government. They preferred to keep their freedom and independence unencumbered at whatever the cost to protect and maintain their honor.

A few years ago some benevolent Hollywood people gathered a carload or two of goods and gifts and shipped it to the Santo Domingo Indians in New Mexico as a Christmas gift. They refused to accept it and told them to give it to their California Indians.

Another thing very much worth noting that reflects upon the Indian's credibility is their attitude towards repaying their loans and debts of extended credit. I have had a great deal of experience of this nature with them over the years, both as a supervisor of their accounts, collection for goods and services rendered and my personal business deals with them. I have personally extended credit to them without taking security. I will have to say that I have lost no money (or only trifling amounts) through non-payments of these personal and business deals. I cannot say as much, in general, for the non-Indians.

The Indian's capacity and will to self-dependence and self-determination, as well as always keeping their word and commitments inviolate, is part of their rich inherited nobleness and pride and their ability to survive.

The Indian nobleness is also manifested in the many rich accomplishments which they have contributed to mankind and our civilization. A partial list of these are cited in the next chapter. Read it and count our blessings.

CHAPTER 2: GIFTS AND CONTRIBUTIONS TO THE WORLD AND ITS IMPACT UPON OUR CIVILIZATION

General—List of Food Plants—Corn—Maize—White or Irish Potato—Sweet Potato—Wild Rice—Tobacco—Pine Apple—Grape Fruit—Tomato—Tapioca—Pop Corn—Beans—Egg Plant—Sweet Corn—Various Other Items—Rubber welding, balls—The Wheel—Irrigation—Medicine and Medical Herbs—May Apple—Cochineal—Amil—Government—First Indian Alphabet—The Talking Leaves—Military Gift—Boy Scouts—The Gift of Versatile Horses—The Appaloosa Horse—Chickasaw Horse—Quarter Horse—The Mustang Horse—The Yokima Pony—The Gift of Literature—Speech of Chief Red Jacket—I Am An Indian—Paraphrase of The Lords Prayer—Old Warrior's Last Prayer—Chief Seattle Speech (1786-1866)—The Indian's Night Promises To Be Long—Debate - Chief Tecumseh and Chief Pushmataha—The Talent is Phenomenal—

George Dorsey, the famous historian, said that by sheer genius in military and civil engineering—her sewers, aquaducts, baths, paved streets, highways, temples, law, a hippodrome, etc., etc.—Rome rose to preeminence in power, dominion, and influence, but her actual contributions to the civilization we now enjoy were less than that of the aborigines of the American continents. John Collier, former head of the B.I.A. and eminent authority on Indian affairs said that the Indians contributed more of material wealth than any other group of people. Few people realize that about fifty percent of the plants grown in America today for food were developed centuries ago by Indians, according to Dr. Raymond B. Farnsworth, a Brigham Young University agronomist.

It is said that about fifty percent of the volume of plant-food consumed in the entire world today comes from plants unknown to other parts of the world prior to the coming of Columbus and Lief Ericson. Seventy percent in volume are grown and consumed or exported in the United States.

The white man has not developed a major agricultural product from its wild growth, with the possible exception of guayule; whereas the ancient Indian developed more than twenty important products. The development of corn remains one of the most difficult and important achievements in genetics to this date, according to Edwin T. Walker of the SW Museum in Los Angeles. In addition, according to Walker, the Indian cultivated or utilized a great number of wild growth all of which, acquired by the world, aggregate more than half of our present agricultural wealth.

Physicians, botanists, pharmacists, and others have repeatedly reported that so extensive was the knowledge of the Indians of herbs and the medicinal preparation of them and their prescribed use for specific ailments, that the American and European botanists and physicians have been examining and analyzing the flora of the Americas and have not come up with a single new herb for these purposes which the Indians did not know about four hundred years ago. Some scientists have estimated that at least seventy-five percent of the drugs and cures known to civilized man today were bequeathed to us by the American Indians. Furthermore, the herbs used by ancient civilizations, including that of the American Indian, have been the basis for some of our important drugs used routinely today. Pauwolfia (a blood pressure medicine) is one, according to Dr. Ruble—April 10, 1979—in his column in many newspapers.

By the time their European conquerors arrived in the New World, the Indians of Middle America and Peru had developed civilizations that were, in several respects, superior to what prevailed in the Old World. They knew more about some aspects of astronomy and had a more accurate calendar; they were the first to develop the concept of zero in arithmetic, many of their cities were richer, and one larger, than any in western Europe; they were better farmers and developed crops that now provide over half of the world's food. In fact, they made only one great mistake and it led to their downfall. They failed to invent gunpower.

It was about six thousand years ago that the Maya civilization made an important breakthrough. They had an astronomical method of checking time at least once a year and they were able to check it right down to the very minute. By studying the movement of the stars they determined how long it took to make a year. The Maya civilization probably deserves credit for inventing the calendar year.

The sundial, which tells God's time, is reliable in daylight hours but won't glow in the dark.

The ruins of some of the wagon wheels, made on elevated flat plains by placing rocks to form the wheel and spokes (some of them a quarter mile across) are still visible and intact in the United States. One of these is located near Sheridan, Wyoming. From these the Indians could tell the time when the sun would rise and set. They could also tell the time of the beginning and the end of the four seasons.

As long ago as 5000 BC, cultivation of squashes, avocadoes and pumpkins had begun in the highlands of Mexico. Ultimately, the Indians harvested more varieties of plants than were used or even known in any other region of the world. Others included corn, potatoes, tomatoes, beans, chilies, nuts, fruits, manioc (for making a kind of bread), and others. A list of the more important ones is given.

Archaeological evidence indicates that the South and North American Indians were the greatest domesticators of food and fiber plants in the early history of man.

A List of Gifts to the World by Indians

Corn and popcorn	Peanuts
White Potatoes	Cashew nuts
Sweet potatoes	Pecans
Squash	Brazil nuts
Pumpkins	Butter nuts
Beans—many varieties	Tobacco
Chili	Chocolate
Peppers	Sunflower seeds
Wild rice	Maple sugar
Tapioca	Coffee
Tomatoes	Vanilla
Artichokes	Chewing gum
Pineapple	Sweet gum
Cultivated strawberries	Various kinds of dyes
Plum	Several precious balsams
Wild cherry	Sagrada, oil of winter green
Berries, arrowroot	Ornica, petroleum jelly
Avocado	Quinine and drugs

Indigo Indian dyes	Varieties of cotton
Glue from buffalo hoofs	Long staple wool
Sarsaparilla	Rubber-rubber balls and toys
Turkeys	Fibres from sisal
Llamas	Ropes and mats from hemp
American bison	Parkas
Alpacas	Canoes
Vicunas	Snow shoes
Guinea pigs	Tobaggans
Muscovy ducks	Hammocks

In addition to the list above the Indians used a wild Indian turnip and a wild cabbage and many other plants for food.

Looking over the list one may wonder what plants were foreign to America. Here are a few: barley, onions, radish, (although the Indians probably had some radishes), lettuce, spinach, beets, chard, cabbage, broccoli, collards, carrots, parsley, turnips, peas, asparagus, soybeans, mustard, alfalfa, and sugar beets. The watermelon is a native of Africa and is greatly loved by our Indians.

Corn, the "gift of the gods," remains the great mystery plant, and has become the backbone of American agriculture. There are various theories which concern themselves with the origin and development of this great plant. Even the scientists cannot agree on this.

Did some ancient Indian genius plant breeder create it or was it purely an accident of nature? It is a true hybrid—a cross between two different species. The only other hybrid I can presently recall is the mule. The two are different in one respect—the mule is sterile and cannot reproduce itself, whereas corn can both cross-fertilize and self-fertilize.

There are different kinds of varieties developed down through the ages and big improvements have occurred. Today our corn is the only cereal that cannot survive in the wild state. Unlike other cultivated crops, it requires domesticated environment. The seed is such that the plant will not distribute and reseed itself. This indicates that corn has been a domesticated and cultivated crop from its beginning. Prior to the coming of the European, only the Indian was here to carry on the job. Since this plant cannot survive in a wild state, one might conclude that it had to be created by some plant breeder and nurtured from the very beginning.

Scientists believe that corn may have been developed from the annual *tesosinte* plant, but none have been able to duplicate the original work which is believed to have been done by the Indian in the basic development of corn.

Corn was grown in prehistoric times from Canada to Patagonia and from sea level to heights of 14,500 feet. It is considered the most remarkable achievement in agriculture history.

Historians say that corn may be the oldest domesticated cereal, with a continuous history behind it on American soil of 10,000 years and that corn is the only cereal found in a fossilized existence.

This "gift of the gods" went from America to Europe and thence spread all over Africa and Asia. It ranks today as one of the top three in terms of production and consumption in the entire world. Its impact on the world's commerce is tremendous, amounting to three billion dollars annually in the United States.

The Irish potato—the Irish or white potato, the "poor man's food," ranks about fourth in volume of the staple foods in the world today. It is our most economical and nutritionally balanced staple food. The USDA reports that the potato with whole milk will supply almost all of the food elements necessary for maintenance of the human body. We would get along pretty well with this as our sole dish for a considerable time. It is said that during World War II millions of people in Europe and Scandinavia lived almost entirely on potatoes. They not only survived, but in many cases their health improved, as sugar and other refined foods became scarce and they had to rely more on the potato. It would provide good quality, easily digested protein. There are seventy-six calories in a medium sized potato, about the same as an apple or pear. It is bulky, packed with vitamins, including vitamin C, minerals and would be valuable in a balanced reducing diet. Whole milk adds animal protein and fat lacking in potatoes.

Allen R. Magie, PH. D. has said that the potato is a relatively inexpensive source of protein and other nutrients essential for the body's proper growth and maintenance. It's 99.9 percent fat-free, contains no cholesterol, and has no additives. It's just natural goodness!

The potato's protein and starch are easy to digest, and it combines well with other foods. It keeps well in storage. Contrary to what many calorie-conscious people think, says doctor Magie, it is low in calories. Unlike some foods on a dieter's menu, potatoes tend to "stick to the ribs." Even though it has only a few calories, a potato is satisfying. "Of course, if you add butter, margarine, sour cream or gravy the potato very quickly becomes 'fattening.' In addition, it loses some of its fine nutrition when it is french fried, chipped, puffed, powdered and flaked."

The potato came from South America. The Incas of Peru first cultivated the potato in about 200 B.C. The looting Spanish Conquistadors first found the potato in the Andean village of Sorocota in 1537.

When the Spaniards, some forty years later, introduced the potato to Europe it immediately became a victim of myths and slander. Since it was not mentioned in the Bible, it was thought to be unfit for human consumption. And because it was not from seed, it was said to be evil, responsible for leprosy, syphilis, etc. The French said it would destroy the soil.

We wonder, since the potato is a member of the nightshade family, some of which are deathly poisonous, if the fear of poison may have had something to do with the slow acceptance of it as food. Little was grown in England until the latter half of the 17th century. It was introduced in Ireland about the same time (1663), but the Irish started eating it and produced much before England did. In fact, when England started general use she obtained her seed stock from Ireland, as did some of the colonies in N. America. Indications are that some Irish who settled a colony at Londonderry, N.H. brought the potato with them in 1719.

The potato became quickly adopted by the Old World. In fact, it was Ireland's ideal "potato climate" that soon supplied most of the world's potatoes.

If memory serves me correctly, Ireland at one time prohibited the exportation of potato seed stock to protect her monopoly of the lucrative export trade that she had acquired.

It must be that these events account for the white potato getting its name of Irish potato. Otherwise, why wasn't it called the Indian potato, the Inca potato or the American potato?

In some instances, the potato saved many Europeans from famine and it began to replace wheat in England and Germany. It was not found in North America until 1719 when the colonists brought it with them from Europe. Today, the potato produces great commercial wealth for us and throughout the world. What a valuable gift it turned out to be for the whole world so aptly called the "poor man's food!" What can you buy that gives you as much for your money and health? It has saved millions of lives from starvation, in times of famine and war. It is said to produce more food value per acre than any other crop.

Sweet potato—The American sweet potato came to be a favorite in the Far East. It was received with great joy in China, Luchu, Japan, and under the Spaniards spread over the Philippine Islands. The yam has long been a favorite staple food for the peoples of the Orient. The American sweet potato has largely replaced the yam throughout that part of the world.

It seems to produce better for them and several times it has saved many Orientals from starvation. It spread like wildfire. During the famine years of 1832, 1844, 1872, and 1896, the sweet potato was their sole means of subsistence.

Both the sweet potato and the white potato have been valuable famine crops in Ireland and in Central and Southeast Asia.

With America's corn, white and sweet potatoes, peanuts and tobacco, the earth is richer than it used to be. The European white man is responsible for this richness because he put it to this great expanded use. The sweet potato ranks about sixth or seventh in consumption throughout the world.

Wild rice—The Mahnomonee Indians long have used wild rice as the basic vegetable in their diet. They considered wild rice a perfect food because it is highly nutritious and delicious. It is an excellent source of niacin, thiamine and riboflavin. It has more than four times the iron, magnesium, and phosphorous of the white rice, twice potassium and protein, plus one-hundred percent more fiber. And O, how tasty and delicious with fowl, game, fish, and beef—the perfect touch at any meal!

At one time, wild rice grew from the Gulf of Mexico to Hudson Bay and from the Atlantic to the Rockies. Today it grows only along the Minnesota-Canada border.

Tobacco—Purely American, tobacco has come to profoundly influence our national economic and social customs. It is said by B. Laufer, the German-American anthropologist, to be the world's greatest maker of peace, tranquility, comfort, and happiness. In an incredibly short time, the tobacco business found its way across all parts of the world. It has had a considerable impact in the economic world. Tobacco is over a billion-dollar-a-year industry, plus related uses of nicotine in insecticides and medicines. It is used for many things including religious ceremonies and the peace pipe to seal treaties. The first snuff factory started in this country and had an annual output in 1931 of 41,000,000 pounds. Laufer, after long investigation, found only one tribe in the world that does not use the weed in some form, and all have adopted it since 1492.

To the Indian goes the dubious honor of having outstripped his white brothers in devising all the known ways of using tobacco, but he is not the one who spread it to all parts of the world.

Pineapple—Pineapple, queen of the fruits, is a native of South America and was a thoroughly domesticated plant in pre-Columbian Brazil, Guiana and Columbia. It is cultivated practically out of its seeds and is propagated only by crowns, slips, or suckers. According to Laufer, the pineapple is first mentioned in English literature in 1568. Before the seventeenth century it had reached the East Indies and soon thereafter China where it is cultivated in enormous quantities. Fiber from the leaf is the staple dressgoods of the Philippine Islands.

Tomato—Tomato, another member of the nightshade family, was considered, in North America, to be a poisonous plant as recently as 150 years ago. More tomatoes are now canned in the United States than any other vegetable.

It is one of America's favorite foods. I believe South America (probably Peru) gave the tomato to Europe. Yet there is some thought that tomatoes came from Egypt centuries ago. The name is derived from the Aztec word *itomate*. It was first introduced into England in 1596. At that time, the prevailing opinion was that they were poisonous to man. The first record of this fruit being regularly quoted on the market was in New Orleans in 1812.

Tapioca—Tapioca is made from the roots of the deadly manioc plant. The Indians in South America learned how to press and squeeze out the deadly juices and made the remaining pulp into bread. Tapioca has become one of the top ranking items of food in the world.

Popcorn—Popcorn was sweetened with maple sugar by the native Indians several thousand years ago (It is used as a confection for Cracker Jack's or caramel corn.)

Beans—The Indian varieties of beans are native to tropical America and were cultivated and used for food many years before its discovery by the white settlers. Both the lima and kidney bean have been found in ancient Peruvian tombs at Anton. The Indians of both North and South America were well acquainted with the species and according to tradition the cliff dwellers of the Southwest desert countries grew beans as a food thousands of years previously. Shortly after 1500 AD, the kidney bean began to expand extensively in Europe where it entirely supplanted the common bean for garden purposes.

Eggplant—The eggplant, a native of South America, was introduced into England. It was cultivated in the United States for less than a century. A myth claimed that it was poisonous and to be utterly forsaken.

Sweet corn—Sweet corn is a native of Peru and was grown in North America when it was discovered. A fossilized ear of corn was found in Cuzco, Peru, in 1914; tangible evidence of the geological existence of the species. It has many of the characteristics essential to the domestic varieties still being grown in Peru and Bolivia. It is one of the first pieces of evidence that vegetables were transferred from prehistoric to geological times, possibly taking it back 100,000 years.

Grapefruit—The grapefruit originated in the West Indies. It was there before the Spaniards discovered and took over the islands. Practically all of the Indians are gone from the islands but the grapefruit still remains and has spread to other parts of the world. It was some time before the grapefruit appeared in the continental United States. It is now grown most abundantly in the U.S. and Israel.

Some think it may have emerged as a hybrid or a mutation. Perhaps the Indians of long ago created it or found or created a mutation. Or was it a direct creation by the Creator of all? In any event it was a gift of the Indian to the whole world.

Various other items—The Indians invented the moccasin, snow shoe, parka, canoe, and tepee, and taught the early colonists how to use them. The Indians had the hammock developed to perfection, but it took the white man many years to appreciate the fact that it was a practical sleeping device for a rolling ship—or for a lazy afternoon on the lawn.

They passed on to us their knowledge of how to make cocoa, baked beans, tamales, maple syrup, teas, canvas snowshoes, cornbread, some types of drugs, and many other things.

They were the first to vulcanize rubber and to make rubber balls and other toys. Today the rubber industry is in the over five-billion-dollar class.

Indian women made their own "rouge" by grinding up minerals and used herbs to make many perfumes and other toilet articles. Manufacturers cannot even lay claim to cold cream. Indian women first used animal tallow.

All of these things and many more did not just happen, but came as a result of intelligent and orderly agricultural development, the arts, and democratic government.

The Indian domesticated the honey bee. They caused them to swarm and then by beating on instruments caused them to settle on some limb or object (as we used to do when we were kids) and coax them into a hive instead of flying off to some hollow tree.

The Aztecs made a kind of paper from maguey fiber and hollow rubber balls for their children.

The Tuscarora Indians taught the immigrants from Europe how to make rope and mats from hemp which they cultivated and harvested.

America's first skyscrapers were not in New York, but in the Pueblo lands of the Southwest.

The wheel, with all the ingenuity and skills the Indian possessed and the many things he accomplished, is one thing we would think he would have invented, he did not. This invention along with the discovery of fire are considered the two most important inventions of mankind. The wheel would be relatively simple to make and would have been so useful to them. Why did they not think of the wheel, especially when the circle played such a prominent place in their lives? We tell the story of the circle in the chapter on religion. Suffice it here to recount a few of them. They believed that there was power in the hoop and their flowering tree that grew within it. When their hoop was broken their power was lost. Nature operated in cycles and circles—the days, the seasons, the years, the sun and moon, the stars, the animals, and other things.

Irrigation—The Indians constructed extensive irrigation systems from Arizona to Peru. Our culture cannot even take credit for the idea behind our ever-growing and efficient irrigation systems. Several of the tribes, particularly the Pueblos of the Southwest and several Mexican tribes, had complete and effective irrigation systems in operation when the first white settlers came.

Some of these projects were of monumental proportions, when we consider that they evidently had to excavate their miles and miles (hundreds of miles in some cases) of canals and ditches by manual labor, using crude tools.

Medicine and medicinal herbs—The medicine man did a great job for his race in the Americas, but has given to the rest of the world and to civilization a greater heritage by passing his knowledge on to them and posterity.

The Indians believed that the Great Creator endowed every plant with something of value to man. They searched diligently and thoroughly to discover them. They did not possess or develop

34

scientific processes and guidelines, nor did they have elaborate laboratories and equipment for research, but they had the qualities of keenness and aptitude and an understanding of the harmony of nature which served them well. Healers, the native medicine men or their doctors, explored every part of the plant (such was their native nature) including the roots of herbs, bark, leaves, flowers, fruits, and juices. They came up with cascara and quinine, coca as a pain killer and fatigue easer and many other remedies.

For at least 1500 years, Indians of Peru and Bolivia chewed leaves of the plant *Erthroxylon coca*, or rolled them in lime, and held them in their mouths during long treks. The leaves enabled them to go without food, water and sleep for many hours.

Coca was discovered by the white man in the 1850s. The active ingredient was isolated by a German organic chemist in 1855. He named it cocaine.

Cascara, derived from the bark of a tree with the botonical name of *Rhamus purshiana*, was used as a cathartic by Indians of the American Northwest.

Malaria has ravaged humankind since the earliest times. The Collahuya Indians, "druggists of the Amazon," are believed to have been the first people to discover a treatment for it. For years they drank a potion made from the bark of one or more species of cinchona evergreens found on the eastern slopes of the Andes.

Powder from cinchona bark was widely used against malaria from about 1645 until 1820. In that year, two French pharmacists, Pierre Joseph Pelletier and Joseph Biewaime Caventou, isolated an essential derivative of cinchona bark. It was named quinine. for the treatment of malaria.

May apple—May apple, commonly found in the U.S. and Canadian woods, showed promise as an anti-cancer agent. May apple had been used as a cancer remedy by the Penobscot Indians of Maine, probably long before the white man came to North America. Private practitioners in the U.S. are known to have used May apple in the treatment of cancer during the nineteenth century. Recent trials have given encouraging results, particularly showing evidence of activity against various forms of leukemia.

Cochineal—One of the world's most prized dyes, cochineal was used in prehistoric Mexico and Peru.

Amil—Amil is used in almost every dye and coloring agent known today. The Indians learned about it hundreds of years ago. They willingly taught us and asked no patent rights or royalties.

The Indians scraped the bark from the cinchona tree and boiled it into a tea to cure malaria; used capaiba oil for healing of sores, ipecac for stomach ailments, and abatus for dropsy. They made and used several precious balsams, such as balsam of Peru, Tolu balsam, copaiva balsam, and sweetgum. Also the therapeutic and medical qualities of witch hazel, jalapa, hydrastic, ipecac and cocaine, sagrada oil of wintergreen, arnica and petroleum jelly, indigo Indian dye, and glue from buffalo hoofs.

There are many more, especially in southwestern North America, that we civilized Americans have not yet "discovered."

Scientists have estimated that at least seventy-five percent of the drugs and cures known to civilized man today were bequeathed to us by the American Indian (taken from the Pipestone pageant).

"In recent times, with the emergence of psychiatry and psychosomatic medicine, attention has been paid to the practices of Indian curers that were designed to restore a patient's health by ministering to his mental state and bringing him back into the harmony of his universe" (from *Indian Heritage*).

Government—Most tribes of Indians lived by a true democratic form of government dating back before the coming of the Europeans. Their chiefs led them, but only with the consent of all members of the band or tribe. Decisions were arrived at on important issues at tribal council meetings.

They stayed in council until a unanimous decision was attained. Some tribes assigned designated tribesmen to head individual projects, such as leading in a war and organizing work units.

The Iroquois Federated Nation is the most prominent example where tribes united themselves for mutual protection, stability, and harmony but there were others. Iroquois council members emphasized strength through unity, leadership by concensus rather than authority and decision-making by unanimity rather than majority or by authority in cases of treaties.

It is very apparent that our founding forefathers investigated at considerable length the Indians' form of government and especially that of the Iroquois Federated tribes. Each tribe had its own home rule, but granted certain authority and power to their central federated government. Certain specific duties were assigned to each of the tribes. The Onondagas were elected to be the capital and they voted only in case of a tie.

I quote from the Iroquois display in the Chicago Field Museum of National History: "The family is the Basic Social Unit. Members of families make up a band—the largest social unit. Iroquois were chiefly farmers, also hunters and skilled craftsmen (as early as the twelfth century.) The culture is a rich diverse blend of the old and the new."

The pattern of states within a state, a federation and the habit of treating chiefs as servants of the people instead of their masters are factors that have led students of the Indian life to hold that the very form of our federal government was patterned after the great Iroquois Confederacy.

It is out of a rich Indian democratic tradition that the distinctive political ideals of American life emerged. For example, they had universal suffrage for women as well as for men.

The Onondaga village with its long-house (Capitol) was centrally located in Iroquois territory so the Onondagas became known as the Keeper of the Council Fire. The others were categorized as follows:

1— The Mohawks, the easternmost tribe were the Keepers of the Eastern Gate.

2— The Oneidas—the People of the Great Stone.

3— The Onondagas—Keeper of the Council Fire.

4— The Cayugas—the People from the Place of the Locust.

5— Senecas—Keepers of the Western Door.

"We constitute but one house, we five Iroquois Nations. We build but one fire and we have through all of the time dwelt under one roof."

Each tribe had its appointed number of representatives or *sachems*: the Senecas—8: Mohawk—9; Oneidas—9; Cayugas—10; and the Onondagas—14.

Fifty *sachems*, wearing the antlers of their office, met in the long-house of the Onondagas and pondered the grave decisions—inter and intra tribal problems. To reach a decision the delegates voted as a representative of a tribal unit, not as individuals. The Onondagas, as moderators, would cast the deciding vote in event of a tie.

War between fraternal tribes was outlawed. They could not war on non-members either. They had to show just cause at a general Council meeting and then the Council would vote on the matter. If the vote was affirmative, the Five Nations were obligated to fight as a single tribe.

Within each tribe, selection of the representatives to the Great

37

Council rested with the *ro-gah-ners*, the wise women.

An Oneida *sachem* voiced the thought that had been running through the minds of some of the white colonists. He suggested that since the league worked so well for the Iroquois, an organization patterned along similar lines might be a possible solution to the many problems which beset the young and struggling colonies.

Benjamin Franklin was one of the men who investigated and studied the Iroquois organization thoroughly in anticipation of forming a federated government for the various colonies.

Our resulting political structure, based upon a respect for rights of the individual, was truly representative in form. It functioned upon compromises in council, but a decision reached was final and binding on all parties. Its total aim was of peace among the nations of Red America.

When it came time for the colonists (America was a country of Red people at that time) to make up a set of procedures of their own, where would it be better to look than to the Iroquois Nations?

The Constitution of the United States is one of the greatest, if not the greatest, political documents created by mankind. We were so fortunate to have had so many dedicated and brave people at one given time.

Members of a proud race can be truly proud of its contribution towards the founding of our great nation with the enduring motto "Under God."

First Indian alphabet—the talking leaves—Sequoyah was probably the greatest of all Cherokees. He is the only man in the history of mankind to invent a complete alphabet, without being able to read or write any other language. He was a great man of letters. The alphabet brought to the Cherokee people a way of writing their language so that they could have their own newspapers, books, and Bibles. It was a great day that would bring everlasting fame to Sequoyah.

We need to preserve the heritage of our Indian citizens because it is so rich and has contributed enormously to our nation and the world's civilization.

Boy Scouts—It should also be more generally known that one of the persons largely responsible for the beginning of scouting in the U.S. was a full-blooded Dakota Indian, Dr. Charles A. Eastman. Dr. Eastman was born in a buffalo hide tepee in the winter of 1858, the fifth child of a Dakota warrior named Many Lightnings. He was christened Ohiyesa (One Who Wins) and by

1890 had graduated from Boston University, where he was class orator with an M.D. degree. After serving many years as a physician in the government service, he achieved renown as a writer and interpreter of Indian life.

The military gift—It has been said of Chief Joseph, Nez Perce tribe, that he set such a high standard of military skill that many of his tactics and techniques have been included in the training program of the American military forces.

Their tactics included surprise, hit and run, scatter, melt away, and hide out, with little chance to run them down or corral them. Their signals and camouflage were the best in the world.

It is said that very few Indians were drafted in W.W. II because they all enlisted ahead of the draft. They excelled in all branches, but especially brilliant was their service in the Signal Corps because of their use of the Indian languages that baffled the enemy decoders.

The Indians fought with us in all of our wars, even against other Indians in the Revolutionary War, the Civil War, wars with the Canadians, the French, the Spanish, and the Indian Wars, but they also fought in the opposition armies. In fact, there was always more fighting on the side of our enemies than on the side of the colonies and the United States, according to recorded accounts.

The gift of versatile horses—The horse was introduced to the Americas by the Spaniards. Horses spread rapidly over Mexico and North America. They were a great boon for the Indians everywhere. The early Indians apparently bred-up their horses through selecting for type and ruggedness) and culling. They soon had great herds and bartered many of them off to other tribes, the military, explorers, and settlers. The final types varied from area to area, according to conditions and primary purposes. Some wanted the rugged and enduring kind; others tended towards a general purpose horse that could be used for draft; others, such as the Nez Perce, wanted color and beauty along with speed, soundness and conformation.

While the Indians did not possess certain formal scientific knowledge such as genetics, pedigrees, etc., they did possess an uncanny eye and a keen sense of observation to select superior individuals, develop them, fix type, and standardize the same. They developed horses to best suit their particular needs. These varied from area to area, including the Northern Plains tribes who needed hardy, rugged, swift horses which could survive their

39

severe winters, and had great endurance. I have never heard of them ever developing heavy draft horses. The reason is because they did not need them. The Indians developed great skill as horsemen, especially the hunting and roving tribes.

The Appaloosa horse—The Nez Perce Indians are credited with the origin of the Appaloosa breed of horses. The Appaloosa descended from the Spanish spotted horse which dates back to before the time of Christ. After standardizing and fixing the breed, the Nez Perce improved their Appaloosa horses through selective breeding by either castrating the less desirable males or trading them off and hence developed the popular Appaloosa. The Nez Perce were more or less isolated at the time, which made it easier for them to maintain purity.

After the Nez Perce succumbed to the military in 1877, their horses were confiscated and the Indians were removed and scattered to remote places, including Oklahoma. The Appaloosa horse almost became a lost breed and deteriorated greatly in quality. From Oklahoma some of the horses worked their way north to the Great Plains area along with the cattle herds.

Some years later, some white men horse lovers set about to restore and improve the breed. Some of these breeders were in South Dakota, where good Appaloosa horses can again be found, as well as throughout horseland. The Appaloosa is noted for his stamina and endurance, as well as for eye appeal because of his heritage as a war, race, and buffalo horse.

Chickasaw horse—The early settlers of Virginia and the Carolinas and the eastern Indians needed a horse to work their fields, pull their wagons and double as a saddle mount. The Chickasaw horse met this need. The Chickasaw Indians had selectively bred a short, thick, versatile horse. They also wanted to race him. To improve the speed of their horses, English stallions were imported and crossed on the Chickasaw mares. These stallions and the Chickasaw mares became the progenitors of the quarter horse, and the quarter horse became the most valuable horse in America today.

Quarter horse—The history of the quarter horse parallels that of this great country. The offspring from these Chickasaw mares, sired by imported English stallions, were superb, and exactly what the colonial Americans and the Native Indian people needed.

They became known as the American Quarter Running Horse because of their lightning speed for a quarter of a mile, usually the only straight distance available in those days.

As more and more horses were imported and used on the quarter horse mares, longer races evolved and became popular. Quarter horses moved west with the pioneers and relocated Indians, finally making their home and fame in the Southwest as "cowponies." Sam Houston not only helped make Texas an independent country but his horse, Copper Bottom, was an important sire of quarter horses.

Known by their unbeatable speed for a quarter mile and impeccable ability as a cow horse, quarter horses are heavier muscled in the chest, forearm, quarter, and gaskin than other breeds. Their quiet, gentle disposition has made them the most popular horse in America today with over 60,000 individuals registered during 1967. While famed as pleasure, roping, and cutting horses, and now as hunters and jumpers, they excited millions of people annually with their terrific speed at the race track. The world record for a quarter-mile (440 yards) is 21.5 seconds (at least up to the middle 1960s.) The world's richest horse race at that time, was run at Ruidoso Downes, Ruidoso, New Mexico, in 1968 over a distance of four-hundred yards with a purse of $602,000.

The mustang horse—descended from escaped Indian horses.The Northern Great Plains Indians took to the horse like a duck to water. The horse invaded this country even before the white man did. They came up from the south—New Mexico, Texas and Oklahoma—from tribe to tribe and later with the migration of the white man and his herds of cattle, they multiplied rapidly. Herds of wild horses roamed the country.

For their hunts and wars these Indians needed horses with speed and endurance that were tough and rugged and able to survive severe winters and droughts. They did not have to be a large horse, but able to carry a man well. The mustang was intelligent, easy and quick turning, and sure footed. He was also a good cutting and all around cow horse as well as superior in holding a bunch of cattle together in a small bunch. His natural gait was mostly trotting, which made him a rough-riding horse.

This horse descended from the early Spanish imported horses, was developed through selective breeding by the Indians and early cattlemen, and was truly an early pioneer and builder of the West.

The Yakima pony—The Yakima Indians of Washington state had a small type that was strong and comparatively speedy and easy to keep. They were useful for riding and pulling wagons.

Other Indian horses—The Indians of the wooded areas selected a smaller breed that were sturdy and could get around well in timber and rough terrain.

The Nez Perce set up a profitable business as horse traders, restocking emigrant trains as the pioneers prepared for their last haul before they dropped down into the rich and verdant valleys of the Oregon Territory. They also sold horses to the military, settlers and other Indian tribes. Appaloosas were held at a premium.

We can see that the Indian played no small part in breeding superior breeds and strains of adaptive horses for our country.

The gift of literature—Good literature is for the ages. Indians are noted for their gift of oration and speech making.

So eloquent was the oration of the Indian that President Thomas Jefferson remarked that he wished that the men of Congress could orate half as well.

There are many speeches of note made by Indians on the various aspects of their life and experiences, including speeches before Congress. Many of these speeches will compare with the best in terms of substance, organization, balance, choice of words, profound and analytical thinking, and effectiveness of delivery. They will compare equally with the greatest made by any man or statesman in our colonial and national history.

Our history books have infamously ignored these valuable assets and gifts of the Native American Indians to our nation and to our world civilization, as it has even of the other outstanding contributions.

It is high time that we recognize these facts, give credit where credit is due, and save these gifts by recording them in history and literature for posterity.

In this chapter, I shall quote only a few samples and refer to others in each of several catagories from chapter to chapter, scattered throughout the book, where they also serve another purpose.

Red Jacket Speech

Speech of Chief Red Jacket of the Iroquois made at a conference after a missionary addressed his tribe at a meeting in Buffalo, New York, in 1805.

A good example of their power of reasoning and eloquence of delivery and their spirit of Christian love follows: Friend and brother, it was the will of the Great Spirit that we should meet together today. He orders all things, and he has given us a fine day for our council. He has taken his garment from before the sun, and caused it to shine with brightness upon us; our eyes are opened, and we see clearly; our ears are unstopped, and we have been able to hear distinctly the words that you have spoken; for all these favors we thank the Great Spirit and Him only. . . .

Brother, listen to what we say. There was a time when our forefathers owned this great land. Their seats extended from the rising to the setting sun. The Great Spirit had made it for use by the Indians. He had created the buffalo, the deer, and other animals for food. He made the bear and the beaver, and the skins served for clothing. He had scattered them over the country, and taught us how to take them. He caused the earth to produce corn for bread.

All this he had done for his Red Children because he loved them. If we had any disputes about hunting grounds they were generally settled without the shedding of blood.

But an evil day came upon us; your forefathers crossed the great waters, and landed on this island. Their numbers were small; they found friends, not enemies; they told us they had fled from their own country for fear of wicked men, and came here to enjoy their religion. They asked for a small seat; we took pity upon them, granted their request, and they sat down among us. We gave them corn and meat; they gave us poison in return.

The white people had now found our country, tidings were carried back, and more came among us; yet we did not fear them. We took them to be friends; they called us brothers, we believed them, and gave them a larger seat. At length their numbers had greatly increased, and they wanted more land, they wanted our country. Our eyes were opened and our minds became uneasy. Wars took place; Indians were hired to fight against Indians; and many of our people were destroyed. They also brought strong liquor among us.

Brothers, our seats were once large, and yours were very small, you now have become a great people, and we scarecely have a place left to spread our blankets. You have our country, but you are not satisfied, you want to force your religion upon us.

Brother continue to listen, you say that you are sent to instruct us to worship the Great Spirit agreeable to His mind, and if we do not take hold of the religion which you White people teach, we shall be unhappy hereafter; you say you are right and we are lost. How do you know this to be true? We understand that your religion is written in a book.

43

If it was intended for us as well as for you, why has not the Great Spirit given it to us, and not only to you, but why did He not give us, and our forefathers, the knowledge of that book, with the means of understanding it rightly? We know only what you tell us. How shall we know to believe, being so often deceived by the White people?

Brother you say there is but one way to worship and serve the Great Spirit. If there be but one religion, why do you White people differ so much about it? Why not all agree as you can read the book? . . .

Brother the Great Spirit has made all of us, but he has made a great difference between his White and Red Children. He has given us a different complexion and different customs. To you he has given the arts; to these he has not opened our eyes. We know these things to be true. Since He has made so great a difference between us in other things, why may we not conclude that He has given us a different religion according to our understanding? The Great Spirit does right. He knows what is best for His children. We are satisfied.

Brother you have heard our answer to your talk. As we are going to part, we will take you by the hand, and hope the Great Spirit will protect you on your journey, and return you safe to your friends.

The chiefs and other Indians drew near the minister, but he arose hastily from his seat and told them there was no fellowship between the religion of God and the works of the devil and that he could not shake their hands.

This speech by Chief Red Jacket is very analytical, thorough, well balanced, and includes well chosen words. We certainly can not call these people ignorant and savages. While they could not fully accept the precepts of the white man's interpretations and his violations in the practices of the Christian gospel as expounded by many white people, they had a more Christlike attitude towards life and toward one's human brothers than did the minister. The minister, in his arrogant way, was a poor witness for Christ.

The Indian's forgiving and friendly ways represents qualities of a superior race and a superior religion as they practiced it.

The minister made no attempt to answer the questions asked by the enquiring chief.

The chief wanted to know why God had not revealed to them

this religion if it was supposed to be the only one for mankind.

The minister could have explained that God and His universe are universal and is always in the process of evolution and always aimed to a higher and more perfect kingdom and that in this world man must make his own individual decisions and as a nation, its people must make decisions—for good or bad.

We have freedom and are the architect of our future and place in the coming Kingdom. God himself does not convert man, but He beckons him. He establishes the way and provides the light for man's guidance. He selected a disciple nation (Israel) and the disciples as a nucleus, for the leadership, and gave them the positive instructions to carry the message to the outermost parts of the world. God does not do this simultaneously and immediately for everybody. Christ's coming and going provided the light, the way and the instructions in a very short period of time and then charged man with the responsibility of getting the job done. Yes, the white man BROUGHT CHRIST TO AMERICA! All things are not revealed suddenly and completely. We must grow in the knowledge of God.

Our next article will show a different attitude by the Indians and his appreciation for the gift of Christ, even at such a price which it cost him. No doubt time itself wrought the difference.

I am an Indian. Born here ages before the white man came, we had the entire country to ourselves, its lakes, streams, forests, mountains, and game of all kinds. We were a happy and carefree people. Our school was the great out-of-doors, and Mother Nature was our teacher.

We saw the Great Spirit in the starry heavens—His painting in the glories of the sunset. We loved the green carpet of the plains decorated with the colors of countless flowers, we worshipped Him in the majesty of rugged mountains topped with snow, in the sun and moon, and in the great animals like the bear and birds, like the eagle. He was everywhere.

We wondered about Him when lightning flashed. We trembled when we heard His voice in the boom of the thunder. We were touched when a star fell and bewildered when meteors sprayed the sky with fire and even once when we saw a longtailed comet which we did not understand.

When the white man came, some righteous and godly men of your people answered our questions and told us about the true God. These good men taught us that this God was our

Creator and Maker of all. They told us about Jesus, the Godman, and now some of us are Christians too.

Will you train us, so that in our own language and in our own way we can share these joys with our own people until they all have a chance to learn English?

I am an Indian, and want my people to know Him who is our Master and our true Great Spirit Father. You will help us, won't you?

Paraphrase of the Lord's Prayer

(Written by Virginia Wilder, former English teacher in the Bureau of Indian Affairs. She caught the spirit, style, and thinking of the Indian.

> Great Spirit whose tepee is the sky
> And whose hunting ground is the earth,
> Mighty and fearful are you called.
> Ruler over storms, over men
>   and birds and beasts:
> Have your way over all-
> Over earthways as over skyways,
> Find us this day our meat and corn,
> that we may be strong and brave.
> And put aside from us our wicked ways as
>   we put aside the bad work of them
>   who do us wrong.
> And let us not have such troubles
>   as lead us into crooked roads.
> But keep us from all evils,
> For yours is all that is-
>   the earth and the sky:
>   the streams, the hills,
>   and the valleys, the stars,
>   the moon and the sun, and
>   all that live and breathe,
> Wonderful, shining Mighty Spirit!

Old Warrior's Last Prayer

By Harold Watson, a Cherokee member of the Oklahoma Veterans Center in Talihina—Taken from *Indian Life*—Mar./Apr. '77.

O Great Chief and Chief of all Chiefs:

I speak these last words from my heart in humble thanks for all you have given me during the many moons I have camped and hunted here in this land.

—For the forests and the buffalo that provided food and shelter during the long moons of winter.

—For the rain, and the sun that gave light and beauty to all growing things.

—For your mercy and guidance on our many trails together.

But now my body is frail; my eyes are dim and I can no longer see the trails ahead.

Like the tall oak of the forest, I have reached the horizon and bid farewell to the setting sun.

I am weary, for the trail has been long, the hardships many; and my pony and I seek now only for rest in the long sleep that must come to all that have lived here.

I can hear the rustle of the winged ones, and the hand that once held the bow is reaching out now to take your hand that will lead me into your camp where the campfires glow in the golden forest, and the chant of the drums, speak of peace and contentment forever.

Chief Seattle — 1786 - 1866

Governor Stevens visited the town named after the Suquamish and Duwamish tribe's Chief and addressed the settlers and Indians gathered in the small community. After his talk, Chief Seattle made his reply which was delivered through an interpreter. Dr. Smith carefully wrote it down on the spot—Indian Oratory. Compiled by W. C. Vanderwert, U. of Oklahoma Press.

THE INDIAN'S NIGHT PROMISES TO BE DARK

Yonder sky that has wept tears of compassion upon my people for centuries untold, and which to us appears changeless and eternal may change. Today is fair. Tomorrow it may be overcast with clouds. My words are like the stars that never change. Whatever Seattle says the great Chief at

Washington can rely upon with as much certainty as he can upon the return of the sun or the seasons. The White Chief says that Big Chief at Washington sends us greetings of friendship and goodwill. This is kind of him for we know he has little need of our friendship in return. His people are many. They are like the grass that covers vast prairies. My people are few. They resemble the scattering trees of a storm-swept plains. The great—and I presume—good white Chief sends us word that he wishes to buy our lands but is willing to allow us enough to live comfortably. This appears to be just, even generous, for the Red Man no longer has rights that he need respect, and the offer may be wise also, as we are no longer in need of an extensive country.

There was a time when our people covered the land as the waves of a wind-ruffled sea cover its shell paved floor, but that time long since passed away with the greatness of tribes that are now but a mournful memory. I will not dwell on, nor mourn over, *our untimely decay*. Nor reproach my pale-face brothers with hastening it as we too may *have been somewhat to blame*.

Youth is impulsive. When our young men grow angry at some real or imaginary wrong, and disfigure their faces with black paint, it denotes that their hearts are black, and they are often cruel and relentless, and our old men and old women are unable to restrain them. Thus it has ever been. Thus it was when the white man first began to push our forefathers westward. But let us hope that the hostilities between us may never return. We would have everything to lose and nothing to gain. Revenge by young men is considered gain even at the cost of their own lives, but old men who stay at home in times of war and mothers who have sons to lose, know better.

Our good father at Washington—for I presume he is our father as well as yours, since King George has moved his boundaries further north—our great and good father, I say sends us word that if we do as he desires he will protect us. His brave warriors will be to us a bristling wall of strength, and his wonderful ships of war will fill our harbors so that our ancient enemies far to the northward—the Hydas and Tsimpsians—will cease to frighten our women, children and old men. Then in reality will he be our father and we his children. But can that ever be? Your God is not our God!

48

your God loves your people and hates mine. He folds his strong protecting arms lovingly about the pale face and leads him by the hand as a father leads his son—but he has forsaken His red children—if they really are His. Our God, the Great Spirit, seems also to have forsaken us. Your God makes your people wax strong every day. Soon they will fill all the land. Our people are ebbing away like a rapidly receding tide that will never return. The white man's God cannot love our people or He would protect them. They seem to be orphans who can look nowhere for help. How can we be brothers? How can your God become our God and renew our prosperity and awaken in us dreams of returning greatness? If we have a common heavenly father, He must be partial—for He came to His paleface children. We never saw Him. He gave you laws but had no word for his red children whose teeming multitudes once filled this vast continent as stars fill the firmament. No, we are two distinct races that separate origins and separate destinies. There is little in common between us.

To us the ashes of our ancestors are sacred and their resting place is hollowed ground. You wander far from the graves of your ancestors and seemly without regret. Your religion was written upon tablets of stone by the iron finger of your God so that you could not forget. The Red Man could never comprehend nor remember it. Our religion is the traditions of our ancestors—the dreams of our old men, given them in the solemn hours of night by the Great Spirit; and the visions of our sachems, and is written in the hearts of our people.

Your dead cease to love you and the land of their nativity as soon as they pass the portals of the tomb and wander way beyond the stars. They are soon forgotten and never return. Our dead never forget the beautiful world that gave them being. They still love its verdant valleys, its murmuring rivers, its magnificent mountains, sequestered vales and verdant lined lakes and bays, and ever yearn in tender, fond affection over the lonely hearted living, and often return from the Happy Hunting Ground to visit, guide, console and comfort them.

Day and night can not dwell together. The Red Man has ever fled the approach of the White Man, as the morning mist flees before the morning sun.

However, your proposition seems fair and I think that my

people will accept it and will retire to the reservation you offer them. Then we will dwell in peace, for the words of the Great White Chief seem to be words of nature speaking to my people out of dense darkness.

It matters little where we pass the remnants of our days. They will not be Many. The Indian's night promises to be dark. Not a single star of hope hovers above the horizon. Sad-voiced winds moan in the distance. Grim fate seems to be on the Red Man's trail, and wherever he goes he will hear the approaching foot-steps of his fell destroyer and prepare stolidly to meet his doom, as does the wounded doe that hears the approaching footsteps of the hunter.

A few more moons. A few more winters—and not one of the descendants of the mighty hosts that once moved over this broad land or lived in happy homes, protected by the Great Spirit will remain to mourn over the graves of a people—once more powerful and hopeful than yours. But why should I mourn at the untimely fate of my people? Tribe follows tribe, and nation follows nation, like the waves of the sea. *It is the order of nature, and regret is useless.* Your time of decay may be distant, but it will surely come, *for even the white man whose God walked and talked with him as friend with friend,* cannot be exempt from the common destiny. We may be brothers after all. We will see.

We will ponder your proposition and when we decide we will let you know. But should we accept it, I here and now make this condition that we will not be denied the privilege without molestation of visiting at any time the tombs of our ancestors, friends and children. Every part of this soil is sacred in the estimation of my people. Every hillside, every valley, every plain and grove, has been hallowed by some sad or happy event in the days long vanished. Even the rocks, which seem to be dumb and dead as they swelter in the sun along the silent shore, thrilled with memories of stirring events connected with the lives of my people, and the very dust upon which you now stand responds more lovingly to their foot-steps than to yours, because it is rich with the blood of our ancestors and our bare feet are conscious of the sympathetic touch. Our departed braves, fond mothers, glad, happy-hearted maidens, and even our little children who lived here and rejoiced here for a brief season, will love these somber solitudes and at eventide they greet shadowy returning spirits. And when the last Red Man shall have perished and the memory of my tribe shall have become a myth among the white men, these shores shall swarm with the invisible dead of my tribe, and when your children's children think themselves alone in the field, the store, the shop, upon the highways, or in the silence of the pathless woods, they will not be alone. *In all the earth there is no place dedicated to solitude.* At night when the streets of your cities and villages are silent and you think them deserted, they will throng with the returning hosts that once filled them and still love this beautiful land. The white man will never be alone.

Let him be just and deal kindly with my people, for the dead are not powerless. Dead, did I say?

There is no death, only a change of worlds.

Who among us could have said all of this so well in a speech without benefit of script or notes?

One of the Nation's greatest?

Chief Tecumseh and Chief Pushmataha Debate Policy

Tecumseh is outstanding among Indian orators and warriors. His Shawnees attempted to crystalize opposition to the encroachment of the whites by forming a coalition among the Wyandottes, Delawares, some of the Algonquins, the Chippewas, Nanticokes, Creeks, and the Cherokees. They would fight on the side of the British in the War of 1812. Pushmatsha, a Choctaw (Push), took the position of fighting on the side of the Americans.

Tecumseh and Pushmataha, two great Indian orators, expounded on two divergent courses at a point of national crisis. It is eloquently expressed by two orators, like a Lincoln and Douglas debate.

This is part of a speech Push made in debating Tecumseh following one in which Tecumseh was trying to get the Choctaws to join his rebellion. This is the reasoning of Push, as he spoke in 1811:

Attention, my good red warriors:

Hear Ye my brief remarks.

The great Shawnee (Tecumseh) orator has portrayed in vivid picture the ravage of the paleface. The candor and fervor of his eloquent appeal breathes the conviction of truth and sincerity and, as kindred tribes, naturally we sympathize with the misfortunes of his people. I do not come before you in any disputation either for or against these charges. It is not my purpose to contradict any of these allegations against the white man, but neither am I here to indulge in any indiscreet denunciation of him which might bring down upon my people unnecessary difficulty and embarrassment.

The distinguished Shawnee sums up his eloquent appeal to us with this direct question:

Will you sit idly by, supinely awaiting complete and abject submission, or will you die fighting beside your brethren, the Shawnees, rather than submit to such ignominy?

These are plain words and it is well they have been spoken, for they bring the issue squarely before us. Mistake not, this language means war. And war with whom, pray? War with some band of marauders who have committed their depredations against the Shawnees? War with some alien host seeking the destruction of the Choctaws and Chickasaws? Nay, my fellow tribesmen. None of these are the enemy we will be called on to meet. If we take up arms against the Americans we must of necessity meet in deadly combat our daily neighbors and associates in this part of the country near our homes.

If Tecumseh's words be true, and we doubt them not, then the Shawnee's experience with the whites has not been the same as that of the Choctaws. These white Americans buy our skins, our corn, our cotton, our surplus game, our baskets, and other wares, and they give us in fair exchange their cloth, their guns, their tools, implements, and other things which the Choctaws need but do not make. It is true we have befriended them, but who will deny that these acts of friendship have been abundantly reciprocated? They have given us cotton gins, which simplify the spinning and the sale of cotton; they have encouraged and helped us in the production of our crops; they have taken many of our wives into their homes to teach them useful things, and pay them for their work while learning; they teach our children to read and write from their books. You all remember the dreadful epidemic visited upon us last winter. During its darkest hours these neighbors whom we are now urged to attack responded generously to our needs. They doctored our sick; they clothed our suffering; they fed our hungry; and where is the Choctaw or Chickasaw delegation who has ever gone to St. Stephens with a worthy cause and been sent away empty handed? So in marked contrast with the experiences of the Shawnees, it will be seen that the whites and Indians in this section are living on friendlier and mutually beneficial terms.

Forget not, O Choctaws and Chickasaws, that we are bound in peace to the Great White Father at Washington by a sacred treaty and the Great Spirit will punish those who break their word. The Great White Father has never violated that treaty and the Choctaws have never been driven to the necessity of taking up the tomahawk against him or his children. Therefore the question tonight is not the avenging of any wrongs perpetrated against us by the whites, for the Choctaws and Chickasaws have no such cause, either real or imaginary, but rather it is a question of carrying on that record of fidelity and justice for which our forefathers ever proudly stood, and doing that which is best calculated to promote the welfare of our own people. We do not take up the warpath without a just cause and honest purpose. Have we that just cause against our white neighbors, who have taken nothing from us except by fair bargain and exchange? Is this a just recompence for their assistance to us in our agricultural and other pursuits? Is this to be their gracious reward for teaching our children from their books? Shall this be considered the Choctaw's compensation for feeding our hungry, clothing our needy, and administering to our sick? Have we, O Choctaws and Chickasaws, descended to the low estate of ruthless breaking the faith of a sacred treaty? Shall our forefathers look back from the happy hunting grounds only to see their unbroken record for justice, gratitude, and fidelity thus rudely repudiated and abruptly abandoned by an unworthy offspring?

We Choctaws and Chickasaws are a peaceful people, making our subsistence by honest toil; but mistake not, my Shawnee brethren, we are not afraid of war. Neither are we strangers to war, as those who have undertaken to encroach upon our rights in the past may abundantly testify. We are thoroughly familiar with war in all its details and we know full well all its horrible consequences ... War is an awful thing. If we go into this war against the Americans, we must be prepared to accept its inevitable results. Not only will it foretoken deadly conflict with neighbors and death to warriors, but it will mean suffering for our women, hunger and starvation for our children, grief to our loved ones, and devastation to our beloved homes. Not withstanding these difficulties, if the cause be just, we should not hesitate to defend our rights to the last man, but before that fatal step is irrevocably taken, it is well that we fully understand and seriously consider the full portent and consequences of the act.

Hear me, O Choctaws and Chickasaws, for I speak truly for your welfare. . . .

(The warriors overwhelmingly supported Pushmataha, which caused Tecumseh to declare that Pushmataha was a coward and that the Choctaws and the Chickasaws warriors were squaws. As rebuttal, Pushmataha made another statement, speaking as follows:)   Halt Tecumseh! Listen to me, you have come here, as you have often gone elsewhere, with a purpose to involve peaceful people in unnecessary trouble with their neighbors. Our people have had no undue friction with the whites. Why? Because we have had no leaders stirring up strife to serve their selfish, personal ambitions. You heard me say that our people are a peaceful people. They make their way, not by ravages upon their neighbors but by honest toil. In that regard they have nothing in common with you. I know your history well. You are a disturber. You have ever been a trouble maker. When you have found yourself unable to pick a quarrel with the white man, you have stirred up strife between different tribes of your own race.

Not only that, you are a monarch and unyielding tyrant within your own domain; Every Shawnee man, women and child must bow in humble submission to your impervious will. The Choctaws and Chickasaws have no monarchs. Their Chieftains do not undertake the mastery of their people, but rather they are the people's servants, elected to serve the will of the majority. The majority has spoken on this question and it has spoken against your contention. Their decision has therefore become the law of the Choctaws and Chickasaws and Pushmataha will see that the will of the majority so recently expressed is rigidly carried out to the letter.

If after this decision, any Choctaw should be so foolish as to follow your imprudent advice and enlist to fight against the Americans, thereby abandoning his own people and turning against the decision of his own Council, Pushmataha will see that proper punishment is meted out to him, which is death. You have made your choice; you have elected to fight with the British. The Americans have been our friends, and we shall stand by them. We will furnish you safe conduct back to the boundaries of this nation as properly befits the dignity of your office.

Farewell, Tecumseh. You will see Pushmataha no more until we meet on the fateful warpath.

At the beginning of the War of 1812, Tecumseh went to Canada where he was highly esteemed. The British commissioned him a brigadier general in their forces.

Tecumseh was killed in battle on the Thamas River, near Chatham, Ontario, on October 5, 1813.

We have sometimes wondered how some of those early day Indian speeches got to be in written form. Some of them had to be spontaneous, yet could be so comprehensive and well said. They had developed marvelous memories and power of concentration.

What is the mental phenomenon? A mental imprint is obtained and retained for a time by concentrating and fixing the subject matter firmly in mind, enabling the person to recall and recite perfectly without benefit of script or notes. The Indian's mind had been trained to do this for centuries, which gave him this great and useful faculty.

As an example of what can be done, we recently witnessed a white man take a magazine (*Time*) with 60-70 pages, separate all of the pages into single sheets, hand them out to individuals in the audience and have them call out the number of the page he held. He then would tell what was on the page. He could do this for evey page of the current magazine used.

He said that he did not have a photographic mind, that it was a matter of concentration that any one could do. He would read the magazine and concentrate on it just before he enacted the deed. He was a banker at Freeman, South Dakota; named John Waltner and not a professional at this type of thing.

We have often observed Indians attending a council or meeting, just sitting quietly and perhaps looking at nothing and saying nothing (some would say looking dumb). After a little time they would come to attention and were ready to speak or make a lengthy speech. They were concentrating on what they were going to say and formulating their speech word by word. The white man might think that they were just dumb.

It is remarkable how accurate they could be and the remarkable choice of words and correct English used, when speaking in English or being translated into English.

It is a phenomenal gift or talent which the race has developed to such perfection, perhaps paralleling the accomplishment of the musician or the artist.

The Appaloosa horse was developed and standardized by the Nez Perce of Idaho. Refer to pages 39 and 40.

CHAPTER 3: RELIGION

Religion—Extrasensory Perception—The Case of The Dog—
Harmony With God—God Communicating With His Crea-
tures—Lamb Of God—Yes, The Animals Are a Noble Species—
The Circle—The Number Four—The Family—The Influence of
the Early Christian Missionaries—Influence of The Christians—
Philip Cook—Handsome Lake—The Pauite Wovoka—Black
Elk—Black Elk Laments—Vine Deloria Sr.—Prayer Of a New
Indian—Indian Version Of The Twenty-Third Psalm—Religion
As Chief Seattle Saw It—Ella Deloria-Indians Working In The
Church—Mahpiyato, Blue Cloud—Webster Two Hawk—

One cannot write about Indians without delving into religion,
nor can he properly understand them without some in-depth ex-
ploration into their inherited subconscious minds and the moral
precepts ingrained in them over many centuries. They are a very
homogeneous people, especially within their tribe.

Their concept of harmony with God, which they call the Great
Spirit or Mystery Spirit, who created all things and abides in all
of His Creations, the animals, the trees, the mountains, the lakes,
the sun, the rain, and all earthly things, as well as man himself.
This sense of harmony and its attainment with nature dominates
all of their religious beliefs. They seek to communicate with the
Great Spirit by learning to interpret and understand the animals
and what the Great Spirit says to them and through them. It is
apparent that the Great Spirit has endowed all of His creatures
with certain knowledge and directs them what to do. All forms
of life are born with instincts, directions from God.

This does not mean that the Indians worshipped the animals,
or revered the wild plum bush or the wild rose bush, which for
some reason he came to believe to be sacred. It is to understand
and contact the Creator better. There are other things and events
which they interpret and wove into meanings (holy meanings),

such as the circle or the hoop, the numbers four and seven, the meaning of the different directions, and others all of which we will go into detail later on.

Suffice it to say here that the Indian appeals to the Great Spirit by talking or chanting with uplifted eyes and arms, by ceremonials, dances and sacrifices. He tries to get the attention of the Father, Great Spirit or one of the sub-gods, such as the Rain God, War God, etc. to make his wishes known or to give his thanks for a good crop or good hunting or whatever.

We, the white people, believe that our body is the temple of God and that He dwells within us. The Indians believe that God also dwells within all objects of His creation. He is everywhere and in all things and in our presence at all times. He believes that the Great Spirit Creator loves and directs His creatures in everyday life and that He does communicate with them. The method of communication varies from species to species. At least faculties for sending and receiving messages are inborn, build-in, or, as we may say, instincts. He believes that harmony is necessary if one is to feel the presence of the Great Spirit; to appeal to Him for help, guidance or victory, or to give thanks for good crops and hunting harvests. He must study and seek ways to conform in harmony with the Great Spirit and all creatures. He knows that all creatures and inanimate things dwell in harmony with the Creator. He can learn from the animals, and so devotes much time to the study of them, and to the probing into the mysteries of the Mystery Spirit.

The world was believed to be filled with spirits that could give advice, help and by fasting and solitary vigils, men sought the guardianship of a spirit in a dream or vision. Sometimes, while seeking the supernatural, a song would occur to an Indian, and thereafter he might sing the song to help regain communications with his spiritual guardian.

Many of the great Indian spiritual leaders have claimed to have talked with God on some mountain or secret place, or had a vision or dreams. Some of these became legendary, others wound up in a flop.

If we encounter some of the unusual visions or dreams of our own, can we always understand their meaning and significance or get a positive message? Certainly we are still "babes in the woods" when it comes to communicating or understanding the all-prevailing Great Spirit or lesser spirits.

I should like to quote the wisdom of Ethel Percy Andrus on

empathy. " . . . feeling of projecting oneself into another until we can understand what the other says and thinks and dreams." The interesting thing, perhaps, about empathy is that we know that it is an ability we can learn to develop in ourselves, and that can be successfully cultivated.

"Of some people it is said that their instinctive penetration can detect the feelings of others and so often embarrass their opponents—reading aloud their secret motives."

Extrasensory Perception
(Clairvoyance, telepathy and other psychic)
A Gallup poll released in June found that fifty-one percent of U.S. adults believe in extrasensory perception.

The Case of the Dog
Someone has said that a dog receives, by direct radiation waves of some kind—and knows whether or not a person meeting him is afraid of him, and will react towards that person according to his findings. If the person is afraid of him, he may attack, or run a bluff.

If the person is truly not afraid of him, he will know it and be friendly with that person. A dog will meet some persons with friendliness and another person with threats. But you cannot bluff him. On that score he has your measure for sure.

I know that there are premonitions that come to people because I have seen it happen numbers of times, and I have had experiences of my own, which left a predominant mood or impression of something not of this world. You cannot explain it, a "something" which impresses you and you are not likely ever to forget it—the word spoken which you hear, the quality-sound of the voice, or the direct stare of a person which you see in a dream or vision and which you cannot be mistaken about. It leaves a lasting impression, and leaves no doubt in our mind that it was not an ordinary dream, of this earth.

We recently were very much interested in something our mother explained had appeared to her. She was in her ninety-seventh year and recently confined to a wheelchair due to a broken hip. I know exactly what she meant, when she was so impressed and knew that it was not something of this earth. She said that she had talked to someone, Christ or an angel. She asked him: "How are my husband and three daughters?" who had departed this life, and when would she be going to join them? The answer was, "They are here and the time is soon."

When I was in my early teens, an aunt came to visit us in our home for a week. One day she was deeply disturbed and kept saying, over and over: "I wonder how Elmer is, I wonder how Elmer is?" Elmer was her sister's husband who was a railroad engineer or conductor in Idaho. That evening we got a telegram saying that Elmer had fallen underneath a train, cutting him in two. I know this to be a fact because I heard her myself, before it happened.

I believe that similar experiences occur to many people, but they may be puzzled and never mention it to anyone, and we never hear about them.

Harmony with God

The Indian believes that the Great Spirit speaks to man through all His works—does not speak directly to man but His knowledge and wisdom are with the animals and all created things.

The spirit world of the Indians is a world in which the animals, the birds, all growing things, the sky, and the great earth itself had voices through which they could talk with man. They believed that the Great Spirit may not speak directly to man but His knowledge and wisdom flow from the animals and all created things. Everything is for a purpose. All life is a struggle between the powers of Light and the powers of Darkness, and man must attune his ear to Nature, the only source from which he might hear the truth.

The Indian sees God's translation by the being and manifestations of the Great Spirit in the being of animals. They are created by God and endowed by Him, with certain qualities and characteristics. They think that He manifests Himself through these creatures and they look to them for His revelations and communications for themselves. Therefore their almost and sometimes reverent attitude towards these, His creatures. Some tribes have a similar reverence towards certain plants, as the sagebrush and cottonwood tree.

How do we fathom this reverence by our process of reasoning and logic to get to the bottom of an understanding of the Indian's inner feeling, and perhaps gain something from the experience for our own spiritual enrichment?

Artists and persons with some artistic emotions and understanding of certain arts, such as beauty, rhythm, harmony, order, etc., can sense and enjoy these things which may appear senseless and meaningless to others of less insight or understanding.

Some can see and enjoy it more than others do, as with any work of art. To understand and thrill at this can move us to a great love and desire for same. It can only be a marvel of God and His wonderful creation and we want more of it and be closer bound to it.

Some tribes came to consider certain animals and plants as holy and sacred. They may venerate the eagle or some other animal (as do the people of India who consider the cow sacred and deserving of their protection and veneration).

The late Mabelle Land DeKay, M.A. of the University of Wyoming described and portrayed the Indian philosophy so well in her famous pageant, *Vedauwoo, Earthborn Spirit*:

" . . . for its basic philosophy is: That the Great Spirit speaks to man through His works; that man with every breath of air draws in life from the One-On-High; that man high solitudes communicates with holy spirits to learn holy things; that the One-Above does not speak directly to man, but his knowledge and wisdom are with the animals and all created things, that the earth was made in kindness, covered with love and finished in beauty. So all is beautiful, . . . their poetic phraseology which voices the depth and dignity of Indian thought and feelings about the creation of the world."

God Communicates with His Creatures

The Lord answered Job out of the whirlwind. He used parables of animals to convey His message to Job (Chapter 39). God was telling Job that He and not Job made the animals and caused them to do their thing. He built in His communication system with His creatures and they understand what to do and obey His ordained decree.

The Bible tells us that God, at the completion of the earth, was well pleased with His product. He no doubt loved His animals, as we also do. Yes, we love our dogs, horses and other animals.

God says He tells the animals what to do. He provides for their needs and protects them. The young ravens cry unto God. God's great love is in the animals. His love is greater than man's. I believe that no one understands and appreciates these things better than does the Indian. It is to love God in a fuller sense.

What makes the dog so faithful? He appreciates and feels the love of God and man. He hesitates not to lay down his life for love and faithfulness to his devoted master. (No greater love, has man

61

than this.) Does not this spirit come from God? Who can say that animals do not have a sense and feeling of the presence of a Creator? Can we agree with the "man of cloth" when he says that man is the only creature who can worship God?

Lamb of God

The Bible calls Jesus the "Lamb of God."

Lamb of God has a three-tiered interpretation: (1) the conquering lamb of Jewish literature that will destroy evil in the world; (2) the silent lamb that stands for the suffering servant of Old Testament prophecy, who even though oppressed and afflicted remains quiet and non-violent "like a lamb that is led to the slaughter" (Is. 53:7); (3) the victim lamb of the Passover, whose blood was smeared on the doorposts and lintels of the Israelites so that they might be saved from the bloodshed of their first-born (Ex.12:3–13).

God loves His animals and communicates with them by instinct and perhaps by other means also. He ranks the lamb with Christ and calls Christ the Lamb of God. The lamb represents love and purity, innocence, sacrifice and non-violence.

Can we say that animals do have an inner feeling or consciousness of a Creator? And, in turn, can we say that they do communicate with their maker? What gives them the instinct and fear of death and harm? Do they rely upon their Creator to protect and guide them? Do they render thanks to Him?

Let us think on these things and endeavor to get more understanding and enlightment of same! The mysteries of God are many and fascinating. Can God's love for the animals go unreciprocated?

Many a farmer hears his animals speak and understands what they say. Oftentimes I heard my hogs talking as I came near where they were. I understood their voices—whether they were out of food, were thirsty, or having some other trouble, or if they were happy or if maybe a mother sow was looking for her babies who may have been separated from her for some reason.

One winter day I entered the shed where a bunch of medium sized pigs were. They about filled the place, but as I entered one pig immediately caught my eye. He was about in the middle, just separated enough from the others to standout. His head drooped as did his ears, a little gaunt and sad eyes, he pathetically was saying, as plain as could be; "I am sick, do something for me!" I know that the other pigs were cooperating with him to put across his message, by making him stand-out so I would see him. I got my instrument and gave him a shot of cambiotics. It was not long before he was recovered and going about normally. I think his faith made him well. (The faith that I could help him.)

There are many obvious cases when our pet dogs and cats learn to understand what we say and obey our orders. They also do tell us what they want. Many similar cases can be cited. It is a matter of being in harmony and trying to understand.

Yes, God loves His animals and so do we! And love creates understanding between each other.

Could it be that when people say that they talk to their plants and rocks that is is not necessarily a joke? And that they do respond to TLC?

YES, THE ANIMALS ARE A NOBLE SPECIES!

The Indians evolved and developed concepts and interpretation over many centuries. They had no written language nor a written Bible. They passed their knowledge and beliefs down from grandparent or parents to the children. Their interpretations were imprinted on the young minds with strict and exact interpretation of words and meaning. They had to depend upon memory for recording and preservation. They developed a very strong and unwavering memory.

There is a similarity among most of the hundreds of tribes in certain aspects of their religion. There are also similarities between their religious beliefs and that of the white race. The Indian believes in and worships a "One God" concept. They believed in a Great Spirit or Great Mystery, as they called Him; we call Him the Holy Spirit or Holy Ghost. They had their sub-gods, such as the Rain God, Harvest God, Hunting God, or War God, which they appealed to for specific purposes; as does the white man appeal to his saints, such as to St. Anthony for recovery of some lost article. They tried to make their wants and needs known to the Great Spirit or sub-gods, as does the white man. They tried to attract His attention to their pleas and supplications for help and protection, or to give thanks. They attempted to demonstrate their beliefs and faith in Him, and their worthiness by ceremonies and sometimes sacrifices, including self-torture often to the point of death, and in some tribes they gave a human sacrifice of a member of their tribe. They gave burnt offerings and fasted. Their belief was strong enough to inspire them to make the supreme sacrifice to demonstrate their belief and faith.

In order to demonstrate their beliefs, faith and worthiness of His love, they devised several and various ceremonies which they practiced. These were of the nature of dances or powwows. The Bible tells us that David danced "with all his might" and his musicians played before the Lord. Have not all of our white-man churches and religious organizations formulated ceremonies and formalities for their religious expressions and appeals to God?

The Europeans brought Christ to America. Indians have no firm record of Creation, of an Abraham, a Moses, or a Christ, as we do. They do have legionary concepts of similar events, places and personalities. They do not have any firm record, written historical revelations, and only a few archaeological findings to support their legendary concepts of these things. Whether they are just induced hallucinations and myths or spirit-world communications—who can say?

There is a remote story that Christ visited South America after his Holyland life on earth. However, we believe that Christ at the end of His life on earth charged man, beginning with a nucleus, to spread the gospel to the whole world.

The Mandan Indians had a story of a great flood, and a big canoe landing on a high mountain in the west—and a morning dove returning with a willow bough—and the saving of a family, all others lost.

The Navahos have a myth about a great bird carrying them from their ancient home in Canada to a place in Arizona. There are other references to a flood. Chief Red Fox said that there is found in the folklore of all Indian tribes a legend of a flood. Perhaps they have deducted this from the findings of sea fossils in places high on mountains and the far north—even to the Arctic Circle—a sign that warm water had been there at one time.

Many tribes have a legend that the Great Spirit had His abode in the hills or mountains (the Sioux in the Black Hills), even as gods of ancient Greece lived on Mount Olympus.

The Circle

To better understand Black Elk we should know the significance of the hoop and the flowering tree to the Indians. There are several generally similar versions by the different Indian tribes. Lets hear Black Elk's version:

Hoop—everything an Indian does is in a circle, and that is because the POWER of the World always works in circles and everything tries to be round . . . so long as the hoop was unbroken, the people flourished. The flowering tree was the living center of the hoop, and the circle of the four quarters nourished it. The east gave peace and light, the south gave warmth, the west gave rain, and the north with its cold and mighty wind gave strength and endurance. This knowledge came to us from the Outer world with our religion. Everything the Power of the World does is done in a circle. The sky is round like a ball and I have heard that the earth is round and so are the stars. The wind in its greatest power whirls, Birds make their nests in circles, for theirs is the same religion as ours. The Sun comes forth and goes down again in a circle. The moon does the same, and both are round. Even the seasons form a great circle in their changing and always come back again to where they were. The life of a man is a circle from childhood to childhood, and so it is in everything where power moves. Our tepees were round like the nests of birds, and these were always set in a circle, the nations hoop, a nest of many nests, where the Great Spirit meant for us to hatch our children. The dog circles before he lies down.

But the Wasechus (white man) have put us in these square boxes. Our power is gone and we are dying, for the power is not in us any more. You can look at our boys and see how it is with us. When we were living by the power of the circle in the way we should, boys were men at twelve or thirteen years of age. But now it takes them much longer to mature.

Well, it is as it is. We are prisoners of war while we are waiting here. But there is another world.

The south is the source of life—and does not the flowering stick truly come from there? . . . Man advances from there towards the setting sun of his life, then approach the colder north where the white hairs are. And does he not then arrive, if he lives, at the source of light and understanding, which is the east? Then does he not return to where he began, to his second childhood, there to give back his life to all life and his flesh to the earth whence it came?

The more you think about this the more meaning you will see in it. The circle has no beginning and no end.

The Number Four

The number "four" was considered a sacred number by most tribes in the days of yore—there are the four directions, west, north, east and south; four divisions of time, the day, the night, the moon (twenty-eight days) and the year; four parts of everything that grows from the ground: the roots, the stem, the leaves and the fruit; four kind of things that breathe: those that crawl, those that fly, those that walk on four legs, those that walk on two legs.

Four things above the world: the sun, the moon, the sky and the stars; four kinds of Gods: the Great God, the associates of the Great God, gods below them and the spirit-kind; four periods of human life: babyhood, childhood, adulthood, and old age; and finally man has four fingers on each hand, four toes on each foot and the thumbs and the big toes taken together form four.

Since the Great Spirit caused everything to be done in fours, man himself should do everything possible in fours.

The Family

Black Elk calls the Great Spirit "my grandfather" when addressing Him. All tribes of Indians have a great veneration and respect for their parents and grandparents—they considered themselves as children of God, and that He is a real member of their family. This is a part and strength in their strong adherence to the family unit. Father means greatness and authority. The Great Spirit and Creator is grandfather; the Great White Father sits in Washington; our own father heads the family; men are brothers to each other and children of God. God made His children of various colors like the rainbow—red, white, black, and yellow.

The Influence of the Early Christian Missionaries

One of the greatest incentives bringing the Pilgrims and pioneer settlers to the new continent was to find religious freedom.

The burning sense of mission, coupled with deteriorating economic conditions at their home in Europe and the growing despotism of Charles I and the feeling that the mother country was doomed to "general calamity" led many Puritans to risk the Atlantic.

The Puritans and the Pilgrims were grim, earnest men, disenchanted with the "corruption" of the Anglican Church. They came to practice the positive part of Church Reformation and propagate the gospel in America. They were hard workers, believed in self-denial and preached sermons laced with threats of everlasting fire for the sinner. They planted Protestantism along the Atlantic coast, between the French Catholics in Canada and the Spanish Catholics along the Gulf of Mexico.

Besides seeking religious freedom for themselves they were determined to propagate their faith among the Indians, who were their neighbors, originally friendly and helpful towards them.

It was easy and natural for the Indian to accept the Christian religion and to incorporate it into their own religion. But there were problems for them and some of them turned to reject the white man's attitude towards living up to its tenets. Because of that fact some of them rejected the Christian religion or sometimes only the church while accepting the Christian gospel.

The early day Indian could not understand why the white man preached one thing and then would not practice it. In other words he considered the white man a hypocrite. Even to this day there are Indians, including Christian ministers, who consider the white man as a religious hypocrite. The Indians were a very homogeneous people. They were very united in their ideas and principles. They lived their religion every day—always conscious of the fact that the Great Spirit was always present among them. He never stole from or lied to anyone except an enemy. He did not consider it a sin to steal from or even kill an enemy. That trait is still held by many present-day Indians.

Influence of the Christians

The Spanish missionaries of the Catholic Church were the first invaders. They pushed their way from Florida, west along the present southern border states to California. Their purpose was to win the Indians for the Church and the Spanish Crown. Connected with each mission was a presidio, a small fort whose handful of soldiers were supposed to guard against threats from without and sin from within. Some miscreants and backsliders were forced into slavery, or even executed. These captive Indians were used to do the labor building these missions. The missions were spaced to be about one day's travel apart.

The Catholic Church has claimed converts among the Rio Grande Pueblos for over three-hundred years and most of the Indians make use of some services provided by the Church (baptism, confirmation, marriages, burials) but the importance of the native religion has not diminished. The two religious systems are separate and the Indians find nothing inconsistent in making use of both.

The Catholic Church gave all baptized Indians Spanish names, which they retain to this day, along with their Indian names. All

Pueblo Indians and many others speak Spanish fluently as well as their Indian language. The imprint of the Spanish people and government and the Catholic Church was well implanted in the culture and life of the Indian people of the Southwest. But they still retain much of their native culture and religion.

The Southwest tribes have not been disturbed too much by the intruding whites as were the Indians of the other parts of the nation. They had their differences and uprisings, wars and killings. But they still occupy practically the same ground, for the last thousand years. They have taken advantages of parts of both cultures for their own benefit, and it has resulted pretty well in their stability—to live among the whites.

Pueblo Indian life is based on the fundamental religious conviction that they must live in harmony with the natural world about them. So strong is this belief that it is not possible to separate religion from the everyday life of the Pueblos. The dances and ceremonies that are performed throughout the year are enactments of this philosophy.

Societies headed by priests within each pueblo are responsible for maintaining harmony with the supernatural world. Properly conducted ceremonies will control the weather, effect cures, bring rain, mature crops, and insure success in hunting.

John Collier said: "These men (Taos) were at one with their gods."

Philip Cook (Mohawk), on the St. Regis Reservation in the early colonial days, was one of the several, interested and investigative leaders. He contributed to a paper written by Mad Bear, and titled "Does a Small Nation Have the Right to Exist?" It contains some caustic remarks on the behavior of the "so-called" white father in his relations with the Six Federated Indian Nations.

There was a time, he said, "when I wasn't a human being, I didn't have a heart here—I had a piece of lead! When I'd see a white man on the reservation, my hair would stand up on my head."

He knew then that he must break with the Catholic Church. He had, besides, come to realize that whole races of men, including the great Indian civilizations of Central and South America, had flourished over periods of thousands of years and then became almost extinct before God had provided solutions through Christ—and what kind of God was that?

Many Indians were embittered so deeply that they said, "If this be an act of a Christian nation, we will cling to the faith of our fathers and reject Christianity forever." The strength of the non-Christian part of the Six Nations dates from the fraudulent treaty, and to this day, they recite the frauds of Buffalo Creek as a reason why Christians should not be trusted. He blamed the missionaries and the white schools with liquor as a cause of his people's deterioration.

There are a large number of Iroquois who still live in the Indian world and for whom the Great Spirit, the Tadodaho, Deganawida, and the Hayowentha are more real than the Christian Trinity, the President of the U.S., George Washington and Thomas Jefferson.

It is of interest to note how the career of Philip Cook developed. Though still repudiating the Christian cult of the whites, he fulfilled a religious vocation which was deeply and strongly felt. (Only two men at St. Regis were able to recite the code.) (Handsom Lake's dream.)

Philip Cook, with his scholarly turn of mind, recognized the Christian influence in the Handsome Lake religion, but in turning his back on the Church, he had not rejected Jesus, and this was primarily an Indian cult which had never been a cult of the white man.

Cook told a couple of Mormon missionaries about the Handsome Lake religion.

He told them that what was needed was a faith that was founded upon the primary truths (such as human brotherhood), and which did not allow itself to be alienated from them. He asked them when the Mormon's religion had broken off from the Catholic Church—the Mormon missionary replied that it had never done so, that the Mormons did possess the fundamental religion, which had never been connected with the Catholic Church, that the revelation from heaven had come direct to Joseph Smith at Palmyra, right here in New York State: that their holy book dealt with the Indians and showed how they had come from Jerusalem. They were descendants of the lost tribes of Israel. When he dictated the Book of Mormon, he put into it the story of the prophet Lehi, who left Jerusalem in Ad 600 and sailed to America in a kind of ark. Lehi and his family were originally white, but some of them turned out so badly that God cursed them by making them red.

At the end of the eighteenth century, a prophet and religious reformer arose among the Senecas. He was known by his English name as Handsome Lake (1735-1813). He had been influenced by the Quaker missionaries. He apparently had repented of the errors of his life, and was seeking, so to speak, to find the "Way" (or find himself, as many say today). He claimed to have had a vision, and thought he heard voices calling to him. They told him that the Creator was much displeased at the drunkenness of his people. That he, who had been a hard drinker himself, had been forced by his illness to abstain from drinking and to think about the Creator. They announced that a fourth person would later arrive. When in a further dream, this fourth person did appear and declare to Handsome Lake that he pitied him and was going to take him away, he felt that he was talking with the Creator himself.

Handsome Lake recovered from his illness. He declared that the four divine messengers had made him a revelation in which he was ordered to preach to his people to save them from corruption and degradation.

From these visions he was instructed to form a moral code and to perpetuate it. The vision process was somewhat like that which produced the Koran. Like Mohammed, the Iroquois prophet simply repeated the message, never writing anything down. His grandson became his disciple, and his English name was James Johnson. Johnson established an oral text—"Good Message"—which had circulation almost everywhere in the Iroquois world and has survived to this day from the early nineteenth century.

The "Good Message" is recited in the long-house (Church of the Old Remnant of Indian Cult) every other year, in three or four installments for successive mornings. It has retained the authority of scripture for those Indians who are seriously religious but who have not accepted Christianity.

The Pauite, Wovoka, Author of the
Ghost Dance, and the Man Who
Talked with God — 1888

Was the Pauite visionary a master of hypnotism who inducted his own beliefs into the minds of others? Were his tribesmen, and later thousands of other Indians, caught up in an auto-suggestive mass hypnosis? Perhaps, but no one can say for sure.

It was a form of religious ectsacy brought out of the abasement and suffering of a racial minority, but probably the deepest and truest meaning of the Ghost Dance must always remain a mystery to us. Divergent beliefs arose from many interpretations. Many representatives from most if not all other tribes went to see this

70

man for themselves. Each tribe saw the movement in a different light and worked the teaching of the biblical Messiah into their own lore. The movement developed around one basic thought— the time was coming when the entire Indian race, both living and dead, would be brought together upon an earth which had grown new again. There would be no more disease, no want and no death, and the regenerated earth would provide, out of her great bounty, for the needs of the Indians.

Some said the white man would disappear and the Indian would be restored to his domain. And that the buffalo would come back.

By this time, the latter quarter of the nineteenth century, all of the tribes had become exposed to the Christian religion, and many of them related Wovoka to the Christ of whom they had heard. In their eyes, the white man had not followed the teachings of the Bible. They believed that Christ had returned as an Indian to his chosen children and became the true Son of God to thousands of them. Wovoka said many times that he was merely a prophet of divine revelation who had talked to God and who had returned with a message of peace and promise (similar to Moses).

The fanaticism of the movement was smothered by the debacle at Wounded Knee, when the Ghost Shirts had not prevailed against the thunder sticks.

Thus the mighty Sioux Nation was crushed and with it perished the bright hope of the Indians from the Navaho country north to Canada and from California eastward to the Mississippi River.

Wovoka had misread the signs or he had misinterpreted the vision, or did he have a pipe dream? Whatever we believe he received, it was a divine message but those of an adverse mind brought about its distortion and defeat.

In any event the Sioux, a misguided people, took over and doomed the movement to destruction and failure.

Wovoka had returned from his vision from heaven with a message of peace and promise. He preached industry and non-violence in conjunction with the Ghost Dance. He said God told him to go back and tell his people they must be good and love one another and not fight, or steal or lie. The desperate Sioux took a course to the opposite. They did not follow the teaching of this man who claimed to have talked to God.

Was he a false prophet or one whose teachings fell into the power of the Evil Spirits or the Spirit of Darkness?

The Bible says there will be many false messiahs and not to be misled.

71

The Jews wandered in the wilderness for forty years—punishment for forsaking God's teaching. The Indians of America have been wandering in the wilderness of despair for two-hundred years.

God's hand is a hand of correction. Man sometimes gets to thinking too highly of himself and gets out of harmony with his Creator. We need some corrective policy to bring us back into harmony. We may need our balance wheel readjusted.

What might have happened had the Indians followed Wovoka's teaching? Could it have started Black Elk's tree to blooming again and resulted in happiness for all? But it would not have sent the white man back to Europe and repopulated America with buffalo and deer as they thought might happen.

The Sioux distorted Wovoka's movement. They did exactly what Wovoka's message said not to do. In desperation they resorted to violence. The voice of the Great Spirit fell on deaf ears for them.

Was God warning the Indians as he did the Jews? Think what He did to the people of Noah's time for not heeding His words and His warnings to them.

Does the Indian's Original Christ Like but Christless religion, suffice him now?

I am the way and the life. No one can come to the Father except by me.-Bible.

Black Elk

Black Elk, whose complete life—from a small boy to his long life—was trained and educated to be a medicine man, became one of the most famous spiritual leaders in the Indian kingdom. He ended up dejected and filled with a spirit of defeat.

Black Elk's religion was made up of many of the Indian's concepts and rituals, such as the sacred number four, the hoop (circle), the sacred pipe, the sweat lodge, etc.* It was not exactly the Christian concept and style of worship. It may have served as a sufficient means for the aborigine in his time. But in Black Elk's time, religious troubles were overtaking them. Their gods and the Great Spirit were not protecting them or bringing them the victory and success they were longing for.

Black Elk explains the hoop:

Why we always go from left to right—The South is the source of life—and does not the flowering stick truly come

* For those who would pursue further study of the origin and meaning of these Indian rituals, the books *The Sacred Pipe, Black Elk Speaks,* and others are recommended reading.

72

from there? Man advances from there towards the setting sun of his life, then approach the colder north where the white hairs are. And does he not then arrive, if he lives, at the source of light and understanding which is the East? Then does he not return to where he began to his second childhood, there to give back his life to all life, and his flesh to the earth whence it came?

Such theorizing is very logical but God's way transcends pure human-limited theorizing. The Way of the Cross supersedes all other ways, since Christ led the way for all mankind.

The Ghost Dance ceremony, which developed from the vision of Wovoka, the Pauite, turned out to be a craze that swept the western Indian nations as their last great hope to save their homeland and their Indian world. It collapsed and left them in despair.

The final curtain came down for the old man (Black Elk) as he stood at their Holy Spot on Harney Peak in the Black Hills of South Dakota for his last appeal and confession to the Great Spirit. It is a classical portrayal of a noble episode.

Black Elk Laments: With tears running O, Great Spirit, my grandfather, with running eyes, I must say that the tree has never bloomed. A pitiful old man you see me here and I have fallen away and have done nothing. Here at the center of the world where you took me when I was young and taught me, here, old, I stand, and the tree is withered, my grandfather! Again, and may be the last time on earth, I recall the great vision you sent me. It may be that some little root of the sacred tree still lives. Nourish it then, that it may leaf and bloom and fill with singing birds. Hear me not for myself but for my people; I am old. Hear me that they may once more go back in the sacred hoop and find the good road, the shielding tree.

For some minutes the old man stood silent, with face and arms uplifted, weeping in the drizzling rain. In a little while the sky was clear again.

These episodes should be preserved by history and literature, in memory and honor of a noble race's passing culture, and for what it has contributed to the culture and honor of our country.

Did Black's Elk's lifelong sacrificial religion fail him and his people? Is it an indication that the Indian's Christ-less religion needed to change and advance to a better one with the process of evolution and progress? Had the time come for them to embrace the religion of Christ to replace their own? Was that the message God was telling them? Was their religion dying also of old age? Better the new Indian recognize this fact and direct his effort's to finding God, the Great Spirit on a different level—conform or die is a universal law!

The old medicine man felt defeated and humiliated, tearful, sorrowful, and in a state of repentance and appealing for guidance. Humiliation itself is the Spirit of God. Christ's whole life and death on earth exemplified this fact. God surely heard his prayer and answered it in a way He knew to be best. Perhaps, his experiences lead his people to a better communication and life with God—and fulfilled His life purpose after all.

Vine Deloria, Sr.

Reverend Vine Deloria, Sr. Archdeacon, was a son of a Yankton war chief, who was one of the earliest Christian ministers among the Plains tribesmen at the time of Sitting Bull. By heredity he was both a war chief and a minister. In his many years in the Episcopal Church he has brought the faith to hundreds of hamlets and backcountry villages of the Dakota Sioux. He said: "I live in fear! Fear that the white man will kill himself and all of us. Can he be saved from himself? Will he be damned? Go to hell before he is saved? I wonder. The white man is going to hell right now." (He, himself is a white Indian.)

This retired minister of the Christian gospel had devoted a lifetime to proselytizing Christianity. From parish to parish and village to village to preach "the gospel of the white man to my Indian people."

He had come to doubt not the gospel but the white man, and his thoughts returned more and more to the gospel of the Indians. The minister had retreated behind the curtain of his suburban home to prepare for the religious battle: "with my own soul" he said.

I live in fear! I live in fear! he said once more. There is no man I hate, no matter who he is or what he is. But I live in fear of the white man, I fear the death he possesses. I fear the violence that is in him. And I would not be surprised if one day the white man killed himself, and all of us. I live in terrible fear of that.

The white man hates himself. And he hates the Great

Spirit. I think of that sometimes. Why else would the white man do the things he does? The things he has done to the Indians? To everyone? I do not believe that the white man feels guilty, as they say: he is too full of hate.

Can the white man be saved from himself? I wonder. Will he have to be damned? I wonder. Will he have to go to hell before he is saved? I wonder. The white man is going to hell right now!

(One fellow Churchman, a long-time friend, said gloomily! "I just do not know why the old man says things like that. He's half white you know.")

The retired minister said further: The ways of our fore-fathers have not passed away. My father is in my heart often these days. Religion is strong in the hearts of my people. It is in my heart too. Sometimes I despair of the white man's ever becoming a Christian. Some times the Holy Bible does not seem to teach people anything. And the Lord seems to have foresaken us. I go down in the basement of my home when I feel that way. I pick up my drum and beat it quietly. Quietly so the Lord will not be offended. Though I think the Lord will not mind the drum.

I feel better then, I feel Indian—Taken from the *Rosebud Sioux Herald*—Eyapaha) May we advise him?

Put away your fears. Revive your faith. Replace the fear with reposed confidence and joy. Let the Great Spirit dwell in your heart and being. That will serve you and others better. The power of God and His fatherly love encompasses all things and cannot be broken as can the power of the hoop. The white man may be on track towards hell. But he did most to make you what you are today. Love is the antidote for fear. Praise God from whom all blessing flow. We know you will.

Vine Deloria, Sr. Spoke at Cook (Christian College for Indians) Tempe, Arizona (1977).

The Reverend Vine Deloria, Sr., retired Episcopal priest who now lives in Pierre, S.D., was the guest speaker for this year's Spiritual Emphasis Week at Cook Christian Training School, Tempe, Arizona.

The warmth of his smile and the sparkle in his eyes belied the 77 years of combat against the forces of evil in this world. The love of God shone through this old Dakota warrior and touched the heart of each and every person present.

When he opened his mouth, it was the traditional Indian Orator who spoke, weaving the magic that gripped his listeners like a spell, bringing them to the verge of the lump in the throat with tender memories of days and people long gone, leading them along the dark and shadowy trails of deep and meaningful thought, pushing out into the sunshine of the love of Jesus Christ.

Fr. Deloria indicated he felt he could find those things in the Dakota culture and situation that could speak to all American Indians regardless of their own tribal origin.

Over the years he declared, something has happened to the Indian and the Christian religion.

Fr. Deloria emphasized Jesus' development along the four potentials (The figure Four again)—mental, physical, spiritual, and moral—and pointed out the marvelously balanced development, "The Church," he said, "has forgotten this aspect of the Christ—the balanced development."

Notice that Fr. Deloria says something has happened to the Indian and the Christian Religion over the years. Notice also that he emphasizes balanced development. Balance in all things, is one of the most fundamental factors in God's universe.

LONG MAY HIS TREE BLOOM!
PRAYER OF A NEW INDIAN

Our Indian people are a praying people. Down through the centuries they have always believed in prayer. They pray beautiful prayers, prayers that touch your heart and make you cry. They are sincere when they pray. Most of their prayers are prayers of thanksgiving to the Great Spirit, prayers for the healing of the sick and prayers for their children.

It is so important to know how to pray. How to get in touch with God. Prayer brings to us faith, forgiveness, peace, assurance, joy, healing, wisdom, provision, protection and many other gifts from God. To receive these gifts we must learn to pray.

First, when we pray, we must come before God with a pure heart. God is holy and cannot look upon sin. If our heart is filled with sin, He will not hear. We must sincerely ask Him to cleanse our heart from every sin. Then and only then, will He hear us when we pray.

Psalm 66:18: "He would not have listened if I had not confessed my sins."

Isaiah 59:2: "But the trouble is that your sins have cut you off from God. Because of sin he has turned his face away from you and will not listen anymore."

God will hear you when you pray to be saved from all your sins. This is the first step in prayer. You must ask Him. You call upon His name. He will save you. He will save you now.

"For everyone who calls on the name of the Lord will be saved from the punishment of sin" (Romans 10:13).

Second, we must pray in Jesus' name. God will not hear us in any other way. Jesus Christ is the Son of God. He is the One we must go through to reach the Father.

He wants all people to be saved from punishment of sin. He wants them to come to know the truth. There is one Man standing between God and men. That man is Christ Jesus (1 Timothy 2:4,5).

Jesus said "I am the Way and the Truth and the Life, No one can go to the Father except by Me" (St. John 14:6).

Third; we must pray in faith, We must believe God's Word and trust Him for the answer to our prayer. He has promised and will not go back on His word. He will do all we ask in His perfect will.

"We are sure that if we ask anything that He wants us to have, He will hear us. If we are sure He hears us when we ask, we can be sure He will give us what we ask for" (1 John 5:14,15).

"—I say to you, whatever you ask for when you pray, have faith that you will receive it. Then you will get it" (St. Mark 11:24).

By Thomas Claus,
Editor Indian Life Sept./Nov. 1976

Another quote from Thomas Claus:

Do you know why the Bible is such a precious book to our Indian people? Because now we can hold the Word of God in our hands. We can read the complete plan God gave to us—for the past, present, and the future. It is truly marvelous to our eyes.

In our old ways, we had no book to guide us. The ceremonies were passed on from generation to generation by word of mouth. Therefore, they were constantly changing. We were never sure if our worship was acceptable.

But, now we can be sure our worship is acceptable because we have God's written Word, which tells us the message of Jesus—His love and forgiveness, and of His gift of eternal life.

Inscribed on a stone tablet in the Chapel at Bacone College, Muskogee, Oklahoma.

We have been broken up and moved six times. We have been despoiled of our property. We thought when we moved across the Missouri River and had paid for our homes in Kansas we were safe, but in a few years the White man wanted our country. We had good farms, built comfortable houses and big barns. We had schools for our children and churches where we listened to the same gospel the white man listened to. The white man came into our country from Missouri and drove our cattle and horses away, and if our people followed them, they were killed.

We try to forget these things, but we would not forget that the White man brought us the blessed gospel of Christ, the Christian hope. This more than pays for all we have suffered. What a NOBLE Character and a Christian spirit!

This great spirit of forgiveness which has been said and demonstrated on other occasions, truly reveals the Indian's great love for Christ—a big price he has paid: Truly a noble people from a noble race!

What Some Indian Youth are Thinking

We Can Never Forget.
It would be much easier
Just to fold our hands
And not make this fight—
To say:
I, one man
Can do nothing—
I grow afraid
Only when I see
People
Thinking and acting
Like this.
We all know the story

78

A man sat beside the trail
Too long
And it grew over
And he could never find
His way again.

We can never forget
What has happened
But we cannot go back
Nor can we just sit
Beside the trail—Poundmaker

The above was written by a Navajo Student at the South West Christian School in Peoria, Arizona.

The youth realizes his plight, and what will happen if he just sits and takes the easy way. He realizes what he must do.

The last five to ten years have been a near miracle for the Indians. The 1975 Civil Rights Act and opportunities for self-determination have aroused him to action. Both men and women, youth and even the elderly, are doing a wonderful job of resurrecting themselves for a new age and for their race. Long live America and our Indian heritage! (But far too many Indian youths are committing suicide.)

An Indian Version of the Twenty-third Psalm

The Great Father above a Shepherd Chief is. I am his, and with him I want not. He throws out to me a rope, and the name of the rope is love, and he draws me to where the grass is green and the water not dangerous, and I eat and lie down and am satisfied.

Sometimes my heart is very weak and falls down, and he lifts me up again and draws me into a good road.

His name is "Wonderful." Sometimes, it may be soon, it might be a long, long time, he will draw me into a valley. It is dark there, but I'll draw back not. I'll be afraid not. For it is in between those mountains that the Shepherd Chief will meet me, and the hunger I have in my heart all through this life will be satisfied.

Sometimes he makes the love rope into a whip, but afterwards he gives me a staff to lean upon. He spreads a table before me with all kinds of foods. He puts his hand upon my head and all the "tired" is gone. My cup he fills until it runs over. What I tell you is true. I lie not. These roads that are "way ahead" will stay with me through this life: and afterwards I will go to live in the Big Tepee and sit down with the Shepherd Chief forever.

(The above version was found in a guest book by Miss Isabel Crawford.)

Compare this version with the actual version of the Bible and get the Indian's way of saying the same thing. The beauty of language, the spirit, and the meaning are all there, said in the Indian's way of expressing his thoughts.

The writer is trying to show, in an abbreviated way, the progress, development, and problems encountered along the course from the earliest exposure of the American Indian to the gospel to the present day. We have cited a few typical examples at the different stages.

At the beginning many Indians were interested. They listened, pondered and studied it. They sought to understand it and incorporate acceptable portions of the gospel, its rituals and ceremonies, into their own worship. They rejected parts and some rejected all of it. They accepted the moral precepts which they claimed they already had and lived by.

As time moved on and the Indians came more and more in contact with and under the influence of the Europeans and their religion, the Indians gradually and progressively came closer into the white man's religion—until today most of them are as Christianized as the general population of the United States. Of course there are always a certain number who do not believe or perhaps tend to revert to the old.

When people are thrown together they absorb some of the ways of others. We have noticed this happen in the cases of the Hindus and Buddhists. Theirs are the most primitive religions of record. They started with no supreme God or Creator. But as they expanded outward and came in contact with others of the world they began to adopt some changes in their beliefs and in their seeking to find a universal life. The writer's studies indicate that Buddhism still does not recognize God. The Hindus believed in reincarnation. The Hindus believed in multitudes of deities. They believed in spirits of their ancestors.

They had their prophets or teachers. Buddha was the Enlightened One, but had no claim to divinity. Hinduism has no founder or uniform dogma. Buddhism and Hinduism were passed along orally.

80

After thousands of years these two groups of people have made very little progress—spiritually or materially. The Indians have done far better in their four-hundred years.

Indian Religion as Chief Seattle Saw It

Our religion is the traditions of our ancestors. To us the ashes of our ancestors are sacred and their resting place is hallowed ground, you wander far from the graves of your ancestors and seemingly without regret, your religion was written upon tablets of stone by the iron finger of your God, so that you could not forget. The Red man could never comprehend nor remember it. OUR RELIGION IS THE TRADITIONS OF OUR ANCESTORS—The dreams of our old men given them in solemn hours of night by the Great Spirit; and visions of our sachems, and is written in the hearts of our people.

Your dead cease to love you and the land of their nativity as soon as they pass the portals of the tomb and wander way beyond the stars. They are soon forgotten and never return. Our dead never forget the beautiful world that gave them being. They still love its verdant valleys, its murmuring rivers, its magnificent mountains, sequestered vales and verdant lined lakes and bays, and even yearn in tender, fond affection over the lonely hearted living, and often return from the Happy Hunting Ground to visit, guide, console and comfort them.

Chief Seattle (1786 - 1866 Speaks More
on the Plight of the Indian's Religion

Our God the Great Spirit, seems also to have forsaken us. Your God makes your people wax strong every day. Soon they will fill all the land. Our people are ebbing away like a rapidly receding tide that will never return. The White man's God cannot love our people or he would protect them. They seem to be orphans who can look no where for help. How can we be brothers? How can your God become our God and awaken in us dreams of returning greatness?

Answer to your prayer will come in God's due time, in a way He decrees, for our Indian brothers. But it will make him a new Indian brother, better prepared for God's Kingdom instead of the backward look of your dreams.

Ella Deloria

Ella Deloria (part Indian) seems to be a person who has mastered and understands equally and fully both the Indian and the white man's philosophy, culture and ways of life. In true perspective, she sees and properly evaluates the differences and similarities of both races.

Here is something she says about accepting and working in the Christian Church:

Falling in with the Church year Calendar, with its sequence of feasts and observances, starting from Advent, the Indian people were already familiar, and with Dakotan translations for the seasonal names, used them freely and understood what they represented. They followed through with the proper collects, epistle, and gospel selections and read their teaching very carefully, for many had by this time learned to read. They sang appropriate hymns of the church seasons, some of which their own religious leaders had composed.

They emphasized Kinship being a good thing; God devised it: let us all remember to live according to it. They said it identifies Christian brotherhood with the old Dakota kinship system and its laws of interpersonal responsibility and loving kindness.

Missionary work was not neglected either. As Christian missionaries progressed westward, the Indians sent their missionaries on to the next tribe, and eventually they in turn sent them on to the next—So, their part to spread the gospel to other Indians.

These Christians, at their own expense, enthusiastically made regular journeys to the outlands, where they held meetings and passed on to the people what they knew. The people, in true Dakota style, feasted them royally first and then heard their message.

In all earnestness, and with a genuine desire to help others, the people worked to raise money by making things to sell. And thus, "for work across the water" and "work at home," they sent money. Special gifts were voted for the starving to various parts of the world, as the need arose. It was nothing new, helping others; it was something very new and very wonderful to extend that help far around the world. The most unlettered, retiring Dakota women helped as well as the more advanced. They still do.

82

Ella Deloria's intense devotion to Christianity permeates the work as it did her long life. Her premise is that the European culture forced such rapid change that the Indian society was not able to cope with it. She thinks that further damage was done by those who invariably viewed all tribes as the same without major differences of belief or morals.

In kinship lies one of the major differences which Ella perceived between the white and the Indian cultures. The white system lauded the attainment of goods while the Indian stressed sharing. Complete change to Christianity.

Mahpiyato, Blue Cloud, 1833 - 1918 — Yankton

Blue Cloud was a man of peace and a devout Roman Catholic who remained a staunch supporter of his faith even though his people were without a priest for fifty years. He saw Christianity as a way for peace with the white men and worked all of his life for that end and for what he believed was the good of his people. Blue Cloud Abbey was established in South Dakota and named after him. Bishop Marty bestowed a special religious credential upon him.

That old-time Indian religious spirit—to share what one possesses with the needy—motivated their feeling of honor and nobleness.

This is a brief picture of the transfer from the old religion to the new. We can see that it was no overwhelming problem; that instinctively the people themselves dropped whatever was in conflict with it and retained those fine elements from the past that were fundamentally right as a firm foundation for the Christian life.

The Christian Dakotan dies calm, full of faith and trust. The march of religion for the Indian has kept pace with the times.

One Sin the Indian Did Not Have

He never took the name of the Lord in vain. He had no swear word in his vocabulary.

"The Christian Church might do well to adopt some of the ancient religious philosophy of the American Indians, of the South Dakota Sioux"; thus spoke Webster Two Hawk, full blood, Sioux Indian Episcopal minister.

At the annual convocation of the United Theological Seminary, at New Brighton, Minnesota, which trains ministers for various protestant denominations, Webster Two Hawk suggested that the

Indians belief that people belong to the land and are sojourners on earth is more Christian than saying "This land is my land."

"We can't go back to the blanket and buffalo," Two Hawk said. "We can't practice the Indian religion as we used to. But we can still retain the principle on which it was based—*that the Great Spirit is part of everyday life.* Indian people know the Great Spirit will never forsake us."

Chapter 4: HISTORY OF INDIAN POLICY

Dominant Factor—Land Hungry Settlers: Corrupted Our Treaty Obligations—Nature And Credibility of History—Policy Milestones And Landmarks—Pre-Colonial And Colonial—Removal Act 1830—Indian Country—Beginning To Lose Their Sovereignty—The Indian Trade And Intercourse Act. 1834— President Jackson "Right of Conquest"—President Jackson Defies U.S. Supreme Court And The Law of The Land—Cherokee-Trail of Tears—Congress Fights For Indian's Rights—The Ultimate Outcome For the Cherokees—Indian Not A Person-Standing Bear VS General Crook 1879—Standing Bear's Historical Speech—Standing Bear Inducted Into The Nebraska Hall Of Fame 1979—Reservation System 1834—The Allotment Policy 1887—Government Treaties Guaranteed Food, Clothing, Blankets, Medical Aid Etc.—The Last Indian Wars And The Pursuit Of Extermination—The Indian Reorganization And The Meriam Report—Indian Claims—Indian Relocation, Training Program And Employment—Capital Development—Termination And Self-Determination Indian Leadership For Indian Programs—

History is for the enrichment of our present and future. Accuracy, truth and comprehension are exceedingly important. Much of the value of our history has been wasted, despoiled, distorted, and been misleading, especially as it has been recorded of our Indian people.

In the main, the chief factor in the American government's overall policy towards the Indian—from the beginning and from generation to generation—has been to take the Indians' land, homes, resources, means of subsistence from him and push him out. It has ranged from assimilation to extermination, to rehabilitation, self-determination, self-sufficiency and self-government.

85

The government has tried about everything imaginable, at one time or another, constantly jumping from one thing to another—and sometimes back and forth with many programs and regulations. About all most of it ever accomplished was to create confusion and despair for everyone, especially for the Indians. Seldom was any general policy continued long enough to make it successful. One prominent Indian leader expressed it as a self-defeating zig-zag course of constantly altering programs. When someone would complain to this writer, when he was with the BIA, about some new policy or regulation, I would tell them to just wait, that it might change again—perhaps back again to where it previously had been. At times the BIA reminded one of a chicken with its head cut off—a lot of jumping and flopping around and getting no place.

The dominant practice was always to take the land and its resources from the Indians, and give it to the white man for his sole use and the policy of the government was "ways to dispose of the Indians."

In the recent years, the actual practice in the field was to preserve the Indian reservations and the Indians as government wards, and to keep them in the status of incompetents, for the purpose of perpetuating the jobs for the Civil Service employees. Many times they did this in defiance of the central office in Washington, DC, and sometimes Congress and by subversion of the government's policy.

The Indians had their problems too with the several groups of the European invaders. There were the English, the French, the Spanish, the Dutch, the Quakers, the Canadians, the colonists, and then the United States. The Quakers seemed to be the most considerate and helpful for the Indians. The French and Canadians had a more conciliatory attitude towards the native Indians than did the colonies and later the U.S. government and its people.

Many times when Congress initiated legislation for a new policy they felt it would result in a solution of the problems arising over the conflicting interests of the native Indians and the invading colonists and settlers. It seemed to be the logical thing to do at the time. Many times the interest and concern of the Congress and the President for the welfare and just treatment of the Indians were unquestionable. They were well meaning in the keeping of their treaty obligations.

Many honest, well-planned efforts were made by our national leaders in the early days of our nation to help and protect the

Indian and his interests in his country. Included in the efforts were presidents, senators, and representatives in Congress, military officers, church leaders, congressional committees, Indian traders, and civilian citizens. They deserve a lot of credit, even though what they did may have eventually turned out to be mostly failures to accomplish their aims. They were sincere and gave it the best thought and planning that could be conceived by them, at the time. Of course, there were always others who were enemies to any progress suggested or attempted.

Inter-misunderstanding and the covetiveness of the aggressive white poeple are doubtless root causes of the long and brutal struggle between the white and the red men. The first clashes between the Indians and the settlers came from quarrels and misunderstandings over land. In most cases, the New England colonists had honorably paid the Indians for land, which they then considered their own. The Indians, however, did not understand such European ideas as exclusive land ownership, and continued to hunt and fish where their ancestors always had. To the English this was trespassing, and trespassing meant arrest, trial and conviction. Tensions increased between Indians and settlers.

There were many of this type of misunderstandings between the two races. Only time could abridge it.

It was the land hungry settlers who corrupted our treaty obligations. However, there were times when the national policy, with the concurrence of the President, the Congress and the courts, was to exterminate the Indians. The records show that orders were given to kill all male Indians twelve years of age and over. The generals reported to the War Department on their results in carrying out the orders. These reports and the policy of extermination are found in the archives and the history of Indian policy. The records show that generals reporting from the field actually carried out the orders; sometimes they killed all and sometimes they reported a few escaped. There were some instances, when all men, women and children were run down and killed. In some instances a few escaped alive. This action included the Sand Hill Massacre and the famous Wounded Knee, where women and their babies crawled in their attempt to escape a distance of two or more miles before they were run down and shot—where their bodies were found later. The bodies of the whole massacre were unceremoniously dumped in a single grave. We sometimes sanctimoniously forget these deeds when we are shocked by the atrocious crimes of some other peoples and nations.

Have we, our nation, repented our sins? Have we tried to demonstrate it by compensating the injured?

Yes, I think we have, at long last. In recent years some of the tribes have brought suit against the government for claims which they claimed were owed them for taking their land. The courts have been awarding them hundreds of millions of dollars, which they acknowledge is justly due the Indians. At one time they could not bring claims in the courts. The contention was that "the Indians were not persons" and not protected by the 14th Constitutional Amendment. The case that finally abrogated this attitude is reported in this book under the heading "Indians Not a Person."

The recent legislation granting the Indian citizens self-determination, planning, and management of their own affairs has brought a great change in their lives. These millions of dollars which were reclaimed have been a great asset for them.

Many of our white citizens do not understand this fact, even in this enlightened day, and spread many false conceptions. They are continuing the two-hundred-year-old psychological atmosphere degrading these persons. The Indian has endured it for a long time.

Many people continue to think that this money that they have been getting is a complete "handout." Some people have long thought that all Indians got a monthly check from the government—just an across-the-board payment. This, of course, is not and never was true.

Let us not forget and be uncharitable in mind and deed when thinking these racial-damaging thoughts. The results may persist for generations.

Nature and Creditability of History

I believe it was Al Smith who said, "History is bunk."

Alan D. Crown, senior lecturer in Semitics at the University of Sydney, Australia, said of the nature of history: "Historians might never mention any single incident in common. Though both would tell the truth and write history; we might wonder if they lived in the same century, let alone in the same country. This is the nature of all history. It is not an objective chronicle of events that have been found to be worth recording. History differs from historian to historian according to attitude and outlook."

John Collier, ex-Commissioner of Indian Affairs and noted authority on Indians and Indian affairs said: "Powerful nations and empires have always been alike in one way: They brush the records of their mistakes and misdeeds under the rug, where they remain until the search-light of history uncovers them. Even then they are never more than footnotes in the records of the country where they occurred."

There certainly must be a lot of "dirt" under the rug in the U.S. history as it concerns her Indian people. This writer and researcher has reviewed our school history textbooks of 1900 and the 1970's. The total number of pages mentioning Indians amounts to a half dozen, revealing practically nothing of the factual truth of importance. The real history of our nation's Indians is buried in the files of the Bureau of Indian Affairs, the War Department and the archives.

More of this buried material is coming out in print and circulation such as the Department of the Interior's 1973 book titled, *A History of Indian Policy,* and other publications. Much is revealed therein, but, of course, not the complete story. This book makes its contents official and no doubt is authentic. The author of the book is no doubt well qualified as a researcher and author.

Chief Red Fox, whose life spanned 106 years, has said that the honest story of the conquest of America is found only in the factual writings of researchers who have looked beyond the limited horizons of textbooks, encyclopedias, and government publications.

History is an encyclopedia of fables, folklore, and fiction. It is censored to sustain and maintain the ego of races, religion, and nations. American history, as taught in school textbooks, pictures the development of a nation from the arrival of Columbus to the present in star-spangled language. Censorship has eliminated all hostile, damaging and inhumane behavior from the pages of our past. The Indian is depicted as a savage and the white man as a good Samaritan.

A study of the files buried in the Indian Bureau, by anyone interested, as others have done, will shock the pursuer of the covered up atrocious and criminal acts of persons in the military and government agencies that occurred. One example is at the Wounded Knee Massacre in South Dakota in 1890. This is the best known massacre of many performed during those years of warfare with the Indians. Now that these atrocities are being brought to light, some violent reactions are occurring by both Indian and white people throughout our land. Many more deaths have occurred as a result and much property destroyed.

Yes, even justice delayed and denied for a long period of time, can and may be brought to the public light. How, so many times, it comes back to haunt us! Now, the descendants of their fore-fathers are receiving hundreds of millions of dollars from law suits awarded them against Uncle Sam.

Is it any wonder that the whole citizenry of our country are so ignorant about the Indians—a complete cover-up for these many years? How did they do it so successfully? Let us hope that the sacrifices we make today will ease our national conscience and put us in an honest and strong position to wage a battle to save other people in other lands from similar injustices.

What our school history books have to say about Indians, is not only grossly inadequate but misleading in substance and in fact. The history books don't say that the Indians were forcefully re-moved by the army, that is those that they could catch. The Trail of Tears is the classical example of what happened. Sixteen thou-sand Cherokee Indians were forced to leave their ancestral home-lands in the southern Appalachian Mountains for new territory in what is now Oklahoma. The army gathered those that they could catch and hauled them, many walked, a distance of seven- or eight-hundred miles, in the dead of winter. (Then they were unwelcome by other Indians already settled there.)

More than 4,000 died along the way from exposure, disease or hunger. Some escaped and took refuge in states through which they passed. Many of the Cherokee Indians fled to the mountain, where they hid until they felt it was safe for them to emerge, a few at a time. Eventually they gained back some of their land by purchase. Many of the Florida Indians hid out in the Everglades until "all was clear" for them to come out. Also the Modoc escaped in the lava wilderness of Washington state. AND SO IT GOES!

Our school's history books are grossly negligent in doing justice to our Indian citizens when it comes to recording such important matters. They give practically no credit to them for their impor-tant contributions to our country or the contributions to the world and its impact upon our present-day civilization, nor allude to the injustices and suffering we have dealt them throughout our his-tory.

To futher demonstrate I quote a paragraph from the govern-ment's own *History of Indian Policy* (page 80): "Indians who did not go willingly to the reservations would be either driven there by force or exterminated in the process."

These statements, and many others like them, are not myths, but their absence or cover-ups leads to many myths. It is a grand-scale brainwashing deal for all of us.

In order to get a clearer overall picture of the progression of the government's Indian policies over the years of our white history, I choose to outline the course with landmarks and milestones headings with a brief description of each, to be followed by a discussion of each more extensively and in detail through the chapter.

Policy Milestones and Landmarks

I. Pre-colonial and colonial—Dealt by treaty and hoped for assimilation. A provision—"The utmost good faith shall always be observed towards the Indian, their land and property shall never be taken from them without their consent and in their property rights and liberty shall never be invaded or disturbed." In 1788 Indian affairs were administered under the Secretary of War. In 1793 Congress appropriated $20,000 to the treaty with the Indians. 1871 ended without the making of any more new treaties. In 1803 it appropriated $3,000 to civilize and educate the "heathens." In 1819 another appropriated $10,000 annually for the civilization fund.

II. Removal Bill—In 1830 enacted the Removal Bill—to Indian Territory. $500,000 appropriated for the purpose.

III. Indian Trade and Intercourse Act (1834)—Organization of the Department of Indian Affairs and regulation of trade and intercourse with the Indians.

IV. Reservation System (1850)—To set aside designated territory for tribal occupation and use.

V. Indians Recognized as Persons (1879)—Chief Standing Bear's eloquent and timely court victory.

VI. The Allotment Act (1887)—To break up tribal estates and individualize Indian land holdings.

VII. The last Indian wars and the Pursuit of extermination. Destroy the buffalo and starve the red men to death.

VIII. Indian Reorganization Act (1934).

IX. Indian claims against U.S. Government (1940s-1980s)—Millions of dollars awarded Indian tribes. The act enabled tribes to organize and deal with the U.S. Government as corporate bodies—They could borrow funds and use credit and bargain for many other and comprehensive benefits.

X. Employment and Relocation (1950s)—Assist younger Indians to get training and finance to relocate where jobs could be found.

XI. Agency termination (1960s)—Independence from bureaucratic control. It failed.

XII. Self-determination through Indian leadership (1968-1972)—
The Indians taking over and planning and managing their own
tribal affairs.

Pre-Colonial and Colonial

We do not intend here to describe in all details nor narrate the
whole history or the policies of the white man-Indian relationship
in the pre-colonial and early colonial area. Suffice it to bring out
the high points and the most important factors. Other factors are
cited in the chapters on "religion" and "literature."

Some historians tell us that "of all the white men, the Indians
preferred the Frenchmen." A paragraph from the U.S. official
History of Indian Policy states a good summary of the difference
in attitude and treatment of the Indians by the Spanish, the
French and the English governments and their colonial people.

In intercourse with them, the French neither treated
them, as did the Spaniards, as minors or "wards," whose
every action and opinion must be supervised, nor did they
despise them as the English obviously did, even while
recognizing their title to the soil and their right to bargain
and make treaties. The attitude of the French was more
like that of an older brother who might coax, scold, punish,
deceive, or seek to impress his primitive kin, but who
never attempted to enslave him or behave contemptuously
towards him.

The Dutch Indian program was of a comparatively short
duration. They tended to live apart from the Indians, both
physically and as two separate cultures. Little effort was
made to do missionary work among them. The Dutch
tended to be more liberal in their land policy and more
sophisticated in their cultural relationships.

The English frontiersmen tended to have a more general attitude of hostility towards the native Americans.
Once the Englishman had learned that the Indian was
going to maintain a separate identity, and that he would
not, by choice, and by a natural course of events, begin to
give up Indian ways and adopt English ways, the Indian
became an undesirable creature and a foreigner. As such
he became a mere obstacle that stood in the way of
securing whatever the Englishman wanted that the Indian possessed. In the face of laws passed by the crown to
protect the Indian, the frontiersman usually found some
way to get around the obstacle.

92

The same can be said of the subsequent colonies and later the United States governments and their frontiersmen, in their attitude towards the policies of the government in dealing with the Indians and the treatment of them down through the generations well into the twentieth century.

One of the basic features of the relationships between Indian and non-Indian was trade. The endeavor was to secure and keep this trade. The competition was not only between the European nations, but also between the different English colonies. Few people of the United States realize the extent and the volume of the fur trade conducted by the Indians. It was a vital part of their economy, and the economy of the whites.

By 1763, as a result of their experience, the English had learned that they got along best with the Indians when they were separated some distance apart. This fact led to the U.S. Government's changes in its Indian policy. One experience led to another and new problems arose at almost every turn. And so from Indian territory to reservations to allotments—and so ran the white man's Indian policy. It was a stubborn and long, drawn-out struggle.

Removal Act – 1830

At first the Europeans dealt with the Indian tribes by treaty as separate nations. It was believed that the Indian would gradually be assimilated, that their communities and those within the colonies would intermix. When this did not occur as soon as anticipated, the Indian tribes were removed farther west. When the western lands were needed for further expansion, the Indians were placed on and confined to reservations.

At that time this western land was called "no man's land." Some early pioneer explorers dubbed the area as worthless wilderness. So when they forced the Indians to go out there, they thought they had them taken care of and all would be okay thereafter. But alas! Their problem only took on a new form. The whites could take over the territory, which they did. But part of the tribe would not go. The concoction was to divide it up with the Indians and organize the reservation system and give the Indians the poorest parts of the area.

Indian Country

The most revolutionary departure from the previous program (the Removal Act) in Indian affairs was the recognition of a boundary line that separated Indian lands from non-Indian lands. The result was the creation of an "Indian Country." This area, generally to the west, was reserved for the Indian. The officials of the established colonies were forbidden "for the present, and until our further pleasure be known," to allow surveys or to grant lands beyond the watershed of the Appalachians. Any persons who had already established themselves in the Indian Country were ordered to remove themselves.

In regard to this proclamation, time soon made a practice apparent that was to recur again and again in the future. In the later years, in the case of the Black Hills area in South Dakota, the army actually rounded up the non-Indian trespassers and hauled them off and away to the Platte River in Wyoming, at Fort Laramie. After releasing them there, many of them returned in a very short time. The army finally gave up and then the government tried to remove the Indians and relocate them in the Indian territory in Oklahoma, which became only partially successful. Then they resorted to establishing reservations in the Dakotas, Montana and Wyoming, and confining the Indians to those areas. The Indians last great united effort to save their homeland and their survival resulted in the extensive wars and massacres, such as the Sand Creek and Wounded Knee affairs.

Established lines, with military power to secure those lines, might keep Indians in the Indian Country, but the military power could not guard the Indians against the political pressures that allowed settlers to invade the Indian Country. Troops could keep Indians in, but they would not be used consistently to keep non-Indians out.

In the controversy that developed between Great Britain and the colonies after 1763, the Indians' causes of complaint almost all came from the colonists' abuses of the Indian trade and encroachment on Indian lands. The British officials had a better record in their dealings with the Indians, and they did not fail to remind them (the Indians) of this. As the controversy heightened, the Indians tended to give their support to the British rather than the colonists and later to the Canadians. They also gave most of their support to the French in our controversy with them and to the South in the Civil War. The English colonists and the United States Government and its people could have done better by the Native Americans all through its history.

Since we assume that independent, established Indian tribes were self-governing and sovereign before the colonization of the

Americas by European powers, we should also recognize that after the establishment of European colonies, and the subsequent continuing expansion into Indian territory, tribal sovereignty and self-government have been gradually but persistently weakened, and in some cases entirely extinquished.

One of the first steps taken by the European nations was to extend their "protection" over the Indian tribes. They then proclaimed to the Indians that they were vassals or subjects of the king of a European nation. Thus, at one, the supposedly unlimited sovereignty the tribe had possessed became, at least in the mind of the European, a limited sovereignty. In order to "protect" the tribe, the European nation established its jurisdiction over the tribal territory.

It was usually understood that local government was a tribal matter, but if a citizen of the European nation that acted as the tribe's "protector" was charged with illegal action and punishment was threatened by the tribal government, the protecting nation would often intervene on behalf of its citizen in spite of the fact that the illegal action occurred within tribal territory. In actual practice, in a variety of ways, the "protector" tended to become involved in the internal affairs of the tribe.

A national criminal jurisdiction over tribal actions tended to follow these practices:

It is noteworthy to note that the United States Congress from its beginning, in various and fluctuating degrees, has continually and to an increasing extent asserted criminal jurisdiction over Indians and Indian territory, irrespective of the fact that Indian tribes were sovereign in the sense that the United States negotiated and concluded treaties with them until 1871. In addition to, and sometimes prior to, this criminal jurisdiction, an economic surveillance was extended over the territory occupied by the tribe. All of this was done, of course, as a part of this role of protector, or guardian. Sometimes it was done in good faith. At other times it was done because it was good politics or good business.

Gradually, as the European, then American nations continued to infringe upon this now limited tribal sovereignty and the rights of the tribe as a self-governing entity, tribal leaders recognized that they were no longer entirely free to make decisions in the customary ways. There was now an outside entity whose interests would have to be considered in a variety of ways. Since these Indian leaders were no longer free, they could no longer be truly responsible.

One of the elements we will need to watch, as we observe the results of changes of policy towards the Indians, is the effect, not only of outright assumption of jurisdiction, but also of the subtle influences that are brought to bear that may have devastating consequences on the economy, the social values, and the way of life of a tribe, or of specific Indian communities.

Thus, we can see how the pattern evolved and was imposed upon the noble and proud race for over two-hundred years, and they were deprived of any recourse to justice, and how it tended to erode and destroy their dignity, their pride, honor, and well-being. Where lies hope for their emerging young people?

Must we strain our imagination to understand why so many of the Indians, and especially the youth, resorted to a high rate of alcoholism and suicide? And they still do.

How can a people survive without hope and justice, without power or recourse for justice? In light of their miraculous response to recovery in recent years, they are proving that they are as durable as the Jew and the raccoon.

The Indian Trade and Intercourse Act

June 30, 1834, is considered a significant date in the history of Indian legislation, and of the creation of Indian policy. Two comprehensive statutes were then passed that in large part, "form the fabric of our law on Indian affairs to this day." One stands as the final act in a series of acts "to regulate trade and intercourse with the Indian tribes." The other is an act "to provide for the organization of the Department of Indian Affairs." The House Committee on Indian Affairs dealt with these two statutes in one report that "contains an illuminating analysis of the entire legislative situation with relation to Indian affairs." These measures define Indian Country, prescribe methods of making contracts with Indians, empower the commissioner to appoint traders and to regulate the kind, quantity and prices of trade goods to be sold to the Indians with whom they trade. They provide that interests in Indian lands, by lease or purchase, can be acquired only by treaty or other agreement formalized under the direction of duly constituted authorities as described therein. Penalties are provided for trespassers on Indian holdings.

One passage from the committee report seems particularly significant in the light of current efforts to involve the Indians more in the management of their own affairs. (Even then, they had thoughts, as ours today.) But it took nearly a century and a half before it came into full fruition. The education of the Indians is a subject of deep interest to them and to us. It is now proposed to allow them more direction in it, with the assent of the President, under the superintendent or the governor, so far as their annuities are concerned; and that a preference should be given to educated youth in all the employments of which they are capable as traders, interpreters, schoolmasters, farmers, mechanics, etc.; and that the course of their education should be so directed as to render them capable of those employments. (Why did it take so long to accomplish these conceptions?) The government already realized and was concerned about the need of protection for the vulnerable Indians against the thieving whites.

President Jackson — Right of Conquest

We have stated previously that many times the U.S. Indian policies have been reversals, flip-flops and inconsistencies. There have been those who worked to defeat the official or established policies, and it is still so to this day in some cases. President Jackson had been a military Indian fighter. One time an Indian who was in battle against Jackson saved Jackson's life when he would have been killed. Jackson appreciated this and was more concilitory towards Indians after that, until he got into the White House, when he turned again to a hardline attitude towards the Indians. He took the attitude that the Indians were a conquered people and assumed the policy of "right by conquest." It was held that peace was granted (notice they said "granted") to the Cherokees in 1785 as a "mere grace of the conqueror." A conflict of opinion quickly developed between the missionary groups that worked with the southern Indians and the government. President Andrew Jackson advised (later gave orders and threats) the Indians to either emigrate beyond the Mississippi or submit to the laws of the state of Georgia. He returned to the argument: "If the Indians remained in contact with the whites, they would be degraded and destroyed."

President Jackson Defies the U.S. Supreme Court
and the Law of the Land

A deluge of debate on the subject of removal, both pro and con, was lost by the press. Much of this was ordered printed in the congressional documents and may be examined in the serial set. By sheer volume of printed matter those against removal and for the position of the Cherokee Indians won the debate. But when the votes were counted in the Congress, the Act of May 28, 1830, governing Indian removal, passed by a small majority.

Jackson won the political battles but lost in the Supreme Court and before the judgment bar of history. Chief Justice Marshall upheld Vitorie's position that the Indian tribes are true possessors of the soil against that of Vattel. He pointed out that the official acts of the United States to regulate trade and intercourse with Indians, and the treaties we had made with them recognizing their rights, had obligated the United States to support the cause of the Cherokee Nation.

All these acts, and especially that of 1802, which is still in force, manifestly considered the several Indian nations as distinct political communities, having territoral boundaries, within which their authority is exclusive. This is not only acknowledged, but guaranteed by the United States.* President Jackson refused to enforce Marshall's decision. He justified his position by a variety of arguments, but the net result in terms of the application of Indian policy is that the United States followed a coercive policy in its relations with Indians during this period that *would have its effect on the application of Indian policy for the next hundred years.*

This amounted to a reversal of administrative policy. Representatives of the United States had previously at least recognized that the cause of the Indian against the frontiersman was just, although they could not enforce the laws that had been passed to protect the Indians. Jackson's action, in failing to support the decision of the Supreme Court, became a precedent that told the frontiersman that his case would be heard in high places to the detriment of the Indian. It told the Indians that the forces arrayed against them were too powerful to be withstood, when the chips were down, and he must eventually acquiesce *or be destroyed one way or another*, in the face of the advancing settlements of the United States. But 150 years later, the conscience-stricken United States is paying out hundreds of millions of dollars to the Indians to partly compensate them for its atrocious treatment of them for these many years. *Yes, Mr. President—history eventually proved that you did not serve your country well!*

The worst of all—it was unfortunate that the immediate object of this change of policy had to be an Indian tribe that had accom-

*See *Cherokee vs. Georgia*, 5 Pet. 1 (1831); and *Worcester vs. Georgia*, 5 Pet. 515.

plished as much as any other in the realization, by way of civilization and education, of the goals that past policy makers had set for the Indians (See 'Trail of Tears" below).

The official Indian policy of the United States as reflected in the treaties, however, continued to uniformly guarantee Indian rights. "The tremendous weight of the argument put forth in the 1830s by the supporters of the Cherokees stirred the conscience of the Nation." And as to the effect of this national sentiment: "What new authority it gave to the traditional principles behind American Policy cannot have been insignificant."

Morally, Jackson's political success had been a *"victory at too high cost."*

Cherokee — Trail of Tears

In spite of the fact that the Cherokees had so successfully attained their intercourse into the Anglo-Saxon civilization which had encompassed them, they were forcefully and brutally expelled from their traditional, and United States legally established, country and homes. The President of the United States was the leader and prime mover of this brutal lawlessness.

At this point of time and place we should consider what the Cherokees had done.

A Cherokee, known by the alias of Boundinot, completed the course at Andoves Theological Seminary and in 1826 traveled through the North speaking to church groups to build support of the Cherokee people in the crisis already shaping on the horizon. He wanted the white people to understand what his tribe had accomplished and why they were entitled to remain unmolested while they worked out their adjustment to the new order.

Speaking before the First Presbyterian Church in Philadelphia in 1826 he told them: "It is a matter of surprise to me, and must be to all those who are properly acquainted with the condition of the aborigines of the country, that the Cherokees have advanced so far and so rapidly in civilization. But there are yet powerful obstacles both within and without, to be surmounted in the march of improvement. . . . In defiance, however, of these obstacles the Cherokees have improved and are rapidly improving. At this time there are 22,000 cattle, 7,600 horses; 46,000 swine; 2,500 sheep, 1,662 looms; 1,488 spinning wheels; 172 wagons; 2,948 plows, 10 sawmills; 31 grist mills; 62 blacksmith shops; 8 cotton machines; 18 schools; 18 ferries; and a number of public roads. In one district there were, last winter, upwards of 1,000 volumes of good books . . . most of the schools are under the care and turtion of Christian Missionaries of different denominations, invented an alphabet in 1821 (the first alphabet for an Indian language) and plans were afoot to issue a mewspaper, and the Bible translated into a written language for them."

In 1827 a written constitution proclaiming a "sovereign and independent nation" was drafted, providing a principal officer called the "Chief," a bicameral legislature, a supreme court, and a code of laws, adopted July 4, 1827, and first election, quite orderly along with a growing prosperity (author's note: with some opposition, of course).

In 1829 the Georgia legislature extended state law to Cherokee territory and at the same time annulled Cherokee laws. (What a blow to these deserving people!)

The whites were determined to take everything the Indians had including their bank accounts and drive them away. A long bloody and costly fight ensued. Of course, the Indians eventually could not win when there was no justice for them and no courts of appeal. Petitions began to pour in to Congress urging a due regard for the rights of the Indians. Civic groups, religious organizations and private citizens of Massachusetts, Ohio, New Jersey, Pennsylvania, Virginia, New York, and Maryland expressed their concern.

There were senators and congressmen who fought for the Indians' rights. A senator from New York talked for two days against a Senate bill.

His argument ran: "By immemorial possession, as the original tenants of the soil they hold a title beyond and superior to the British Crown and her colonies and to all adverse pretensions of our confederation and subsequent union. God in his providence planted these tribes on this western continent so far as we know, before Great Britian herself had a political existence. I believe that the Indians are men, endowed with kindred faculties and power equal with ourselves—with this conceded, I ask in what codes in the laws of nations or by what process of abstract deduction, their rights have been extinquished—Is it one of prerogatives of the white man, that he may disregard the dictates of moral principles, when an Indian shall be concerned?"

(Senator Frelinghuysen's speech is in Thomas H. Benton, ed., Abridgements of the Debates in Congress, 1789-1856, Vol. 10 Washington, D.C. 1839, page 519-26. See also the editorial in Niles Register, 38 March 20, 1830, p. 67) On the House side,

Congressman Starrs of New York spoke of the fallacy of pretending to remove the Indians for their own good from a community where they had pleasant homes, churches, and schools to a wilderness where hostile tribes would be their only neighbors— The law against the Indians passed on May 28, 1830.

It was at this point that the Cherokees, seeing themselves defeated in every effort to adapt themselves to white civilization and to obtain protection from the Executive (Jackson administration), turned to the white man's court. For the Cherokees, more than legal principles were involved. It was as if they were giving the white man every opportunity to prove how treacherous he could be.

The Ultimate Outcome for the Cherokees

The ultimate outcome was the Trail of Tears.

The eventual results—Part of the tribe worked their way back and re-purchased and re-established themselves where they remain to this day, over a hundred years later. Great credit is theirs, members of a noble race and proud citizens of the United States. (For more complete coverage, read the book, *The Trail of Tears,* by Gloria Jahoda.)

Indian Not a Person—Standing Bear vs. General Crook—1879

The government kept trying to relocate the Indian tribes in Oklahoma Territory, the last place left where they could be pushed and be out of the white man's way. This country was considered, at the time, to be no good anyway. The effort started in the 1830's and ended in 1879. The government succeeded in getting part of the several tribes moved there. One group became known as the Five Civilized Tribes. These were the Cherokee, Choctaw, Creek, Seminole, and Chickasaw from the southeastern states. These tribes became quite successful there. The Cheyenne of the Northern Plains were removed to the territory but many of them filtered their way back to Montana where they remain on a reservation. Other tribes from the Northwest and the Great Plains were among those forcibly removed to the Indian territory. So the relocation policy was partly a success and partly a failure.

The duplicity and contributory rulings of the courts and the reversal of policy by the administration made a shambles of policy and the enforcement of law to cause confusions that kept arising for a hundred years.

We found in the archives that on July 7, 1876, the *New York Times* reported: ". . . that there were those in the War Department, mostly "high officers" who advocated "the policy of extermination of the Indians and think the speedier the better its accomplishment." That was the period of "Wars of Annihilation" and was during the final years of the Indian Wars and three years prior to the court case of Chief Standing Bear—the story follows:

The peaceful and loyal Ponca tribe who lived and occupied territory on the Missouri River in what is now Nebraska, in the middle and late 1870s, were ordered out of their traditional home and transplanted in the Oklahoma Territory. Some obeyed; others refused and resisted. Chief Standing Bear took his case to court in the case of *Standing Bear vs. General Crook*. The hearing began April 30, 1879.

The crux of this case was whether or not the Indian could be considered under law, a "person." The district attorney declared that the Indian was not a person within the interpretation of the 14th Amendment of the Constitution.

The hearing lasted three hours. Taghabut, another chief, spoke first: "I sometimes think that the white people forget that we are human, that we love our wives and children, and prepare not only for the winters as they come, for old age when we can no longer do as when we were young. But one Father made us all. We have hands, feet, head and hearts all alike. We are also men. Look at me. Am I not a man? I have no others. But I am a man."

Webster gave his rebuttal for Standing Bear and sat down. Judge Dundy paused a few moments. He was thinking about Standing Bear's request to address the court. One solution would be to adjourn and give him that privilege. He rapped for adjournment and told the Ponca he might now speak.

Standing Bear rose slowly and held out his right arm. He held it out a long time, saying nothing, so that the spectators grew restless. Then he spoke:*

That hand is not the color of yours (he said, looking at Judge Dundy) but if I pierce it, I shall feel pain. If you pierce your hand, you also feel pain. The blood that will flow from mine will be the same color as yours. I am a man.

The same God made us both. (His next remarks were delivered to the courtroom.)

I am standing on the bank of a river. My wife and little

*For more on this Indian phenomenon see previous treatment under "Gifts."

102

girl are beside me. In front the river is wide and impassable, and behind are perpendicular cliffs. No man of my race ever stood there before. There is not tradition to guide me. . . . A great flood begins and there is nowhere for us to go but climb the cliff. We climbed for many days.

At last I see a passage through the rocks and I turn to my wife and child and shout that we are saved. We will return to the Swift Running Water that pours down between the green islands. There are the graves of my fathers. There again we will pitch our tipi and build our fires. He paused-But a man bars the passage. He is a thousand times more powerful than I. Behind him I see soldiers as numerous as the leaves of the trees. They will obey that man's orders. I, too, must obey his orders. If he says that I cannot pass, I cannot: the long sturggle will have been in vain. My wife and child and I must return and sink beneath the flood. We are weak and faint and sick. I cannot fight.

This time he paused much longer, lowering his head. When he lifted it again, he was staring at the judge. *You are that man.*

Tibbles tells us that Dundy wept openly and that "General Crook sat leaning forward, covering his eyes with his hand. Some women could be heard sobbing in the silence that followed and then there was a great shout in the courtroom and the spectators came forward to congratulate Standing Bear, with General Crook the first among them."

A week later the judge announced his verdict. Said the judge: "During my fifteen years in which I have been administering the laws of my country, I have never been called upon to hear a case that appealed so strongly to my sympathy.

"On the one side we have the representatives of this wasted race coming into this National tribunal asking for justice and liberty. . . . On the other side we have the magnificent, if not magnamimous government resisting this application. . . .

"The Poncas are among the most peaceable and friendly of all Indian tribes, and they have at times received from the government unmistakable and substantial recognition of their long continued friendship for the whites.

"Therefore, I conclude: That the Indian is a person within the meaning of laws of the United States and therefore a right to request a writ of habeas corpus before a federal judge."

This was a brilliant and dramatic victory for the Indians, belying the myths that he is a dumb and insensitive creature. The Poncas remained a peaceful and friendly people, and like the Yankton tribe across the Missouri River in South Dakota, they never went to war with the United States Army or its people—even in spite of the broken treaties by our government, a Noble Race!

To commemorate the one-hundredth anniversary of the trial of Standing Bear, the Ponca chief is being inducted into the Nebraska Hall of Fame and a brass bust of him will be stationed on the main floor of the State Capitol in Lincoln.

This episode is of so much importance that the writer has included it as one of the landmarks in the history of the government's *History of Indian Policy.*

I also list Standing Bear's speech as one of the great orations and pieces of American literature of our nation.

For perhaps the first time a federal judge concluded and ruled that the Indian is a person within the meaning of laws of the United States and therefore has a right to request a writ of habeas corpus before a federal judge.

The Author's Summary Comments

—The political reasons used by human persons for enslaving, dominating, robbing and brutally treating other fellow human persons was to contend that they were not a person and implying that they were some kind of sub-species. Such a contention is not supported by either reason or science.

—The same contention was used against the black people. They were considered chattels and it is memorialized historically by the Dred Scott case. It cost us a bloody and costly Civil War to resolve that situation.

—The ignominious claim about the Indian people was legally dispelled by Judge Dundy in his decision in the Chief Standing Bear case.

—When such an evil can exist and continue to exist and reappear some other place and time in the face of the facts and background as that of the Indian race, it is a strong indictment against the intelligence, character and honesty of the white man. As proof of their equal or superior human qualities, the Indians had their ancient contemporary civilizations with that of Europe, Egypt and the Middle East. We have cited some of their contributions and gifts to our present civilization, which some scientists claim are greater than that produced by the Roman Empire.

104

—And now, we have those who apply the same inhuman argument against the unborn babe, of our own kind, so that they can legally and brutally destroy the yet unborn human babe—their own flesh and blood, possessing the spirit and breath of God.

Reservation System

The Indian Trade and Intercouse Act of 1834 which looked towards the concentration of Indians in "Indian Country" west of the Mississippi River and barring unauthorized non-Indians from encroachment on their lands gave way to the reservation system in the 1850s. Pressure to break up the tribal estates and individualize Indian landholdings developed in the 1880s and was formalized by the Allotment Act of 1887.

The refusal of the United States to adequately protect Indians in their rights against non-Indians played an important part in the failures of the concentration policy, the reservation policy and the allotment policy.

The old "permanent Indian frontier" broke down before the westward march of our population. The Indian Country was organized as the territories of Kansas and Nebraska. With their organization the old policy of maintaining a large, unorganized, and "permanent" Indian Country came to an end. But a new policy was at hand. The system of establishing reservations, of relatively small geographical extent, in the midst of the white man's country, had been tried in California and from there it spread ultimately over the entire country.

President Grant described an Indian reservation as a definite area of land set aside for the exclusive use of Indians and surrounded by thieving whites. Those thieving whites were there for nearly a hundred years. We cite some representative examples in the Chapter 6 titled "Thievery and Corruption." These reservations were likened to islands. They were surrounded by privately and federally owned land, but they became permanent fixtures on our national landscape.

The pioneers regarded Indians with contempt and subjected them to wrongs, harassments, insults, and petty annoyances, which sometimes stirred them to retaliate. We cite a few typical cases in the chapter titled "Thievery." Justice was usually unobtainable for them. Sometimes they were treated as foreign nations, at other times they were not recognized as persons; eventually they were treated as incompetents, as children and wards of the government.

105

The Reservation System remained permanent to this day. All other intervening policies, great and small, were within the reservations.

The Allotment Policy

The Allotment or Dawes Act was made a law on February 8, 1887, and considered a great step in advancement in our Indian policy, and was called the "Indian Emancipation Day." It was thought, at that time, that it would give the Indians the opportunity to become a man instead of remaining a ward of the government. It would afford him the opportunity to make for himself and his family a home, and to live, among his equals, an independent life. It offered him the protection of law and all the rights and privileges and immunities of citizenship.

The allotment designation, the name of the original allottee and the allotment number, still is retained to this day for all of the allotments still held in trust. During the allotment of land period, the majority of Indians receiving the allotments did not write or speak the English word. After the allotments were made, guardians were appointed. This led to many abuses and disposals of Indian allotments for the benefit of those appointed. The Bureau of Indian Affairs subsequently assumed the power of attorney for twenty-five years, then renewed for another twenty-five years.

The ultimate purpose of the bill was to abrogate the Indian tribal organizations and to abolish the reservation system. The system was a failure, as far as achieving the results the government planned for it to do. The land-hungry whites still robbed the Indians and stole their lands and created more trouble for the government. Another purpose was to replace tribal culture with white civilization and a desire to protect the individual Indian allottee from further depredation by covetous individuals, by the railroad, and by the federal government itself. During the 1870s and 1880s, it was thought that it would be easier to protect the Indian as an individual than as a member of a tribe. As usual, their conceived idea turned out to do exactly the opposite.

In practice relatively few Indians actually farmed their allotments. Because of this, provision was made for the leasing of Indian allotment land in 1891. It thereby became used by the whites.

In the 1880s and 1890s, Indian landholding shrunk rapidly, as a result of pressures from speculators and land-hungry white settlers eager to buy Indian land. The top governmental officials and congressmen used what appeared to be sound logical solutions to the Indian problems, and they usually were sincere in their efforts. But always the programs fell short of achieving success, even down to the 1950s.

It is the judgment of this writer that D'Arcy McNickle said it correctly when he said: "In the heat of a discussion, it would not have occurred to any of the debaters to inquire of the Indians what ideas they had of a home, of family, and of property. It would have assumed, in any case, that the ideas, whatever they were, were without merit since they were Indians'." That was also the attitude of most of the agency and bureau people.

"Cram it down their throats" was far too long the actual policy. It was also the policy of the Civil Service employees to keep the Indians down to promote their own jobs and in some cases fraudulent rip-offs for themselves. When was it ever possible to bring about a successful program of rehabilitation, with any group of people, without bringing them into the decision-making, planning and consummating of the program? It has been proved by many past experiences of failure and the recent change in that respect, after the self-determination policy and civil rights legislation, started along about the 1960s which has brought about a successful Indian policy for nearly all of the Indian people. Their standard of living is greatly improved and in many cases they are doing an outstanding job for themselves. That fact had been demonstrated before in some few cases, but then slapped down and destroyed when jealous, incompetent and self-seeking Civil Service employees got themselves in sufficient power to do so.

The success of the Cherokees before the forced "Trail of Tears" is an example of success by the Indians to adapt themselves into the new civilization. It is proof of what the Indians could do. The problem was the covetous and brutal white people and their supporting government. It was perish for the minority. What a travesty of justice!

The history in the East was one of indifference to the Indian. These Indians, more or less, are still centered in their native areas, which dates back prior to the coming of the Europeans. While their numbers decreased greatly they managed to survive in the midst of the encroaching whites. They have successfully adjusted to the new way of life, enjoying and profiting by it, and at the same time they have been able to retain some of their Indian culture and their Indian homeland.

107

The West, as a rule, was openly hostile. The Indians fought many bloody wars to preserve their way of life, but inevitably had to surrender to a numerically much superior population and military might.

It was claimed by some that the allotment policy was forced upon the Indians, so that any unallotted tracts of land would then be thrown open to claim and settlement by the whites. No more treaties were made after 1871. Some treaties are still in force to some degree.

J.P. Kinney's chapter on "Experimentation with an Allotment Policy," gives many examples of the pre-1887 assignment of lands to Indians in severalty.

Administration of Indian affairs sought to deal with the problem by providing in treaties for teachers, farmers, blacksmiths, and carpenters who were to educate the natives. This became common during the fifties and sixties. Agency posts were established within fixed reserves. The agents and their employees were made responsible for both the discipline and the instruction of the Indians.

Commissioner William P. Dole thought this procedure was right in theory but admitted that when the reservations became surrounded by white settlers there were glaring weaknesses in application. He expressed regret in 1862 that the small tracts of land which had been set aside for the original inhabitants should have become objects of the white man's inordinate desire. Pioneers looked upon Indians with contempt and subjected them to "wrongs, insults, and petty annoyances," which oftentimes stirred them to retaliate. Justice was usually not obtainable because, to begin with, rights by treaty or under federal law were wholly unintelligible to a vast majority of the Indians. Conversely, Indian crimes against members of the white race were met with swift punishment, and whole tribes suffered because of individual acts.

During the mid-1850s the agent on the Upper Platte made an interesting report on the nature of the Indian and the resulting relations with the relentless white invaders of his territory;

. . . There is not to be found among any people a more cheerful, contented and kindly disposed being than the Indian, when he is treated with kindness and humanity. His friendships are strong and lasting, and his love for and attachment to his children, kindred and tribe, have a depth and intensity which place him on an equality with the civilized race. His love and veneration for the whites amount to adoration, which is only changed to hatred and revenge by oppression, cruelties and deep wrongs and injuries inflicted upon the poor Indian by the white man, without cause or reason. By his education on the war path, which leads to honor, fame and distinction, the Indian is a relentless, a terrible enemy, he spares neither age nor sex, nor condition, but slaughters every one that falls in his path indiscriminately. He neither knows nor heeds the laws of modern warfare, as practiced and observed by an enlightened civilization. As a consequence, the first yell of war whoop has scarcely died away in its distinct echoes before a war of extermination is begun and waged against the poor Indians. The innocent and the guilty alike perish, and their bones are left to bleach on their own happy hunting grounds. This is but a faint picture of the Indian wars that have waged for short periods in every State and territory of the union, and which will burst forth constantly, until the power of the government is exerted to remove lawless and desperate whites from the Indian country, and change the habits of the Indian from a roving and hunting life to one of agriculture and fixed habitations.

There were those who thought this report was of a doubtful nature and character. But to this writer he appears to have been an honest realist among questionable characters.

Match these judgments with the history of the brutal, inhumane, and infamous removal by the story of the Trail of Tears.

After there was no longer land of any consequence for the covetous white people to steal or wring from the red people, the government's Indian policy and the relationships with each other changed. The wars and massacres were over. We could probably say peace prevailed—but stress, which kills and erodes the inner peace, still prevailed for many.

Since the invaders destroyed the source of the Indian's subsistence, he "manfully" agreed through his government, bound by treaties, to supply the Indians with food, clothing, medical aid, etc., for as long as necessary. But it was also stipulated as a part of the treaties that government agents and teachers would teach them the art of farming and livestock raising. It was also agreed to give them an education that could serve them well in their new world. But there were those who taught them bad things also. Some, like Chief Red Fox, made good use of their acquired education. Others became demoralized and a state of low ebb prevailed for many years to come. Their suicide rate escalated greatly as did alcoholism and ravages of diseases. They took a terrific beating. At times there were government agents, army generals, missionaries, traders, and others who worked diligently to help the Indian people—to serve their needs and protect their interests.

After the end of the wars several of the generals, such as Generals Miles and Crook, resigned from the military service and went to work to help the Indians and to protect their interests.

Finally, in the period from 1917 to 1920, excessive pressure was used to force patents and fees on Indian allottee's allotment land. This seemed to be a trick to get rid of the allotted land and the allotment policy. The white man could then buy or steal the land from the Indians. The administration was finally convinced that the allotment policy, as it had been applied, had not accomplished goals hoped for in the 1880s.

The next Indian policy was the Indian Reorganization Act, coming as a result of the Meriam Report (1928).

The Last Indian Wars and the Pursuit of Extermination

Hundreds of thousands of buffalo roamed the Great Plains and had always provided the "great and indispensable" life—sustenance for the many Indian tribes thereon. It became the policy of the government to get rid of this great natural resource by a ruthless campaign to totally destroy all of the buffalo and starve the red man to death, so that the white man could take the Indian's country and home. William Cody won the dubious title and distinction of "Buffalo Bill" for his massive destruction of the beasts. How would we respond if someone deliberately destroyed all of our meat animals? What a tremendous waste of "good eats!"

In desperation, the Indians, to save their homes, their country and their very lives, fought their last battles and surrendered to the invaders. The infamous massacre of Wounded Knee stands as a hallmark of an epoch. The government had willfully set about to exterminate the buffalo and thereby the Indians also by starvation.

For years the Army had tried to coax them, and then extended their efforts to forcefully remove them to the Oklahoma Indian Territory—that is, all they could round up and catch. In all cases part of the tribal members would hide out and escape, to emerge later when they thought it safe to do so, and start to resettle in their old homes. It was those on the Great Plains that the armies were attempting to corral on reservations, and/or finally to exterminate the remaining resistors.

A few tribes, such as the Poncos, Yanktonians and others, settled down on their designated reservations established by treaties and remained peaceful.

A policy of ruling these reservation Indians was started by appointing agents and a staff to handle the job. To reward the Indians for accepting this lot, treaties provided for the government to supply their food and other needs, including education and training for farming. This was for replacing that which the whites willfully destroyed, a part of their policy of extermination.

As a sample of the hatred of the Army personnel towards the Indians, it is reported that three days after the massacre at Wounded Knee a detachment was sent from nearby Pine Ridge to bury the massacred Indians. One trench, which still stands as the grave, marked off, was dug and some two-hundred bodies were unceremoniously dumped into it. There were some missionaries and an Army chaplain who offered to perform last rites for the dead. It is reported that Colonel Forsythe, who commanded the forces at Wounded Knee, said that no Mass or Army burial would be given those "savages and red devils," and that he stated, "Let the red devils go to hell without a prayer."

For many years the Department of Indian Affairs was a political bureau through which appointments were made to satisfy henchmen of the party in power. In some cases, Army generals were appointed at the end of the wars.

In most cases, the appointees, including the reservation agents, were illiterate and unscrupulous and had no comprehension of the Indian as anything more than a savage who could be plundered without fear. This idea persisted among some government employees and local citizens up to the early twentieth century. Those henchmen had votes and were more important than the welfare of a group of painted savages who could not vote and whose rights could be violated with impunity.

There were countless occasions when Indian agents cooperated with trading companies who wanted to stop immigrants from settling in the West so that they could keep control of the lands where they were entrenched as long as they could do that, and there were few laws. They could trade, jump claims, sell liquor to the Indians; and in fact do just about as they pleased. Often the field men of those trading companies committed felonies against the settlers, for example, stealing horses or setting fire to their homes, then blaming the Indians for it.

Many of the reservation agents enriched themselves by selling food, clothing and blankets, and other commodities that the government had issued for distribution among the Indians. When the Indians protested the wrongs, the agents would cry to the government that the Indians were on the warpath. The government would send troops to quell them, and that would be the last heard about the atrocities and robberies. If the Indians raised crops or livestock, the agents, whose control was arbitrary, marketed the surplus at a profit for themselves.

Another typical example of a trader cheating the Indian—Jake Kills In Sight raised wheat in the Norris area in South Dakota. They had to haul it to Nebraska where it was sold. He had a white neighbor who also raised wheat. The distance to market was forty to fifty miles. They hauled it in wagons with four-horse teams. They made the trips together but the buyer gave Jake less money for his wheat. Both were exactly the same kind of wheat. Then Jake and his white neighbor got together on a scheme. A mile or so out, before getting to the little town, out of sight, Jake would remain behind with his load while the white man went on with his and sold it. He would then return to where Jake was waiting. The white man would then take Jake's load on into town with his team, sell it and get the same price for it as he received for his own wheat. It is amazing how so many white people, everywhere one went in Indian country, seemed to think it was their right and duty to cheat the Indian. This writer found that to be the case up to the 1940s. It took considerable effort for him to break them of that habit and thinking. (My good friend, Jake Kills In Sight, personally told me the above story.)

Under the Coolidge-Curtis administration conditions improved, and the Indians were granted citizenship, but it was not until F.D.R. was elected President that the old order was thrown out and a better life made for the Indians.

F.D.R. appointed John Collier as Commissioner of Indian Affairs to reform the service and relieve it of the inefficiency and corruption that had made it a disgrace to the nation and a disaster for the Indians.

As we have said before, Collier was a noted authority on the history and culture of the Indians and the nation's treatment of them after they were conquered. He was able to rid the service of the riff-raff that had dominated it since its beginning. New employees had to be obtained through Civil Service examinations and possessing a good education. Collier improved education facilities and health service on the reservations. He instituted regulations and laws to protect the Indians in their property and to provide opportunities for him to become more active in the affairs of the nation.

The New Deal for the Indians begins.

The Indian Reorganization Act (Wheeler Howard Act) — 1934 and the Meriam Report — 1928

The Meriam Report is probably the most significant report, out of many others before it and since, that has been made on Indian affairs—at least from the standpoint of accomplishments after the enactment of the Indian Reorganization Act (IRA) in 1934—under the New Deal of F.D.R. Other acts have been legislated out of its framework and guidance. After over forty-five years of constructive progress, it appears to be well on the way at last to culmination of the Indian problem in the white man's civilization.

Time alone, will tell how successful and conclusive this policy will become and how long it will take.

John Collier, who served as Commissioner of Indian Affairs from 1933 to 1945, can be called the father of this policy and its programs. Ben Reifel, a Pine Ridge Ogalala Sioux was the prime mover in getting the Sioux Nations to accept reorganization under this act.

The twelve years under Collier were an eventful period of general growth for the Indians of the U.S. Most tribes became better prepared to manage their own affairs, after their experience under reorganization. They were also more capable of making their voices heard in Congress. They could assume corporate power, establish credit and borrow money, and conduct their affairs in the white man's society in a businesslike way.

Probably neither the Congress nor the general public fully understood to what extent the IRA was a reversal of the assimilation policy of the allotment period. The allotment policy was to break up the Indian's clanishness and make them operate more as independent individuals. They could be handled more easily as individuals instead of in groups.

There was a belief that the reestablishment of Indian community life and support of local Indian leadership would help prepare these communities to eventually be included in the family of local communities in the various states throughout the United States and bring about the eventual termination of the Bureau of Indian Affairs.

The tribal constitutions and corporate charters actually alluded to the Meriam Report, which was an outstanding report.

While many good things could be said for the Indian Reorganization Act, in 1945 the Congress was tired of the conflict with the act's foremost champion, John Collier, Commissioner of Indian Affairs. He resigned in February, 1945. Mr. Wm. Brophy, who succeeded him, promised to work with the Congress and do their bidding.

Threats were made to liquidate the bureau. Congress refused to authorize new appointments and withheld funds. Programs were requested from each superintendent, looking to the possibility of other federal agencies, the states or themselves assuming responsibilities that were then a part of the so-called "monopoly" held by the BIA.

Shortly after Mr. Brophy became commissioner, a reorganization of the BIA set-up was made, which delegated more authority to subordinates who would be able to reach decisions closer to the point where Indian problems originate. The bill was enacted on August 8, 1946.

Indian Claims

For two decades or more, recommendations had been coming to the BIA and the Congress to set up a special Indian Claims Commission to hear the many unsettled tribal claims against the United States. It was deemed necessary that such action should precede any attempt on the part of the nation to divest itself of the responsibility for an Indian tribe. In 1946 Congress established a joint congressional committee to make a study of claims of Indian tribes against the U.S. and to investigate administration of Indian affairs.

As one studies the hearings relative to the creation of an Indian Claims Commission it becomes clear that one of the reasons the Congress considered it favorably was because it saw claims settlement as a necessary step to prepare Indian tribes to manage their own affairs and to accept the eventual responsiblility for their own welfare. The U.S. Government needed to square its obligated account with the Indian tribes before turning administration of their affairs over to them.

114

Since that time many claims have been awarded and hundreds of millions of dollars paid on these claims. Many more are still in process.

A certain portion of the money is then paid directly to the individually enrolled Indians. Part is used for constructive purposes and a certain other portion is invested in new projects and beneficial things for the tribe. Another designated amount is invested in interest and dividend bearing investments. The income from same is used to pay the tribal administration costs.

Indian Employment and Relocation

This program was to relocate Indians from the reservations to places where employment could be obtained.

This relocation attempt differed from the old forced removal to the Indian Territory, back in the nineteenth century, in that this relocation was voluntary and the government financed them to move, obtain housing and found jobs for them. Training and educational programs were set up for them. Many of them were successfully relocated, but others gave up and returned to their old homes on reservations. The program was well worth what it cost.

Before W.W. II and the disappearance of farm labor jobs, a certain few jobs were provided by the Roads Department, the CCC, WPA, SMCO, Indian Police, and a few other jobs around the Agency and schools. After the war, improved economic conditions helped greatly.

From the time relocation services began, in 1952, until the end of fiscal year 1967, over 61,500 Indian people had been given help towards direct employment. During the same period, more than 24,300 Indians received the benefits of the Adult Vocational Training Program. By 1980 the number of Indians enrolled in colleges and holding responsible jobs had increased tremendously.

One of the amazing things to me resulting from the Adult Training programs was the number of elderly Indians starting out on a new life by taking advantage of this training and then getting good jobs with the bureau and tribal governments. Many had never had a job before. Some of them rose from alcoholism and a wasted life to render valuable service thereafter—even in universities and colleges.

The bureau estimated that between 1967 and 1968 approximately 200,000 Indians moved to urban areas.

Capital Development

Tribes that received awards as a result of Indian claims were encouraged to invest funds in ways that would bring long-term as well as immediate benefits. Through fiscal year 1968 more than $216,000,000 in awards had been made to tribes by the Indian Claims Commission. The total sum probably equals a billion dollars by now. Sizable judgments may finance a variety of development programs that will bring income over a period of many years to come. Investments are also frequently made to secure educational benefits for younger tribal members. This also promised to bring sizable income to other than the present generation.

Members of the 1961 Task Force, which paved the way for the employment and relocation program, considered it as a primary instrument of the termination policy which the tribes almost universally feared.

Support for Public Law 959 (1956), enacted to provide vocational training and related employment assistance programs for Indians between the ages of eighteen and thirty, began with an appropriation of $3.5 million and gradually increased. On February 8, 1968, the authorization for annual appropriations was set at $25 million. Commissioner Bennett expressed the opinion that this was "one of the most helpful pieces of legislation ever approved to assist the Indian people."

From Termination to Self-Determination
and Indian Leadership for Indian Programs

In the words of the U.S. official *History of Indian Policy*, over forty years ago (1928), the writers of the Meriam Report suggested:

"The people of the U.S. have the opportunity, if they will, to write the closing chapters of the history of relationship of the national government and the Indians. *The early chapters contain little of which the country may be proud.** It would be something of a national atonement to the Indians if the closing chapters should disclose the national government supplying the Indians with an Indian Service which would be a model for all governments with the development and advancement of a retarded race."

It appears that the closing chapter could be near at hand, fulfilling the recommendations of the Meriam Report over a fifty-

*The underlined is the writer's opinion.

year period. These programs, co-initiated jointly by Indian tribes and the BIA, and administered by the tribes, have greatly uplifted the Indian people and improved their morale and standard of living—over a period of fifty years. Their new houses, education and health facilities, job-training, hospitals, churches, tribal offices, and business affairs, their new self-determination and self-help has better fitted them to survive and fit into the world's present civilization.

Valuable lessons could be taken from the Indians' achievements, and used to develop policies for the blacks and other underprivileged minority groups of people. They could do more to help themselves and attain a better and fuller life for themselves. It would require ingenuity, planning, work, and honest leadership. They would have to learn to respect persons and property and to accept responsibility. THE MERIAM REPORT HAS SERVED ITS PURPOSE WELL.

CHAPTER 5: MORE PROGRAMS AND PROJECTS

Range Improvement in New Mexico—Progress Data 1935-1948—Rosebud Indian Reservation—Two Kettle Irrigation Project—Monument to Blundering Bureaucrats—Indian Progress Programs On The Yankton Reservation—Rising Hail Cooperative—Contour Furrows— CCC Projects—Giant Navajo Indian Irrigation Project—

Range Improvement in New Mexico – Taking a Look at Some Results

What has been the outcome and results from the government projects to improve the economy for the Indians on their reservations? I think we can say, as a whole, they have been successful. Naturally, there were some failures.

Since I started my service career in New Mexico in 1936, I was interested in knowing how our work turned out there. Nearly all of the grazing lands were terribly overgrazed at that time. The problem was to restore them to their maximum capacity to produce meat and wool, under the climatic conditions prevailing there.

The tribes and the United Pueblo Agency contracted with the U.S. Soil Conservation Service to accomplish the job of restoring the productivity of their ranges. Some of the Pueblo tribes entered into the contract and cooperated with us. Other tribes did not. My job was working with the S.C.S. as the representative of the BIA.

Of course educational work had to be done, explaining the program to the Indian people and what would be required of them.

For the cooperating tribes, our next step was to inventory the livestock units owned by the tribal members. These numbers had to be reduced to where the range could recover over a scheduled period of years, and thereafter be maintained to a number that would sustain those numbers to their maximum production level.

The greatest need for these people was to have more livestock. Consequently for them to reduce their numbers was not a pleasant thing to look forward tto, but they could hopefully look forward to improvement eventually.

All of the cattle were rounded up and all were identified by ownership. At the same time we branded, dehorned and vaccinated all that needed it.

A schedule was worked out for each owner—the number of head he would be required to reduce each of the scheduled years. The larger herds took the greatest cuts, those of only a few were spared.

After the season's work was done a big Indian cattle sale was advertised where buyers could assemble and purchase what they wanted.

The sheep herds were reduced also and handled likewise.

When a Pueblo Indian gives his word, you can rest assured that he will keep it. This made it a pleasure to work with them, and you could expect full cooperation from them.

I wanted to see what the results were after forty years. I could get no statistics at either the agency in Albuquerque or the central office in Washington, D.C. So I made a survey on the spot. I was much gratified with what I found. The forage on the participating reservations was good to excellent for the area. The quality and condition of the cattle were greatly improved and I would judge that the pounds of meat produced exceeds what it did before the program was initiated.

I found that wells pumped with windmills were strategically located over the area. The ranges were also fenced and cross-fenced, making it possible to rotate grazing. It was not far down to the water. That water, in the water-scarce area, was always there and could have been made available years before.

I was particularly interested in the Sia Pueblos' grazing country. Their cattle grazed out to the Black Mesa country, fifteen to twenty miles inland from the Jemez River. As I remember it, those cattle came back to the river for water every third day—maybe it was less. They left their little calves back on the range when they went for water. I remember seeing those cattle coming to the river about four or five o'clock in the evening to get their drink. They came in on the trot. Now, these cattle only have to go, I would say, a couple of miles for a good refreshing drink of water. The forage was ample and more productive.

As one travels south on the highway from Gallup, New Mexico, to the Zuni Reservation, he comes to a fence that transverses the highway. The highway has a cattle guard across it which permits vehicles to cross over but prevents livestock from crossing it. As one looks up and down the fence line, the contrasts between the two sides tells its own story. On one side the forage is very good and productive, while on the other side the grass is forced to live an underground existence, with very little opportunity to stick its head above ground or manufacture the necessary food for its growth. When you cross over to the side of the good forage you will enter the Indian reservation. The non-Indians on the opposite side are poor managers. They neglect to practice conservation and good pasture management. We can thank the Indian Bureau and the Indian Cooperators for their progressive management.

The Case of the Navaho Program of Range Improvement and Management

The Navaho Indians have long been shepherds—since the Spaniards introduced cattle, horses and sheep to them. Their later progress started, more or less, after their return to their homeland following the four years of forced banishment by the U.S. Army to Fort Defiance. They gladly agreed to a treaty for the return to their former homeland and desist in their raids on their neighbors. In the treaty the U.S. Government agreed to supply them with seed stock to renew their herds, their orchards, and field crops. As was the case of so many Indian tribes down through United States history, they never violated their treaty obligation. (Sometimes tribes retaliated for breach of treaty when done first by the white people). The Navahos soon had accumulated far too many head of livestock. Their ranges were fast being destroyed by overgrazing.

Soon after acquiring sheep they were weaving wool. Still later they would learn to work silver and set turquoise stones in their jewelry. It seems that every home was the source of some manufactured goods. Navaho rugs were famous, known for their quality and wearing properties as well as their beauty. They standardized their products, especially the jewelry which bore their trademark and in later years marketed the surplus through their cooperatives.

According to statistics which we have found, there were 40,000 Indians on the Navaho land by 1930 which figure grew to 120,000 by 1970. By 1930 they had over a half million sheep, 187,000 goats, 25,000 head of cattle and 50,000 horses. These were the equivalent of 1,111,500 sheep units.

The herds concentrated around the relatively few watering places and the surrounding areas were depleted of forage. In 1893, the problem became so serious that Congress appropriated the first funds for water development. There was no systematic effort made to control grazing, and so no accurate livestock count was made until the problem was attacked jointly by the Indian Bureau and the Department of Agriculture in 1933.

By that time destruction of the range through overgrazing was approaching disaster. Technicians who studied conditions in minute detail found that the maximum carrying capacity of the land was 560,000 sheep units. The land had been carrying double that load for an undetermined number of years. The drought conditions, at that time, were growing steadily more severe, which intensified the destruction. Freshwater lakes and springs, which once were abundant in some areas, disappeared, the lake beds filled with silt and their waters evaporated. Perennial streams expired. Ground water receded until springs and artesian wells no longer flowed.

A 1935 study by range experts reached this disturbing conclusion: "Within the reservation there has been brought about a progressively deteriorating situation which, if allowed to continue, would ultimately make the area virtually uninhabitable and will force the United States Government to remove the Indian population and resettle them or support them on a dole."

To the Navaho Indians, when this information was interpreted to them, the conclusion had a shattering effect. Livestock meant food and clothing, and a measure of prestige. The herds might be over age and not fully productive, but a man's worth was judged by the size of the herds. Horses, which had no economic value to the family except as transportation, and work animals, were a particular mark of distinction.

The livestock reduction program created bitterness and a sense of humiliation, bringing the tribal government almost to destruction. There was no alternative. By invoking the legal authority of the Secretary of Interior the objective was achieved. It turned out to be for the good of everybody concerned. In 1941, on the eve of W.W. II, the livestock load was down to the carrying capacity of the range.

The economic effect of the reduction program, in terms of income, actually made for improvement. The animals taken off the range were the cull animals that had a low or no market value, and emphasis was placed on retaining young breeding animals. Excess horses were removed and families were encouraged to keep

121

only young stuff, limited to the number they actually needed. A sheep-breeding laboratory, established at the very start of the reduction program, resulted in introducing improved breeding strains throughout the Navaho country.

The younger and improved breeding stock produced a higher percentage of lambs. The lambs tended to be heavier and the production of wool increased remarkably. In 1935, for example, 550,000 head of sheep produced just over 2,000,000 pounds of wool. In 1941 when the livestock load had been brought down to the estimated carrying capacity the 434,000 head of sheep produced 3,000,000 pounds of wool. The income from livestock actually increased through the years in which reduction took place.

A very valuable achievement was accomplished in a remarkably short time by the technicians and the Navaho Indians. And the Navaho Indians went on in other ways to improve their economic condition, health and education facilities and adjusting to hard and changing conditions. They have the native talents and nobleness of character for survival.

Program on the Yankton Reservation

The Yankton Reservation in South Dakota is in a principally farming area and farmers have been notorious for overgrazing pastures giving the forage plants little chance to do their stuff. We required our lessees of Indian trust land to comply with our stipulations regarding grazing management. In a few short years our Indian pastures were the most productive in the area, and set examples that became followed by the more progressive farmers and livestock producers of the area.

Statistical Data of Progress

Speaking of statistics, I do have a statistical data compilation of progress of the Rosebud-Yankton reservations for a fourteen year period. (1935-1948.)

This could be more or less a typical example on the reservations in the Great Plains region. All Extension Agents and Farm Agents were required to keep track of all livestock in their jurisdiction and make annual agricultural reports, the records of which should always be kept on file some-where.

122

SURVIVAL OF A NOBLE RACE

Progress Data 1935—1948
Rosebud Indian Reservation

Activity	1935	1941	1945	1948
Gross income from Livestock-products	$31,900	$206,185	$435,967	$1,046,879
Gross income from gardens & crops	$28,000	$21,690	$32,330	$159,591
Livestock Population:				
Horses	2,410	3,672	4,153	4,365
Cattle	3,144	7,724	13,855	17,338
Sheep	1,931	1,572	1,866	160
Hogs	475	670	1,768	1,644
Poultry	12,895	20,451	19,618	22,722
Garden & Crops:	?			
garden acreage		716	581	472
Number gardens	1,439	957	671	516
Production, lbs.	788,360	583,779	606,000	465,000
Cereal Grains:				
Acreage	21,882	9,101	12,025	18,299
Production	193,550	96,192	192,831	231,692
Forage Crops:				
Wild Hay, acres	18,260	17,115	16,720	30,360
Production, tons	12,850	9,678	12,740	25,365
Annual Forage, acres	1,278	3,250	3,165	1,050
Production, tons	0	5,851	2,905	950

The Bureau of Census says that the median family income of the Laguna Reservation in New Mexico was $6115 recently. We have no record of what it was in 1937 when we started the range improvement program. One may conclude, however, knowing that it was far below the $6115, that the improved carrying capacity of their range helped considerably to increase the family income for the Laguna people and that they made a wise decision to go into the program.

There have been failures as well as successes with some of the agricultural and industrial enterprises. The failures can largely be attributed to inefficient and improper management and supervision, and oftentimes thievery.

One example where the planners and supervisors, given large sums of money, squandered it because they lacked the knowledge for the type of enterprise and did not know enough to seek the advice of someone who did. They thought they knew what they were doing. The Two Kettle Irrigation Project on the White River is a case in point. I do not know what the project cost the taxpayers but it was costly.

123

Two Kettle Irrigation Project

The Two Kettle Irrigation Project was constructed at the confluence of the Big White and Little White rivers in South Dakota. As an irrigation project it has remained a total failure for forty-five years. The writer does not know how much of the taxpayers' hard earned and hard to get dollars was wasted but it was a large sum and could have been well spent some other place.

In the first place, most of the soil was unsuited for irrigation. Secondly, part of the main canal traversed a steep escarpment of Pierre shale. Pierre shale holds water like a sieve and the steep slope slushes its dirt after every little rain and clogs the canal to overflowing, causing it to wash out.

One would think that an agriculturally experienced person would know enough to obtain soil tests for both the land to be irrigated and for the canal structure. He had absolutely no experience or knowledge of irrigation, which should have been a good reason for him to enlist assistance and advice from professionals. Too many incompetent persons get the idea that they just naturally know it all. We have encountered more than one.

The officials asked the writer to take over the operation and management of the project, since he had irrigation experience, but after viewing the situation he declined to move in and do so. This was a few years after their initial attempt to make it go.

Elsewhere in this narrative we have covered some of the programs promoted by the BIA. Some turned out to be very good, but others ranged to utter failures. Some were ill-conceived and grossly mismanaged, at a great waste of taxpayers' money. They were completely unqualified, but were given the authority, power and funds to carry out their projects. They failed to consult knowledgable sources and did not possess practical sense to reason for themselves.

We have mentioned elsewhere the results of the range improvement in New Mexico. This turned out to be an outstanding program and a credit to those who accomplished it.

The Soil and Moisture Conservation Organization on the Yankton Reservation had multiple accomplishments—restoring grazing capacity to pastures, building stock water dams, rodent and noxious weed control, conservation of soil and moisture, and good farming practices, etc., etc.

In the late 1950s, a new management group bent on wrecking the operating program came to the Yankton Reservation. After wrecking the organizations and the programs they were unable

124

to reconstruct them. It killed the conservation program and nothing has been accomplished in that line even after twenty years. (We tell the story in Chapter 7 under "Conspiracy.")

Monument to Blundering Bureaucrats

Here is the story of another typical example of the ill-conceived programs wasted on Indian reservations by completely unqualified persons with nothing but authority, federal money and a Civil Service position to keep them in power.

The federal government's Economic Development Administration (EDA) was providing the money.

On the Crow Creek Reservation they built a motel complex at a cost of $900,000. Today, hardly a decade later, the motel lies in ruins—a deserted monument to bureaucratic incompetence. The tribal leaders are embittered, since the complex cost their people $220,000 of that amount.

The Crow Creek complex opened with great expectations. There was the motel with forty rooms, a service station, a restaurant and bar, a liquor store, and assorted shops.

The number of tourists envisioned in the feasibility study never materialized. But trouble did. When winter came, with temperatures dipping to thirty below, water pipes, which had been installed above the ceiling, burst, flooding the rooms. Obligingly, EDA spent another $50,000 to winterize the complex. Construction deficiencies were only one of their problems. The motel bar provided intoxication among Indians, creating an objectionable environment for visiting tourists.

The 1976, and EDA financed study concluded what should have been blatantly clear from the beginning: "The motel operation is not economically feasible."

The following year the tribe closed the facilities. Parts of the facilities were sold, the ceiling collapsed and left the building to vandals.

What happened to those who provided the money for the nightmare? Ray Tanner, the high EDA official who has served as the guiding force behind the tourist projects, was awarded the Commerce Department's Gold Medal for Distinguished Service! The above is a typical example of the BIA's gross mismanagement of Indian affairs during that era.

Indian Progress Programs on the Yankton

On the Yankton Reservation there were several projects managed by committees elected by the members of the tribe. These projects and their committees were the Credit Committee, the Rehab Committee, the Soil and Moisture Conservation Organization (SMCO), and some other managing committees, such as Arts and Crafts and Relief. Each of these organizations adopted their own constitution and by-laws. These executive committees transacted all business of their respective organizations.

The purposes were to conserve their natural resources, make the best use of same, to improve and expand their economy, to provide for the needy, and to distribute commodities. It was also to determine and manage their own affairs. They screened, approved and advised applicants for cash and repayment cattle loans. They managed the financial affairs of their organizations. These organizations were in compliance with the purpose and policy of Indians managing their own affairs and gave them the training and experience they needed.

The directors and managers were honest, dedicated people who served without pay and expense money. They did a bang-up job of which anyone could be proud. Their income and expenditure accounts were always favorably balanced and in good order. All surplus money earned was used for the benefit of the tribe and the tribal members.

For some years the Rehab's income from rentals had to be used to repair and improve the Rehab places. When these needs were satisfied, they extended their operations to place wells in the several communities for domestic use. Before that many families had to buy or haul water for their household use. They hauled this water from the Missouri River or other wells. This was a community service completely financed and managed by their own initiative and under the supervision of the writer as the BIA Farm Agent. Eventually the Rehab Committee was able to allow themselves a small stipend for attending executive meetings. At first it was only a dollar or two to pay for gas but as their bank account increased their allowance was increased by a very small amount.

They were very frugal and unselfish. The tribe owes these dedicated servants many thanks for their personal sacrifices and their contributions to the welfare and uplifting of their people. They were living and exalting their ancestral nobleness and pride . . . true to their race. Far too many of them, in the last ten to twenty years, have let their race down and debased their reputation.

Honest and efficient BIA supervisors tend to inspire and make honest and efficient Indian leaders and directors. The dishonest and corrupt ones breed corruption. This fact has been positively demonstrated numerous times. The writer definitely believes that much of the mismanagement of tribal affairs on the Indian reservations in recent years has been implanted by and crookedness encouraged by the conduct of the B.I.A. officials and supervisors in charge of the various government's programs on the reservations. The top people of these programs and projects usually are white persons and many of them seem to manage it to enhance corruption and coverup.

The striking differences of the period of the 1930s through the 1950s, as compared to the 1960s and 1970s into the early 1980s, is that in the first period the Bureau of Indian Affairs was manned by honest and dedicated officials and employees.

In the later period the Great Plains reservations were plagued with uncontrolled inefficiency and corruption.

Some of the other important programs and projects during the later half of the 1930s, through the forties and fifties were the Arts and Crafts, community irrigated gardens, canning and preserving foods, partial self-help home repairs, wood cutting for fuel, extension adult education with picture shows, and making some art and craft articles to sell.

During the winter months we had community meetings three nights a week every other week. Besides these we had other meetings on other nights. These meetings always lasted to midnight or later. Those were difficult times and people were active and cooperated to solve their problems. All departments of the agency cooperated in these programs.

Rising Hail Cooperative (Chalk Rock Colony)
The "dirty" thirties were very hard and trying times. There were few jobs available. Drought and grasshoppers were present in full swing. Low prices and few markets prevailed. The immediate objective was to provide means for obtaining subsistence as very little hope existed at that time for ways to make money.

One of the projects developed to advance some opportunities along this line, which could provide the most benefits for the most people for the money, was the Rising Hail Colony project. It began in 1938 on a tract of land lying on the Missouri River bottom with some rough pasture land on the adjoining river bluffs. This land was purchased with Rehabilitation funds provided by the gov-

127

ernment. Two sets of farmsteads were already on the place. Eight new houses, a community canning kitchen, schoolhouse, a deep well with water pressure for domestic and livestock use, and a large barn were built, using native chalk rock mined from the nearby bluffs and cut into building blocks. A work project was set up to process the blocks and provide many jobs for a while. Marty Mission built a church in a picturesque setting.

A section of rich river bottom farm land was leveled for irrigation and a gasoline engine pumping-plant was installed. The land for irrigation was staked out in ten-acre plots. The plan was to assign one of these to each of the occupants for their individual family use. However, it never reached the stage to be operated as such. Instead the families who gained assignment to the colony decided to organize an Indian cooperative with a constitution and by-laws. Officers were elected and the chairman acted as the general manager. The writer, a BIA Farm Agent at that time, was the general supervisor.

They obtained a reimbursible loan to purchase machinery, equipment, livestock, seed, operating expenses, and subsistence support for a period of one year. Each family had to perform work to qualify for the monthly subsistence check. It provided that if and when dividends became available for distribution, they would be on the basis of work performed by each member during his tenure.

Several enterprises were set up—a dairy, hog, poultry, beef cattle, community garden, canning, sorghum making, a few colonies of bees, as well as general farming. Certain members were designated to head and manage each of the enterprises.

The going was rough at first, some of it due to unusual losses. The barn burned with loss of harness, some machinery and their dairy equipment. Some of the beef cattle were stolen from the pasture, some lost due to anthrax, including the herd bull and some registered cattle. What makes the cattle lost to anthrax so unusual is the fact that they were vaccinated and supposed to be immune. They say this occurs once in many, many years.

The war brought about changes. With the accompanying good crop years and good prices, the farmers expanded their efforts, raising as much food and feed as possible. Some went to war jobs.

After the war the farming became more than a mere subsistence effort. It expanded into larger operations and more progressive methods. The number of members in the Rising Hail Cooperative Association dropped from the original twelve to three, to two and finally to one operator. It became a one-family sized operation.

The cooperative was eventually dissolved, the debts and loan paid off in full and the assets divided among those remaining in the association at the time. With those assets they were able to continue farming on their own, some in other locations on the reservation where they found sufficient land for a larger operation.

By 1980 this land was being operated by a couple of grandsons, under irrigation and raising bountiful corn crops. A few words need to be said here about the Cournoyers who are still farming the Rising Hail land. Frank and Florence Cournoyer and their family were among the first residents at the colony in the thirties and their grandsons are still carrying on. Many of their children left but son Steve and wife Pearl remained and raised a family of fourteen children at Rising Hail, living in one of the small chalk rock houses. They had no modern conveniences. They had cattle, a hog project, poultry, farmed the land and gardened. They stuck it out through the good and the bad times. More of the story of their hard work and initiative may be found in chapters 6 and 7. They survived plans of new BIA employees to break up their accomplishments and force them to leave. Their success was due to the family endeavor. Even the small children helped with the work and were proud of it. The first irrigation project in the area was due to their efforts—producing big crops of corn, cucumbers, etc. My wife and I loved to visit this family where we found so much friendliness down to the smallest child, which we will always cherish. The setting of peace, among the huge chalk cliffs and lush scenery on the banks of the Missouri River, their courage, resourcefulness and hope have enabled them to live better lives to this day. This was handed down to them by their grandparents whose honest, religious lives were well known.

Only a few vacant chalk rock houses remain at the site but most have been replaced by new modern homes.

Steve's older brother, Jim Cournoyer, moved to a large Rehab farm in another part of the reservation. He and his wife and sons operated a dairy, raised hogs and poultry, corn, hay, other crops, and garden produce. This was also a family effort and where we too enjoyed visiting. We loved Jim and Ethel who commanded respect, were honest and hard working. It was cut short when Jim died in a car accident. None of his sons carried on. They attended college and have responsible positions. Son Larry is the chairman of the Yankton Sioux tribe, also chairman of the United Sioux Tribes covering reservations in North and South Dakota.

Contour Furrows — CCC Projects

Soil and moisture conservation is a noble endeavor. The time approaches when both will be hard to come by to meet our national needs. Our need for sufficient water may soon become a critical problem. We need to constantly plan for its conservation.

One moisture and soil conservation program set up on the Yankton Indian Reservation, and some on other reservations, are worthy of notice. The name of it is Contour Furrows. It was done by the Civilian Conservation Corps (CCC) created in the 1930s under the New Deal. Its purpose was to provide jobs for jobless young people. The project's set up had to conserve and enhance some natural resources.

Many miles of Contour Furrows were built on the Yankton Indian Reservation during those days. The furrows were laid out on level contours at specified intervals. The spacing depended upon the degree of slope. The work was done with hand tools, which made furrows that were more stable and permanent and provided many more jobs.

Viewing the scene from the top of the landscape after a hard rain provided a beautiful sight with the furrows covering the hill slope and all of them full of glistening water. The water was held on the land to benefit the forage thereon, instead of rushing down the hill sides, carrying with it much of the soil and organic matter and winding up in the Gulf of Mexico and causing damage by flooding on its way.

After forty-five years these furrows are still intact and in operational condition. Not one cent has been spent for maintenance of these structures during that time. They stand as great monuments to those people who used good judgment and management in their creations.

There were various other types of projects of similar nature throughout Sioux land reservations. Some of these included planting shelter belts of trees to control wind erosion of soil and break the force of hot drying winds; river bank stabilization, small dams and community irrigated gardens with their community canning kitchens. These gardens and canning facilities were a valuable factor for the subsistence and better diets for the Indian people during that long, dry and depression period. The state and federal forests and parks came in for their share of these CCC work projects. Camps were set up on the sites to provide lodging and board for the workers.

Some of these projects may seem small in present-day terms

but the results have not been small. They served a valuable and timely purpose and the end is not yet in sight.

Giant Navaho Indian Irrigation Project

A $260 million Navaho Indian Irrigation Project on 110,630 acres is being realized. It is scheduled to be developed by blocks of 10,000 acres at a time. It is located in northwestern New Mexico near Farmington on desert-like conditions with a fertile wind-deposited topsoil. The climate is mild and dry with a relative humidity of thirty-five percent and an annual average rainfall of seven and a half inches. The elevation is 5400 feet and the mean annual temperature is 51.6 F. The reservation (largest in the nation) is 19,400 square miles of fertile land with an estimated population of over 135,000.

The Navaho family income has always been very low and their unemployment rate very high. This irrigation project probably offers the greatest economic potential that the Navaho people have ever had since they came to Arizona. The possible exception is the introduction of sheep by the white invaders. Sheep raising became a very important economic enterprise for them. It provided another and no doubt better source for food, clothing, blankets, and footwear. The wool provided the raw material for making articles such as, rugs and blankets which they sold for cash. The Navaho blankets were of superior quality and became widely known and famous.

After the preliminary surveys and studies the project was jointly initiated by the Bureau of Indian Affairs (BIA) and the Bureau of Reclamation (BOR) in 1942. The Navaho tribe was notified in 1953 of a proposed Navaho dam on the San Juan River and of its capabilities. A general agreement was reached in 1956 with the Navaho tribe, state and government authorities. The major points of this agreement were: that the developed lands be used solely for the Indians; that all suitable lands in the Shiprock-San Juan Valley be included in the proposed development; that irrigable farm lands were to amount to no less than 115,000 acres; and that allowable Navaho tribal water be no less than 508,000 acre-feet annually; that the United States was to build the project, and the Bureau of Indian Affairs was to maintain it upon completion. After this the Navaho Tribal Council petitioned Congress to act favorably on legislation to authorize the Colorado River Storage Project and participating projects which included the Navaho irrigation.

The Navaho Agricultural Products Industry (NAPI) was created by the Navaho Tribal Council (dated May 11, 1967) for the purpose of administering the development and farming of the 110,630 acres of Navaho land utilizing the Navaho Indian Irrigation Project (NIIP). They plan and guide the development of NIIP. The Tribal Council appointed a management board consisting of thirteen members to carry out the plan of operation. The NAPI was given full and complete jurisdiction to start operations and development of the agri-business venture on April 16, 1970.

Irrigation water reached the first 10,000-acre block in 1976. A second block was planted and irrigated in 1977. A third block was cultivated in the sumers of 1978 and 1979. The current plan is to add 10,000 acres annually until all blocks of the 110,630-acre enterprise is irrigated and cultivated. The project will feature crops of alfalfa, grain, forage, beans, potatoes, etc.

Four regional headquarters are planned. Each is composed of three and/or four blocks. Each regional headquarters will have warehouses, fuel stations, grain mills, administrative headquarters, and any related support services necessary for the region's varied agricultural operations. An overall Administrative Headquarters has been completed and was occupied in May, 1979.

The NAPI has its own marketing division which has been successfully handling sales on the open market with most products being trucked to its destination. (Many tribes all over the nation have their own cooperatives. They usually standardize their product and market the same wholesale over many states.).

The NAPI has been growing with the San Juan Basin. It employed 450 people in 1980 with a $3.2 million payroll. Over $4 million of goods and services were purchased from local vendors in addition to construction contracts awarded in the area by the BOR and BIA. In ten years the planners anticipate that NAPI will employ 2500 to 3000 people in direct farm and agri-business ventures.

The NAPI farm has been and will be beneficial to the San Juan Basin economy. Local employment increases with each block. In 1979, the community of Ojo Amarillo, located on Block 2, was completed. The master plan for this housing project encompasses fifty mutual help and 150 low-rent units with supporting facilities, roads, a town center, fire stations, police protection, and a school. In addition to existing Ojo Amarillo, 150 new homes were constructed in 1980 on Blocks 1, 2, and adjacent to the Main Headquarters building.

The NAPI management is planning a vertically integrated farming and livestock operation. The Navahos have been shepherds for more than two hundred years. They possess an almost uncanny empathy with livestock. We discuss this uncanny empathy of Indians in another part of this book. They have proved their ability to raise cattle and sheep in an incredibly harsh environment. They won't be Navahos without their sheep.

The Navaho Agricultural Products Industry has the potential to turn the Navaho Nation into a green land of opportunity, no longer haunted by the specters of poverty and hopelessness. And the Navaho, in the words of an ancient chant, " . . . will live long and well, Pollen will shine in his smile and stars will dance like moths over his hogan."

There are other important projects on other and various reservations which we have not discussed herein, such as lumbering, fishing, jewelry making, and many industrial projects. We have stated before that we aim to give a few typical examples and cannot cover all cases. Suffice it to say that these are typical, correct and true.

CHAPTER 6: THIEVERY AND CORRUPTION

The Case of FDR and "Big Hugh"—Thievery—Early Experience With Crookedness—Lease Clerk Steals Funds—Repayment Cattle Program—Land Appraiser—Indian Health Service—Whitlock-Aamodt Administration—The New Deal—News Headlines—Large Scale Thefts From Warehouses—Blow the Whistle—The Episode of An Extension Agent—The Episode of Webster Two Hawk—Pay off "Disabled" Bureaucrats—

Crookedness and corruption abound everywhere and one cannot accept their presence, and must guard against temptation almost at every turn. Many people seem to think it is their right and privilege to cheat or steal from their fellowmen. We find so many guilty people everywhere we go. We can be just as guilty by association, consent, or by silence. We would prefer to pass down on the other side of the street, so to speak, and avoid getting involved or risk losing our job over our efforts to prevent or thwart evil. Few people are willing to pay the price that might be required.

We encountered crookedness in the university, in state and county governments, also in federal bureaus and agencies, private business concerns, their agents and supervisors, and, of course, in individuals.

It may be done by stealing valuables, some one's job or prestige. It may be to steal a position on some competitive team-or to get on a gravy train. If you have something good and worthwhile, there is almost sure to be some one around who covets it. They will connive and pull strings, or whatever, to get it.

The Case of F.D.R. and "Big Hugh"

F.D.R. was a great psychologist of understanding people and how to handle them. In the early thirties the Soil Conservation

Service, in the United States Department of Agriculture (U.S.D.A.), was born. The President was looking for the right man to organize and put into operation this new department of government. He contacted Hugh Bennett, a more or less minor employee of the Department of Agriculture in regard to taking over this task. He later became called the "Father of the Soil Conservation Service."

"Big Hugh," as he affectionately came to be called, questioned the advisability of his taking over as head of the organization. This was an important assignment and would be coveted by others in the department much higher on the totem pole than he. Considering the Civil Service system, jealousy by superiors would make overbearing trouble for someone in a subordinate station. No doubt this is what Hugh Bennett was thinking about.

Then the president said: "They are after you, Bennett." "And when they are after somebody he's usually doing a bang-up job." (Hugh had the backing of the top man, that made a difference).

The only time when a lone worker can successfully resist those "vultures" is when he has the support of the powers at the top. The bureaucracy is so organized and against him, regardless of his record of performance, that his chances of surviving are practically nil. Big Hugh had the backing of a great President, however, and his watchful eye. Big Hugh did a great job and won the respect of a nation, who honored him for his services.

At one time if anyone complained about some government employee to a congressman or senator, the congressman or senator passed it on to the head of the agency. The employee was instructed by his supervisor to drop everything else if necessary, and answer the complaint. But in more recent years this attitude has changed. Now the individual or his agency can just thumb his nose at even a senator and get by with it. At times the Commissioner of Indian Affairs can give orders for corrections or an investigation to an agency under his jurisdiction and they just ignore it. Even some senators have said, "We can't win—they have so many ways of evasion." Yes, evil times have come over our great nation! Only an aroused people can curb or control it.

Thievery

For a long time there has been a certain element on and near Indian reservations who made it a business to seek deals to steal and cheat Indians. Sometimes a little liquor went a long way to help.

When the writer first came to the Yankton Sioux Reservation

135

in 1938 there were still a few scalpers and traders around looking for deals with the Indians. Their attitude was that they had the right and privilege to cheat the Indian and they expected us to accept it as a fact. They took it to be the accepted way. Some of them paid no attention to my disapproval and warnings. They took it to be just a matter of form and to be disregarded. It took a little convincing on my part to put a stop to it. I got two of them into the courthouse to convince them.

I cite here a few typical examples:

(1) An Indian had several head of good Hereford cattle and he came to me to get a permit to trade them to a white man for different ones. The ones he would get had Shorthorn breeding and would be better for milking stock, and he could use them for the family milk. I made my inspection and approved the deal, since it was a good deal for the Indian. In fact, I was surprised that the deal was so much in his favor. The white man was to deliver his cattle to the Indian and pick up the Indian's cattle he was acquiring in the trade.

The white man came and got the Indian's cattle but failed to deliver to the Indian. The Indian notified me after waiting a while. The white man gave some excuse, but the delay persisted after several notices, and it appeared he was avoiding living up to his part of the deal. I reminded him that those cattle were U.S. Government trust property and that he could be charged with illegal possession of government property. He then delivered them within an hour or so.

(2) Back in the late thirties quite a few of the Indians were buying horses, harnesses, wagons, and other things. At that time very few Indians had enough funds in their individual money account, and would obtain small government loans to get the funds. As government representatives we had to inspect and approve the purchases and sign the purchase orders.

One day at the agency office I was busy processing loans. One white man horse-dealer walked into my office and handed me a note. It said he would give me five dollars for every horse we bought from him. He not only made the offer in writing but he was dumb enough to sign his name to it. He must have thought that all government employees were bribable! It was a federal offense to bribe a government agent or employee.

(3) An Indian on the Rosebud Reservation had a new harness which he had never used. They cost ninety dollars each. He applied to the extension agent to get a permit to sell it, probably

because they didn't need it anymore or needed the money for something else. I never heard his reasons for selling it. These deals were supervised by the extension agents and reasons had to be given justifying the deal. The agent was required to inspect purchases by Indians to see that they got value received. He had to certify and sign purchase orders and approve checks written if the purchase was by check. He had to certify that the deal was just and of true value. The same applies to sales by Indians.

The harness was sold to a scalper (white man) for thirty or thirty-five dollars. I don't remember which. In another week or two another Indian wanted to buy a harness. He got a purchase order from the same agent and bought this same harness and paid ninety dollars for it. The agent certified that he inspected the harness and found it to be of reasonable cost. The agent had to know that it was the same harness and he approved both sales at a great loss to the first Indian. One can guess how the sixty dollar profit was split. No one knows how many of these deals were perpetrated on the Indian reservations. But there were many, many of them.

By the way, the FBI finally caught up with this BIA agent and he was fired after more than twenty years in the service. He eventually died after suffering for a number of years from incapacitating physical ailments, blindness, mental depression, loneliness and with few friends who cared any more.

This was the end of a human experience. He possessed great native abilities, had a promising and active life with good prospects of a successful future career, and wide acquaintances of fellow men over the state and beyond.

Another case occurred at Albuquerque, N.M. Several of the United Pueblo tribes put in an order for quite a few wagons. (Wagons were very important to them those days and they took considerable pride in good wagons.) The Agency obtained bids for them. Two firms, A and B, submitted bids. Firm A submitted the lower bid and was awarded the order.

The wagons were delivered unassembled to the Agency grounds. I was detailed to inspect the wagons to see if they were all there and measured up to advertised specifications. I discovered that they were far from meeting specifications. They were heavy, high-wheeled, cumbersome, old-time freighting wagons used in the early days for hauling freight overland. There no longer was a market for these, and the dealer had them left over and was unable to sell them anymore. They presumably took a chance

137

to try and dump them at a very reasonable price and likely get the low bid.

The wagons would not meet the needs of the Indians for their purposes. They would have been very unhappy with them and would probably have rejected the wagons and refused to pay for them.

The superintendent rejected the wagons and the other firm (B) was given the order. Firm A being unable to supply the proper goods went to Firm B and purchased the wagons. They had to pay Firm B the price of Firm B's bid and could collect only the amount of Firm A's bid from the Indian Agency. Firm A had to stand a loss of the difference between the two bids. As a consequence the Indians got good suitable wagons at a very reasonable price.

Tony had gotten several head of repayment cattle on contract and was paying for them as per his repayment schedule. Now the time was due for him to make his last installment. He would have several head left over, which would be his "paid in full."

The extension agent came around and demanded the last payment. He told Tony he owed for a certain number of head. Tony told him that he had made a payment the previous year and owed only a lesser number. Besides being a truly honest Indian Tony had a good memory and was very emotional. When Mr. Jones demanded the larger number, Tony told him he would have no dealings with anyone who dealt that way and that if that was the way he did business he could take the whole works. Well, Mr. Jones did just that! It was called to my attention and I relayed the problem to Mr. Jones. He instructed me to check the records, which I did and found Tony was right. I made a transcript of the ledger record and gave it to him without comment. But he still got the cattle and took all of them.

I took the record from the Agency Auditor's office and I learned later that Mr. Jones also kept a record in his office and no doubt his record failed to have that last transaction entered. In some ways he was an ornery man, very stubborn about admitting a mistake and had no qualms about treating others unjustly. I doubt if Tony ever got compensated for his overpayment. Mr. Jones was fired soon after that-but not for this deal. I will elaborate on that later.

I can cite many, many other similar cases. Eventually we got the practice pretty well stopped on the Yankton Sioux Reservation and it is not the accepted thing anymore.

By no means were the non-Indian "scalpers" the only crooks on the reservations. Many of them, and by far the biggest ones, were among the Civil Service employees who worked for the BIA. Some of these ran into the hundreds of dollars, others thousands of dollars and even millions.

Early Experience With Crookedness

The writer had an experience early in his public career which tended to put him on guard against making mistakes and allowing circumstances to develop which might get him involved unwittingly in questionable situations. So, to protect myself, I developed a certain degree of caution and guardedness, and have always been able to keep myself free of inextricable traps and indicting situations—some of them to the chagrin of others. I have been very fortunate and grateful for my career in the Civil Service through the years and have enjoyed a self-gratifying life and experience therein. However, one experience I endured in the BIA gives me very good grounds to sue the government and certain Civil Service employees for a million dollars, as advised by attorneys. My experience encountered both corrupt and honorable administrations. I shall cite both kinds—and what a difference there is! We can be hopeful and grateful because of the good ones.

Now for the story that put me on the double-guard.

It happened in Cheyenne, Wyoming, in 1935. I was the county supervisor of the newly created and organized government sponsored organization called the Wyoming Rehabilitation Corporation, later renamed Resettlement Administration and today called the Farm Home Administration.

One of the first tasks assigned to us county supervisors was to take over the administration and distribution of the federal government's drought relief hay program.

We were directed to take over the supply of hay from the county director of the Federal Emergency Relief Administration (FERA) and give a receipt for it. In my county the hay was a large volume scattered all over a city block, with irregular piles here and piles there, every which way, broken bales and scattered loose hay. There was no way that I could determine the amount of hay there, and no way to get it done without and until it was moved. Hay was being shipped in and added to the lot and hay was being issued out and removed constantly as need required every week. And more hay shipped in.

The FERA County Auditor prepared a receipt on the proper form for me to sign and accept the amount of hay on hand as indicated in the receipt. I protested signing and assuming responsibility for what would amount to a blind order. A five percent waste was allowed. I was ordered to sign the receipt by my superiors—or else. They provided me with no means for determining the amount that was there, nor did they offer any alternatives.

I told the county auditor that I would do it under one condition, i.e., under protest, and that it would be on the basis of the official record of the amount of hay that was actually found to be there, and not necessarily for the amount on the receipt if subsequent events and facts proved the receipt to be in error.

In moving the hay in the everyday transactions, I soon could see that there would be a large shortage, based on the amount that was listed on the transfer receipt which I had signed. This presented a major problem and concern for me. What could I do about it? This required some exploratory thinking on my part.

The auditor, when he had charge of the books, was required to submit a weekly report to the state office. It included the amount of hay on hand at the beginning of the weekly report, the amount that was issued out and removed during the week, the amount of new hay acquired and added to the supply during the same period, and then the new balance at the close of the report. I went to the auditor and asked to see and examine his weekly reports. He refused to do so, saying it would serve no purpose for me. It was apparent that for some reason he did not want me to see his report. There was a discrepancy in the receipt which I signed and his weekly report to the state office. I found this out by going to the state office, a few blocks away, where I knew my way around because I had previously had my office in the same building. I asked the state auditor if I could see the county auditor's weekly report for that date. The state auditor made a duplicate copy of the report for me and certified that it was a true copy of the county report. The report showed that they had considerably less hay than he charged to me.

Sure enough, shortly thereafter, the federal agency started auditing the books of the state and county offices. I got a notice from the federal auditor to account for the shortage showed by the receipt and the amount of hay actually on hand according to my weekly reports.

I gave him my certified copy by the state auditor and explained the situation to him and how and why it happened.

In due time he called me to come back to his office and told me that it was a good thing for me that I had that copy and asked me to let him know if I found any other irregularities. I still have that receipt after over forty years. Had I not been able to clear myself I would have been blackballed by the U.S. Government and never would have been able to get another government or Civil Service job. My life and career by necessity would have been different.

I understand that the auditor for the government, Mr. Harry Henderson, Sr., had been a director of a bank that had closed during that period of bank failures. Also that he, at his personal expense and time, traveled over the state liquidating the remaining assets of the defunct bank and thus salvaged enough to pay back the depositors—a moral obligation of honorable men but not a legal obligation in this case. There was no Federal Deposit Insurance Corporation at that time to protect depositors as is the case today. It was just too bad for thousands of depositors. How many bankers and directors of banks did as much for their depositors? We need more honorable and honest employees of government and industry today.

I want to give due credit to the honorable people, such as Mr. Harry Henderson, as well as to criticize the wrong doers.

Yes, later I was eased out of that job, where I had made a good record and progress. Another with political pull wanted the job.

A new administrator of questionable character had just taken over the State Office. That entered in the decision for me to give up the job and seek a Civil Service job. Perhaps there would be more justice, honorableness and less throat cutting! (Experience shows there isn't, but there are certain other advantages).

It is always worth noting what happens to these conspirators-usually shortly thereafter-nothing to make a happy life for them.

The wages of sin we cannot escape-

But realize it only too late.

Lease Clerk Steals Funds

In 1938 the writer was transferred from the United Pueblo in New Mexico to the Yankton Sub-Agency under the jurisdiction of the Rosebud Indian Agency in South Dakota. Nearly every Indian was on some type of relief and some of them were getting pretty antagonistic about their economic and social situation. Lease rentals were very low for those who owned land or an interest in some.

Their money from trust interests was deposited with the Rosebud Agency, 170 miles distant. It was managed for them by the farm agent at the Yankton Sub-Agency. The Indian had to make a request for his money to the farm agent. He decided whether they should have it, how much and what for. Much of it had to be by voucher or purchase order designating specific purposes and the purchases approved and the voucher signed by him. This was the policy because the government considered the Indian incompetent and a ward of the government.

A lease clerk made out the leases, collected the lease money and sent it to the Rosebud Agency for deposit in a federal depository in the Indian's Individual Money Account or IMA. When checks were issued they were sent to me (farm agent) for delivery. If no checks came when they were looking for them, the Indians complained to me and sometimes it was necessary to investigate why not or why the delay.

At that time the lease clerk was not required to be bonded.

Very shortly I discovered that the lease clerk was stealing some of the Indian's lease money instead of transmitting it to Rosebud for deposit. The FBI was called in and all leases were audited and the amount stolen determined. Congress appropriated funds to cover the Indians' losses, and the lease clerk was sent to the federal penitentiary. How this was accomplished will be revealed in the next story.

I became suspicious of what was happening to some of the Indians" lease money, and put pressure on my supervisors to check up on the situation. They both took no stock in what I said and made no move to investigate or authorize someone to do so.

Besides the fact that the rental money for some of the Indians was not materializing, the lease clerk bought a better car and spent too much time running around and neglecting his office duties. His neglect interfered with the consummation of some of my work as well as the rest of the agency duties.

Our agency, at that time, was a sub-agency under the Rosebud Agency and headed by an assistant superintendent. He not only failed to see what was going on in his office but he still was not aroused by my suspicion. My supervisor from Rosebud came down in a day or so and spent some time with me on our official duties. As he was about ready to return home, I mentioned the lease clerk deal to him.

Apparently he also took no stock in my suspicion and told me to take no time for it but let the assistant superintendent and the Indian Police take care of it—it was their responsibility—besides, he said, I did not have the time for it.

This was a situation that I could not live with and one of the very few times I disobeyed my boss's suggestions or instructions. I again went to the assistant superintendent and told him I felt sure I could get indicting evidence of malfeasance by the lease clerk. I had asked certain lessees of certain Indian allotments why they had not turned in to the Indian office their lease rentals—the money was past due and the Indian lessors were needing it badly.

They told me that they had paid it and that they had receipts and canceled checks to show for it. I had no reason to believe that they were not telling me the truth. So, the next morning I went back to the assistant superintendent and told him I thought I could get indicting evidence that the lease clerk had collected the lease money but had not sent it to Rosebud for processing and depositing.

He then told me to investigate and let him know how I came out.

I went to the home of Merritt Eitemiller a few miles down the river and he showed me his receipts and canceled checks. I copied the information on a piece of paper, and handed it to the assistant superintendent. This was about eleven a.m. He immediately picked up the phone and called Rosebud. They told him to hold the phone while they checked their records to make sure the money was not paid into the office. It was not there. About four p.m. that same day, the head of the lease department and one clerk from the Rosebud office arrived at our office, 170 miles distant. They went right down to Mr. Eitemiller's home and picked up the receipts and canceled checks. Then, that evening or the next morning, they contacted Jake Buus and got some from him also.

That brought an FBI investigation and auditing of all leases on the reservation with the subsequent conviction and sentencing of the lease clerk to the federal penitentiary for stealing over $3,000 of the Indian lessors' lease money.

This shows how fast action was taken in those days. Congress appropriated funds to pay the lessors for their loss.

Another thing shows the difference in attitude of government employees of that era (1938-39) from what it is today about blowing the whistle on someone. Nowadays they are afraid to, with the exception of a small percent of brave ones who will do so even at the risk of losing their job, get a transfer, and at a cost of losing any chance for promotions. In these later years it has become a Watergate type of coverup or shut up enterprise.

As I have said, my boss had told me not to do anything about it. What happened-the very first time he paid us his next visit, he referred to it and said: "If we (he and I) hadn't exposed it, it would not have been discovered!" He said he went right to the boss (as he called the superintendent) and told him and urged taking action. Every subsequent time after that when he came to see us, he would say "I" and not "we." He wanted to take the full credit. He had done nothing of the kind; it was an obvious lie.

There was another case where another employee wanted to steal the credit for the same act.

A few years later a new superintendent assumed the job at the Rosebud Agency-he came to see us and was accompanied by one of the Rosebud Clerks. The lease clerk incident was brought up-this superintendent had never heard of it. As the three of us sat in a booth at a cafe, the clerk took it unto himself to tell this superintendent that he exposed and uncovered the theft of the lease money. His story was pure fabrication and could not match the events and circumstances involved. I would say that he wanted to make an impression on the new superintendent.

In a very few years later, stealing the credit would not have been coveted.

Ninety percent of them would lay low and keep out of sight rather than expose corruption or irregularities. Some would be forthrightly transferred out of the area-Some would be demoted or lose certain benefits, but some others would be transferred and given promotions to buy their silence and cooperation. We hear and read about such deals constantly.

It is noteworthy to observe this change that has occurred in our government in these last few years. The huge growth of our government no doubt accounts for much of it.

What this writer can not understand is why is it that superintendents can sit at an agency office, for many years, and not see the stealing and corruption going on under their noses. They are supposed to be able, qualified and responsible persons—able to administer the affairs of the agency. They get well paid for it. You can sometimes point it out to them, and they still won't believe you.

We have mentioned a number of cases in this book, occurring in New Mexico and South Dakota. To see how far and to what lengths the BIA will go, read the chapter on "Conspiracy."

Repayment Cattle Program

The BIA had a repayment cattle program for Indians. The cattle used for the program were originally purchased by the government from drought stricken areas in the great drought of the 1930s. The cattle were starving by the thousands. Some were salvaged by slaughtering and canning the meat which was issued to people on relief. Some of the cattle were of good quality. These were saved and added to a cattle pool and issued to Indians on reservations on a repayment-in-kind contract. They would repay an equal number of equal quality over a scheduled number of years, and those repayed issued to some other applicant. These would provide a foundation for others who wanted to get a start.

One of our problems on the reservations in the Northern Plains area was to keep some of the Indians from selling their repay cattle before they had made their payments. It was illegal for them to sell these cattle, which were, or at least were supposed to be, branded with the ID brand, without a permit from the agency official. Some white scalpers sought these illegal purchases for a profit for themselves. This was a considerable problem for us at the agency. Not too big in most cases, but there were instances involving thousands of dollars. We never encountered this problem with the United Pueblo in New Mexico.

Land Appraiser

There came to the Rosebud and Yankton Reservations a land appraiser for these Indian agencies. At that time there were many transactions of Indian lands on the Rosebud, consummated under the Tribal Land Enterprise known as the TLE. The main purpose of the TLE was to consolidate inherited fractionated land inter-

145

ests. The fractionated status of Indian trust land had reached an almost intolerable status—a cumbersome, complex and unmanageable situation. Hundreds of exchanges would be involved. To be workable and just, valuations had to be established on all tracts involved. TLE became a great instrument for facilitating the accomplishment of the program. Credit goes to Superintendent C.R. Whitlock for designing and promulgating this great organization and program. The bureau later promoted the program for other reservations in the Northwest.

The Indians and Indian agencies were also involved in purchasing and trading for non-Indian land.

The appraiser should be an honest, as well as an able and qualified professional. Sometimes, however, under insufficient supervision and control, corrupt appraisals were made.

In the interests of my capacity to protect the interests of the Indians and the government in my jurisdiction, I clashed with one of the appraisers and averted his intended "steal" in a case where I was in co-charge. Even a stupid person could not help but notice that corruption was commonplace practice. Why did he keep on with his job for several years before anyone did something about it? And then only to be transferred to a faraway reservation.

This appraiser, and others too, could appraise a given tract of land twice within a month or two. He could appraise it for an Indian seller to a white man purchaser and then again in a short time for another Indian prospective purchaser to buy it from the white man. This time the appraisal would be considerably higher. This inconsistency paved the way for conniving thieves and rip-offs by prearranged agreement.

I recite here one case as an example:

We were negotiating to buy a small low-value piece of land from a white man for the Indians. When we met to negotiate a deal the government appraiser had already met with the prospective seller, and it was very apparent that they had cooked up a deal between them. They came in together, both times, to the office, negotiated together and hung together like buddies. Their conduct had all the appearances of striving for a mutual rip-off by trying to get a price far beyond all reason. It was illegal conduct for an employee of the federal government. I could not conscientiously stand by and become a guilty participant by silence and consent to an illegal and corrupt deal. So I hung out against paying such an exorbitant price. The superintendent bawled me out for being so stubborn. We adjourned for the day to reassemble the next morning to resume the negotiation. I told the superintendent if he would at least remain neutral I think we could negotiate a fair deal. All we had to do was to put the appraiser in his proper place. He said all right.

The next morning they came swinging in together with a spirit of victory emitting from their radiant demeanor. The spirit soon changed—suddenly they realized that the superintendent was silent—said not a word. The white man prospective seller said, "You win." So the deal was closed at a decent price, and so ended one chapter for the crooked land appraiser.

One reason why such crookedness prospered in Indian country was due to the fact that the citizens were generally indifferent and the cheating practices against Indians were more or less accepted practices. Some of these people who otherwise were considered honest became ingrained with a standard idea that it was proper and all right to "scalp" Indians and "rip off" the federal government when dealing with them.

It took the BIA (Bureau of Indian Affairs) ten years, and after he had stolen over a million dollars, before they caught up with him-and send him to prison. I could have gotten indicting evidence against him long before, had I been authorized and instructed to do so. There is no valid or legal excuse for such corruption to be allowed-and to thrive and grow.

Indeed, an honest conscientious person oftentimes found it impossible to continue to hold a job with the BIA. The establishment had become manned by many inefficient, worthless and corrupt personnel.

Indian Health Service

As recently as the summer of 1979 the Rosebud tribal officials complained (and it has been reported) that the Indian Health Service had broken down and most of their doctors and other personnel had resigned because of the situation. The services owed outside hospitals and doctors millions of dollars for services rendered to Indian patients sent to them by the Indian Service, hospitals and doctors, apparently without legal authority to pay for same—because their funds were all gone.

Congress authorized millions of dollars to operate the Indian

147

Health Services. It is reported that the central office in Washington, D.C. used one third of it for the operation of their office; another third went to the twelve area offices for their administrative costs, leaving the other third for the hospitals and health services for all of the field services, on and off the reservations. The hospital maintenance, doctors and all other salaries and administration costs were paid out of this one-third share. What was left from all of those costs went for the actual health benefits of the Indians—the end object of the program. The central office in Washington, D.C. and the twelve area offices which rendered no productive services to the health of the Indians took up two-thirds of the funds. After the administrative costs on the reservations were taken from their third, is it any wonder the doctors and hospitals had to try to pan off the hospital and medical aid of their Indian patients on some other doctors and hospitals?

Then the BIA was proposing another administrative office to oversee the twelve area offices—a sort of sub-super level. This would probably result in dividing the appropriated taxpayers' money four ways instead of the three ways. We could expect more administrative personnel, more red-tape, more paperwork, more corruption, and less for the Indians' health service.

Whitlock-Aamodt Administration
The writer came to the Yankton Sub-agency, under the jurisdiction of the Rosebud Agency as a farm agent in 1938 and worked under the supervision of Mr. Carl B. Aamodt, Extension Agent, and Mr. John Backus, Assistant Superintendent. Those were hard times for most people and the problems were hard to manage. Mr. Aamodt told me it would either make or break me.

But coming into this administration was like a good big "breath of fresh air." There was no bickering, conniving, uncooperativeness, lying, jealousy, or job stealing.

The administration's attitude and policy differed from so much found too often elsewhere. They worked at achieving a harmonious, non-complaining, positive, and honest attitude and got profound results. There was not that favoritism, fault-finding, lying, and undermining attitude found generally in the extension departments and some of the other departments.

Superintendent Whitlock marveled at the loyalty of Mr. Aamodt's staff to him and he wondered why! I think I can say why, and it is worth exemplifying. He was full of enthusiasm himself

148

and worked hard and long and brought all of his men into a circle. He gave them authority and freedom to make decisions and expected good results. He stood behind his men honorably. If he criticized it would be constructive and helpful. He never failed to tell them they did a good job when they did and that he appreciated it. He called for teamwork.

Another thing that was rare and unusual—each employee got a new official car when his turn came. It had been the practice for the boss to take the new car and hand his old car down to a subordinate, for whom the new car was intended. For the subordinate to get the new car caused him to respect his boss, his job, his work, and inspired him to do his honest best in return. It earned good will and credit for both.

Another good example: One time as Mr. Aamodt was accompanying Superintendent C.R. Whitlock to Washington, D.C. on official business, "C.R.," as he was affectionately called, asked him how would he like it, if he, the superintendent, could arrange to get him a raise in salary. Mr. Aamodt replied: He would accept it providing his staff also got a raise. As I recall, we got our raises.

More of the accomplishments on the Rosebud and Yankton Reservations are told in other parts of this book. A few failures and examples of poor judgment are also told.

The New Deal

The New Deal for Indians was initiated on the Great Plains area for economic survival and the Indians' use of their natural resources (with examples of honesty and progress in general). But adverse human elements entered in and took over shortly after the termination of the Whitlock administration. We shall tell that story too and some of the devastating consequences.

Some Indian leaders had learned too well how to fleece their brother tribesmen and enrich themselves. Corruption took a bow and proceeded to the next act. The BIA officials took no action to stop it nor to protect the interests of the innocent common Indian citizen. They were not of the right caliber or character. Let's examine and compare the performance of these BIA people with that of Whitlock's regime, with some selected cases:

Many of the Indian leaders and BIA employees who grew up in the BIA service were just as crooked as their white counterparts and associates. That is the chief reason why we have so much corruption on the reservations—fed by the BIA with its programs and money scattered all over everywhere, and seemingly with total disregard for control and accountability.

News Headlines
We'll cite a few headlines, which tell part of the story:
—Funds earmarked for Weatherization on Rosebud Reservation went elsewhere.—Nov. 9, 1979
—Solons Report Raps Bureau of Indian Affairs. 4-11-66
—To Study Needs. The Bureau of Indian Affairs will spend $44,000 on a six-months study of the needs for teaching the English language on South Dakota Indian reservations, B.I.A. informed Senator George McGovern D, S.—Dec. 27, 1966

(Only B.I.A. bureaucrats are so dumb that they would need to study and spend money to determine the need to teach English language on South Dakota Indian reservations. But that is the kind of service the tax payers and the Indians get from our notorious B.I.A. and their (mostly) needless and wasteful task forces.)

—Indian Leaders Say B.I.A. Head Admits Some White Favortism 5-24-67
—Climate of Terror Marks Pine Ridge 4-9-77
—Bureaucrats Don't Talk to Indians About Plight.—Jack Anderson 11-14-69
—At DWU Conference-Indians condemn B.I.A. Tell of Despair and Hope on Reservations 1970
—Indian Treatment By Government Shameful-Jack Anderson July, 1976
—Grand Jury to Investigate Money Misuses.-Rosebud, S. D. The Rosebud Sioux Tribal Council has called for a grand jury to investigate allegations that the administration of former tribal Chairman Robert Burnette misused tribal money—7-9-76
—B.I.A. study suggests drastic restructuring—Sept. 1976
Hundreds of studies and Task Forces have been conducted. Almost always one is going on. Probably nine tenths of them are laid up on shelves and never looked at-as told by a former B.I.A. official. (This is common knowledge in the Service.)
—Head of Indian Affairs Says Legislature "Playing Politics."
—Indian Workers Say Federal Agencies Discriminating
—Indian health may have been devastated by finance.

—Rosebud doctors leaving. 1978
—Unpaid bills kill budget:
Hospital looks for help. 7-10-78
—"To a mother whose child has a 103 degree fever in the middle of the night, that is an emergency"—said Fort Thompson PA Burt Marion. He has had his life threatened over authorization for outside treatment.

This situation relates to the time the reservation Health Services ran out of funds, because the Area offices and the Washington, D. C. office took two thirds of the appropriated funds and spent it on themselves instead of the health of Indians. This is a barbaric crime. No wonder the doctors and hospital employees resigned and abandoned their stations. The Arab Islamic's would say "cut off their hands."
—S.D. Task Force discovers financial maze. Bookkeeping compounds reservation money Scandal. Nov. 9, 1979
—CETA regulations, funds violated on reservation. Nov. 7, 1979
—Driving Hawk eyes Washington, D. C. Driving Hawk says he's done all he can for the Rosebud Sioux Tribe, which is estimated $11 Million in debt.—He blames the problem on land purchases and poor management by previous leaders.* (We may add rake offs by those previous leaders in connection with the land purchases—it is stealing) Nov. 8, 1979
—Task force probes abuse of funds on S. D. reservations.—Reservation tax dollars represent question marks. Nov. 6, 1979
—"The Story's the same"
Janklow (governor of S. D.) acknowledges abuse of tribal funds. 11-9-79
—Reservation dwellers recognize need for scrutinizing. 11-9-79
—Rosebud resident wages 30 year battle with corruption. 11-9-79
—Use of Ceta funds on Reservaion questioned (AP) 2-19-80

Independent auditors have uncovered almost $10 million in questionable expenditures, widespread mismanagement and an

*The writer's comments are in parenthesis.

occasional criminal abuse in Comprehensive Employment and Training Act programs for Indians in the Nation.

The audits of Indian CETA programs showed that the great majority of the programs—64 percent of them—violated federal accounting and administration requirements.

Auditors gave a clean financial bill of health to only one Indian CETA program, that of the Mille Lacs Reservation Business Committee in Onamia, Minn.

—Audit finds B.I.A. funds misused. 3-27-80

Federal auditors have found that the Rosebud Sioux Tribe misused nearly $2.2 million it received from the Bureau of Indian Affairs. A draft copy of the audit issued funds amounted to more than a quarter of $7.5 million in B.I.A. funding to the tribe over a three-year period.

The new audit bears out the work of the South Dakota Task Force last fall. The team of reporters from the Associated Press and member newspapers found the millions of federal dollars were misspent on Rosebud and other state Indian reservations.

Of $7.5 million in B.I.A. programs, auditors disallowed $576,607 and questioned $1,589,890 more.

The tribe failed to take bids on its $2.2 million irrigation projects "—And as a result probably paid as much as 100 percent more for the irrigation system than was necessary," the report said.

After the Task Force investigated and found the irregularities, the thieveries, the evidence, and reported the same to the responsible sources, (11-9-79) with all of its publicity—what was done about it? It was very quiet and the publicity seems to have died out. We noted only two cases where indictments were recorded. One indictment was for $150 and the other for less than $600.00—out of several millions of dollars involved.

Is this the final judgment and settlement for the corruption and thievery? O, Congressmen, B.I.A., F.B.I. and the Courts. Where are you? Hiding or lost, perhaps.!!

—B.I.A. failed responsibility says official. 11-15-79 News Media—

The Bureau of Indian Affairs has failed to carry out its responsibility to insure that federal funds are properly spent on Indian reservations, a former tribal official said Tuesday.

Former tribal Councilman, Phillip Byrnes of the Lower Brule Sioux Tribe put in his criticism, too. He said in a prepared statement: "The investigation reveals a glaring example of a shameful and dishonest fiscal irresponsibility which exists in the administration of Indian Affairs on these South Dakota Indian reservations. That's a scandal."—Tribe struggles to Rectify Funds Misused—3-28-80

Recently elected Tribal Chairman Norman Wilson, Rosebud Reservation, said this week. "We're looking at some pretty lean times."

"Investigative reporters in the South Dakota Task Force unearthed evidence last fall that millions of federal dollars had been misused on the Rosebud and other Indian reservations."

The council members asked for the prosecution of persons who allegedly misspent federal and tribal funds.

The Council sought B.I.A. evaluation of the tribal financial system. "The tribe hopes to use this evaluation to develop a tribal system that will never again get the tribal administration and council into a financial hole," the chairman's letter said.

The Writer's Comments:

To turn to the BIA for evaluation of the Indian financial system and to establish an effective and free-from-corruption system will not solve the problems. They were the ones responsible for the use of these funds in the first place. They were partners with the Indians and it was first their responsibility and duty to control those funds. What is the BIA in existence for anyway? Appeal for help should go to some other source. Take it before Congress and demand that they clean out the BIA.

There was plenty of warning of the impending trouble for several years. The papers were full of it. A few Indian tribesmen and councilmen and even some BIA employees made their voices heard. Of course, the BIA conveniently did not hear them! All they did was cover-up. They have too much to hide to expect honest action from them.

What Can We Do, Blow the Whistle?

Must people be aroused to the point where they force Congress to do something about it? Will the people and the government employees have to resort to violence in order to attract sufficient attention to provide some means of protection for the employee who blows the whistle? We are constantly hearing about and reading about some federal employee being severely punished for refusing to go along with, or to cover-up, injustice and corruption. It is inhumane if not barbaric! I shall cite a case in the next Chapter where a career woman cooperated with the conspirators and when they were through with her for their dirty work they double-crossed and discharged her. She became emotionally disturbed and spent the last part of her life in the State Hospital.

May God have mercy on the scoundrels.

Large-Scale Thefts from the Warehouse 6-12-80 AP

Meierhenry, South Dakota Attorney General, who led a raid that shut down a government food warehouse on the Pine Ridge Reservation said he would give Pechot (U.S. Attorney) evidence from a state probe of an alleged $500,000 food theft scheme on that reservation.

$400,000 of the $500,000 worth of food was missing from the warehouse in 1978 and 1979.

It took the independent newspapers of South Dakota to form a Task Force and unearth the scandals.

These Scandals Are Enormous And Congress Is Derelict And Is Losing Its Power And Control Of The B.I.A.

There are signs that the "worm is starting to turn." The news reports that an employee of the B.I.A. Area Office has been indicted. TheAttorney General's Office is investigating and running down thieves and misuse of government commodities intended for needy Indians. They raided the hone of one federal employee and found 400 pounds of U.S. government commodities there. He faces state or federal charges.

According to news reports South Dakota's Attorney General Mark Meierhenry has said food stolen from the warehouses was sold to restaurants, lounges and individuals. As much as $500,000 in food meant for needy Indians on reservations is missing. Governor Janklow said he probably could name eight or ten grocery stores and some ranchers.

Gary Rhead of DESE'S Child and Nutrition Service who administers the program for the state said, "nobody tries to stop it because it is *just a way of life.* The white people who receive it probably think it's okay because its been going on so long."

Rhead said his office (state) was aware of entire truck loads being stolen, and most reservation residents know the thieves.

Rhead agency serves as the middle man between the federal government and the reservations. And the USDA says that role makes the state responsible for the losses. Rapid City, S.D. (AP) 8-13-81

Meierhenry said some of the people who complain loudest about their taxes are buying the government food, which is clearly marked government property not to be sold.

The Governor says "They have been selling commodities for years. You can go down there on the streets and buy it.

The federal government provides the commodities and funds. It charges the state with the job of providing central warehousing and distribution of the goods to the reservations. The tribes should provide the care, distribution to the individual needy Indians and the accounting of same. This makes a three-way management and accounting participation for the distribution and control of the commodities and services. If loosely conceived and poorly controlled, theft and corruption have a fertile and tempting field.

Millions and millions of taxpayers' dollars are involved in this business on the reservations in the Aberdeen area in the Dakotas and Nebraska. The three-way arrangement provides a convenience for buck passing and a wide open field for corruption and mismanagement.

The Indians when involved tend to lean on the excuse that the state has no jurisdiction on the reservation and therefore can not enter on trust land to enforce law and order or retrieve stolen property. The federal government does nothing effectively to correct misuse of government or Indian property. The state sometimes hesitates to do so, but Governor Janklow of South Dakota is taking the "bull by the horns" and may mete out punishment to those found guilty and in some way put an end to this wanton corruption that blights much of our nation.

This situation was many years building up and it will not be entirely corrected in a month's or in one year's time. We can not place the entire blame for the outrageous thefts, wastes and mismanagement on the Indian management. They are the little guys getting some of the trickle-down. The top supervisors are non-Indians. Very likely they plan and want some of the tribal council members to be involved, hoping it may restrain them from "blowing the whistle" on themselves.

Hope Peeping Through

Someone has said that hope springs eternal. History shows that events run their course in time—sometimes for better, sometimes worse. In the long run progress seems to triumph. Sometimes disaster precedes a new start (Noah's flood is one example). Many times whole civilizations have fallen—permanently it seems. But better ones may arise somewhere else in point of time and place.

We think of these events and phenomena as repeating in cycles. It is high time for a general moral change in the world today. Let us do our part on the Indian reservations. It would be a noble gesture for the Indians to assume the leadership and pave the way. They can do it if not prohibited from doing so.

The South Dakota governor and attorney general made a recent move in their drive to straighten out the scandalous handling of and accounting for commodities and funded programs which resulted in a raid on another tribal warehouse. They seized and removed the remaining commodities to another storage place in a nearby town and assumed distribution of the food commodities under a new management.

The state had previously investigated and found mismanagement and misuse of government furnished commodities. This case was similar to that which prevailed widespread over South Dakota reservations, some of which we have cited above. Action by someone was far overdue. It created resentment and opposition by some of the responsible management personnel and supervisors, especially from the top echelons.

The management personnel offered different alibis in an attempt to justify their deeds. These people apparently had been oriented to this way of doing this type of business by the influences prevailing throughout the reservations for a period of fifteen to twenty years. They had been getting away with it, so it became the expected way.

One of the excuses offered by the defense has another significant importance worth noting. The claim was that there was a surplus of commodities and that they were not needed for legitimate purposes. Therefore they were sold or given away, which under the circumstances was illegal.

This example brings out the fact of large scale waste by most of the government's programs on the reservations and elsewhere. It is overdone, kept on even after the need has been satisfied. It continues to provide lucrative jobs and rake-offs for the many bureaucratic fat cats (as some call them).

The Congress can not be unaware of the scandalous business. Perhaps it is their pork-barrel politics and is accepted as a way of life for them, too.

However, our President is aware of and sincerely concerned about the situation as he is honestly doing everything in his power to bring about a change and turn the country around and away from the destruction which may eventually overtake our nation. He has the foresight, the vision and the guts to fight the selfish powers that have become too entrenched in the economic and political life. If the governing officials can't or won't do it—then the people will have to face reality and show them the way or they themselves will be faced with the serious consequences.

If we were to stop the wanton waste and the stealing we could successfully balance our nation's budget and discontinue enlarging and passing it on to our children and now our grand and great grandchildren. Must this debt be the heritage we pass on to them? All of this because of our irresponsible living and fiscal mismanagement. It is over a trillion dollar debt, which grows larger and larger every year, without a stop, to say nothing about a turnabout. The interest alone on the debt may sink us, if we don't turn it back. What will our grandchildren have for themselves if they have to pay off our debts which we have failed to do? How can we extricate ourselves without sacrifices and living within our means?

People, especially the elderly, are fearful and concerned, and they should be, about their security and what could happen to our institutions and way of life. Likely, the only way to force correction is to cut off the life-blood or the funds where waste occurs. Always there are and will be innocent or helpless victims who will suffer as a consequence. This fact we have to accept in many cases and alleviate it as much as possible.

Blow the Whistle

What happens to government employees who "blow the whistle" on corruption, waste and regulatory abuse? Too often they are characterized as troublemakers, then are fired, frozen out of promotions or subjected to personal harassment for the rest of their careers.

Too many Civil Service employees do not want to put forth the effort to do a good job—they just want a good salary and authority and power to do as they like and not be disturbed. They get this power by pulling strings, selling their souls, and catering to their 'higherups' for backing and protection. The 'higherups' do the same and reciprocate, so you have a form of Mafia in operation. If you do not conform you are a marked person and a candidate for sacrifice. Some employees manage to keep their jobs, at least for awhile, by the threat of blackmail. But even some of the conformers later meet up with misfortune or disaster. Some of those disasters are pathetic to behold.

The writer has had more than one former employee of the BIA, when referring to his task-force reports, say something to the effect that it was put on a shelf, gathering dust, never read, but went on creating more task-forces to be treated likewise. Some of them resigned from their job because of the waste of money. Yes, there are still some honest and conscientious people!

Why does it take so long for the government to catch up with theft, corruption, and waste like this? Why do we have so many employees on the job and they can not see it or won't expose it? Yes, I have seen plenty of it in the BIA. I can give you reasons why nothing is done to correct the situation.

Recently the T.V. program, "60 Minutes," cited a similar case of a man who was relegated to isolation and an obscure position because he "blew the whistle" on a corrupt deal. He was given nothing of importance to do and no chance of promotion. He would stick it out there until he reached retirement age. When asked by "60 Minutes" if he had it to do over again, would he do the same thing again, he thought he would not. When we talked to other people who saw the same show, they said they did not blame him and that if they were confronted with the same situation they too would not blow the whistle. Few are willing to pay the price to stay honest. This man had already paid the price. Why not make the best of it and feel glad and proud of what he had done?

The writer has paid his price and suffered much too. I will never yield to crookedness and corruption—not even be guilty of consent by silence, which by God-given moral standards makes one equally guilty with the doer of same. I rejoice for my part in opposing corruption and I am proud of my record. The record is good for morale and mental well-being. I would do it again. Later I shall tell you what happened to certain conspirators. Their's was usually an unhappy end and some times disastrous.

The Episode of an Extension Agent

The main premise, over the years, of our nation's policy with our Indian citizens has been to regard them as children and incompetents, with the government's role as that of trustee. We insisted on making the decisions for them. This has stifled his self-determination, his civil and human rights, and his ability to cope with our society. Especially this is so among our Plains Indians, where most of our Indian problems prevail. Many persons of the proud race resent this attitude and sometimes react to it in individual and defiant ways.

The fundamental policy of the Bureau of Indian Affairs should be to provide the education, training and guidance where needed, through responsibility. Also to aid and provide the means, the credit, and help, to adjust to and become self-sufficient in his present-day society and civilization. All BIA employees should be oriented and sympathic to that policy. As soon as the Indian has demonstrated his ability to handle his own affairs, he should be permitted to be on his own. It would not take a considerable number of them long to attain that status as has been demonstrated over and over again in many areas and instances.

Too many of the federal employees have solely worked to perpetuate their own jobs, and to keep their hands in the money bags, where they can rip-off or steal. Teaching and practicing honesty should be the most important factor involved.

The job of the extension agent is to teach and promote the arts of agriculture and the proper and successful use of credit.

We have already cited a few cases of thievery and corruption and poor management in this field. Permit the citing of a typical case of corruption by federal employees and officials along the pipeline. One wonders how so many people prone to crookedness get themselves into positions of power and control. A pure Watergate cover-up in many instances.

A few winters ago a prominent Indian stockman and tribal politician and sometimes office-holder sold off a considerable number of his mortgaged cattle without getting an official permit of release or applying any of the proceeds on his mortgage debt.

The extension agent became aware of this and, in compliance with his duty and obligation, reported it to the agency superintendent. The superintendent, in turn, notified the area director. A meeting with these officials was called and took place in the Superintendent's office.

Everything seemed to be agreeable and at the close of the meeting the extension agent felt somewhat relieved and pleased that something would be done to recover the loss, and perhaps bring some action against the wrongdoer. The repsonsibility then passed to his superiors.

Instead, in a day or so, the extension agent got a sudden jolt. He got a notice to transfer to a far-off reservation. He was given only a few days time, ordered not to visit any of his friends and fellow employees under his supervision on the Yankton Reservation—not even by taking annual leave and paying his own expenses for doing so. He had to write them from his new station and explain things and say goodbye. Who was it they feared for him to contact on the Yankton Reservation? There is only one likely person, so it is easy to figure out. Then the question is—why? The writer can supply part of the answer.

Ordinarily it takes several months to effect a transfer in the Civil Service. But when there is an urgent cover-up, to hell with Civil Service regulations!

Somebody had a fear of something and ordered a cover-up. So far this writer has not learned exactly what it was. The extension agent thinks it was a certain Indian person with political clout.

Honesty, you know, is what crooks fear most. There may even be a conscience bothering someone.

The extension agent was concerned about never getting another promotion. And he didn't. Not long after he retired and we lost track of him.

The Episode of Two Hawk

The following appeared in the press on Jan. 8, 1970, under the headline, "Two Hawk Says—Rosebud Sioux Tribe Broke, Deeply in Debt."

Rosebud (AP)—Rosebud Sioux Tribal President Webster Two Hawk says the tribe is broke and deeply in debt, livestock herd depleted with no records to show what happened to them and that tribal office employees have been discharged because there is no money to pay them.

Two Hawk took over the presidency of the tribe from Cato Valandra last month.

Two Hawk reported to the tribe that the last records of livestock available went back to 1967 and that since then 266 head of cattle have disappeared without explanation.

In addition, he said, several pieces of equipment are no longer on the reservation, including two tractors. Further bad news on the tribal ranch he said, is that the ranch lost $26,000 last year despite owning all of the land and all of the livestock on it.

Two Hawk said that when he took office Dec. 1 the tribe was more than $104,000 in debt and it is now overdrawn by $27,000 in checking accounts at banks. He said there will be no new money until the leases are paid in March except for a small amount from the Bureau of Indian Affairs, an amount not sufficient to even meet the overdrafts.

Accordingly, he said, effective the first of the year all employees were dismissed except for the treasurer, himself and another official who are working without pay.

Two Hawk said that Valandra, Wilbur Blacksmith and William LaPointe borrowed $25,000 from a bank in Kilgore, Nebraska on Nov. 7 to purchase certificates from tribal members.

Certificates are purchased from tribal members who owed money to the tribe. Two Hawk said that LaPointe cashed in $10,350 of certificates and four other persons cashed in almost $10,000 more.

"As you can see," Two Hawk said, "these five individuals got almost $20,000" of the $25,000 available to purchase certificates. He said that scores of poor Indians who had long awaited the opportunity to cash their certificates were not even considered.

Two Hawk told the tribe that "it has been very difficult to get this much information. The reason is that when Cato Valandra left office, he took with him all of the files of the Rosebud Sioux Tribe."

Valandra was not available for comment. It was announced that Valandra had been invited to Washington to meet with federal officials about Indian problems in the Nation.

There are more cases where herds of tribal and individual Indian owned cattle have disappeared without any accountability of what happened, and very little, if any, investigations made. One case I know of was in Montana—I believe it was a case of ineptness on the part of the extension agent in charge. He was later transferred and demoted. How about the superintendent? I do not know!

One certain extension agent (reported above) I know got transferred to a far place for reporting a crooked deal. He believes it was due to a politically influencial Indian who was involved.

The area office knew all about the deal and ordered the cover-up—that is for sure.

I feel that it is the official knowledge of my awareness and record for honesty that prompted the conspiritors to remove me from the scene. Whether the undertaking had the approval of the Interior Department or was just a case of them being misled, I am not positive yet. The responsibility and guilt would be the same in either event.

Pay Off "Disabled" Bureaucrats

One of the biggest frauds in the government today is the fraudulent claim of disability, then retiring the employee on full benefits, even though he is not old enough to qualify for retirement and/or has less than the minimum years of service required. This is one practice the government has for getting rid of someone they don't want.

It is also one of the ways the employee has of getting out to avoid getting fired or because he is tired of working.

The bureau can sometimes appease the employee by offering this way out or force him out with the fraudulent bait. It's a bribe. All they need is a crooked doctor to certify that the victim is disabled. These doctors should be investigated and the guilty ones sentenced and disbarred from practice. (This could be a job for Jack Anderson—I could furnish him with some evidence and put him on the trail of others.) These cancerous growths will eventually kill our government if permitted to continue to grow and spread.

The government's sixty-three-year-old program to compensate federal employees who are injured or become sick as a result of their work could turn into a "general pension scheme."

That's one conclusion of a new study by the GAO (Oct. 1979), Congress' fiscal watchdog. It suggests that the Labor Department's concept of a comprehensive disability is too generous.

Among the cases cited:

—Compensation was granted to an employee injured on a tractor he was driving for fun. The ruling: Workers can be compen-

162

sated for injuries sustained while "goofing off," as long as they don't do anything they can be fired for.

—Payments went to a woman who lost the tip of a thumb while closing her car door. Officials ruled that she had to shut the door to report to work.

—An employee was compensated after his left knee locked as he arose from a toilet. The government held that he had not intentionally removed himself from his work.

Partly because of rulings such as these, the GAO said annual disability benefits more than tripled from 1970 to 1978, to a total of 548.1 million dollars. Auditors estimated that such benefits soon may total one billion dollars a year. The Labor Department has promised to develop new disability guidelines.

How much longer can we withstand the inroads of this huge, fast growing octopus-like organization invading, taking over and destroying our government and its system of freedom, justice, economic preservation, and national security?

Righteousness exalteth a nation: but sin is a reproach to any people (Proverbs 14:34).

CHAPTER 7: CONSPIRACY AND CORRUPTION—THE CONSPIRACY THAT REACHED HOME

The Conspiracy That Reached Home—The Insidious Creep-up—The Episode of Jeanette Packard—The Episode Of Steve-Forcing Them To Their Knees—The Episode Of Percy-Bringing Him To His Knees—The Episode Of "Poor Terry"—The Episode Of An Honest B.I.A. Employee—The Tragedy Of A Career Woman—Soil And Moisture Conservation Association—Enter The Bull Into The China Shop-The Squeeze Is On—Mr. Bull's General Character—Hypocrisy—The Assault On Productive Tribal Organizations—The Assault Against Tribal Management—Backfire—The Yankton Soil And Moisture Conservation Association-Loses Its Fight For Survival—A Surprising Find-Resurrection—The Roy Lempke Episode—Snubbed—Rendezvous With Civil Service Inspectors—Harassments—A Corrupt Doctor—Mockery Of A Hearing—More Hypocrisy—What Finally Happened To The Conspirators—Zona Worthy Of Her Noble Race—Truth Out Of The Past—Another Example Of Evil Design—Area Director Strikes Back With Threats—Episode Of "X" Area Director—

Suddenly, the awareness of it hit like a bolt of lightning out of a clear sky. The ramifications were so secretive and extended that a pipeline developed reaching down to us from at least the area and Rosebud Agency offices and very probably from the Washington offices. Why was it done and who were the chief instigators? The writer, after twenty years of searching, has not been able, as yet, to resolve the questions. The Office of Personnel Management has been stonewalling for four years, evading their obligation to furnish us with our personnel files that we have requested over and over. The cover-up must be pretty important to some conspirators for them to go to the lengths that they did.

There are two reasons that come to my mind: (1) My record and possibly a reputation for exposing corruption and stealing; (2) The destruction of my progressive work on the Yankton Reservation rehabilitating Indians, helping them to manage their own affairs, self-determination and the successful integration into the white man's economic and social world. Their purpose could be to keep the Indians confined to the legal status of incompetents so that BIA employees can preserve their lucrative jobs and dominating power over them. Then there are the opportunities for rake-offs and continuance of the programs where the managers and supervisors are stealing millions of dollars without cease or accountability. They would eliminate anyone whom they thought might expose their lucrative crooked business.

This conspiracy case is not a petty, small or insignificant travesty of justice. It is a serious, cancerous growth on our Bureau of Indian Affairs and our national government. I expressed it some twenty years ago, not so much because of the hurt and injustice it is doing now to certain employees and the Indians, but for what it will grow to become, if it is not punished and stopped NOW.

It has crept into, perhaps, all departments of government and agencies, even up to the presidency, legislative bodies and the courts. Watergate has made its place in our history. But, as a "species" it is not extinct or dead.

To get a better comprehension and understanding of the "acts of conspiracy" that occurred on the Yankton Reservation, one needs for a background, to know what had been accomplished on the reservation and what it was they were out to destroy. We have told much of the story throughout our discourse in portions of this book.

But remember that these committees and organizations were formulated, planned, administered, and the decisions made by the Indians with the help and guidance of the BIA personnel in charge. The leaders were honest, hard working and dedicated individuals. They served without pay and did a commendable job.

Most of these programs were not federal government handouts. Some of the projects and the managing committees included credit, rehabilitation, agriculture and irrigation projects, Indian cooperatives, home improvement, domestic water wells, Soil and Moisture Conservation Association, extension, adult education, and many others.

What made these projects different from those on other reservations is that we had very little federal funds and no tribal funds for improvement and operating capital. At that time the Yankton tribe was not operating under the Wheeler-Howard Act (IRA).

We earned our own money and had a sound fiscal operation. In fact the BIA policy about that time was to terminate the Yankton Reservation in five years. It was a mark and recognization of the Yankton's progress, and readiness to be completely on their own—or termination. And that was before they got any of their claims money. This is another federal policy that was subverted by certain forces in the bureau. Termination as a policy suddenly terminated.

The following stories are representative of some of the things and the progressiveness that the Yankton Indians had achieved. These were the things that the conspirators used their every efforts and means to destroy.

We are attempting to show and record the insidiousness of their actions and what happened as the results.

Compare their methods with that of the Communists. Destroy the prevailing order so they can plant their ideas—exterminate their opposition.

Perhaps the Bible can supply an answer. It certainly monitors the course of events that occurred-I quote from Psalms.

"False witness did rise up; they laid to my charge things that I knew not (Ps.35:11).

"They rewarded me evil for good to the spoiling of my soul (Ps.35:12).

"But in mine adversity they rejoiced, and gathered themselves together: yea, the abjects gathered themselves together against me, and I knew it not; they did tear me, and ceased not (Ps.35:15).

"With hypocritical mockers in feasts, they gnashed upon me with their teeth (Ps.35:16)."

In regard to my expressed concern twenty years ago about the likelihood of these injustices and crimes growing in our government, I quote news headlines from Oct. 12, 1981, which justify and verify my fears of that time. "Our Losing Battle Against Crime. *Look at the statistics on arrests and convictions, and it is no wonder that a judge says 'Criminals have no fear' of being punished. Increasingly, they are getting away with murder—and a lot else.*

"Since 1960, the number of violent crimes in America has more than quadrupled."

The losses of commodities and funds of other government projects in South Dakota has been going on year after year and running into the millions of dollars. We hear nothing of the guilty getting punished.

The Insidious Creep-Up

When I was the soil conservationist on the Yankton Reservation, in the good years, I would get a new employee entering the service assigned to work under my supervision while he served his one-year probation to attain his Civil Service status. He would then be transferred to a permanent position on some other reservation.

The third one sent to assist me was already a permanent Civil Service employee. The reason for his transfer was because his job position had been terminated on another reservation. He was a good man and I was pleased that he could and would assume equal responsibility with me on our reservation.

He shortly resigned and took a non-Civil Service job with a tribe in another region. I wondered why he would surrender his Civil Service benefits. I think now I know why, with the unsuspected subsequent developments. No doubt he was pressured to make trouble for me and to bring about my replacement. He chose, as a couple of others did later, to resign rather than engage in such conspiracy.

The next man sent to replace him was also a full-fledged Civil Service employee. He attempted to carry out their orders. He failed and got himself fired. He came to me to help him and confessed what the deal was. This is the first indication I had that someone was plotting my downfall. Had I been aware, at the time, of the extent which the conspiracy would reach, I would have tried to get a written statement from him and also later one from another person, a woman whose part turned out so tragically for her. I think we could have made someone "burn."

The last guy sent in to do the dirty tricks was a big ruthless, "don't give a damn" type of fellow. He was a big problem for them too, but they did everything they could to put up with him. He got transferred but not fired after leaving our reservation.

Another new man was sent in as the soil conservationist on our reservation and he did a bang up job the short time he was here. Everybody liked him. But the notorious scoundrels at the area office could not stand that, so they forthwith dumped him.

This is the type of administration of Indian Affairs that the Indians have had to put up with for so many years. They had to possess a great moral fortitude to survive such brainwashing and

167

degrading treatment for so long. Only a noble person or a noble race could have survived it.

The Episode of Jeanette Packard

Jeanette's beautiful masses of flowers in her garden were her pride and joy and the outstanding attraction of its kind in the neighborhood. She lived on her allotment on the hill not far from town. By this time she was widowed and managed the leasing of her crop land, which was the source of her livelihood and for her family. She was fully competent to manage her own affairs. The BIA persisted in approving all leases of Indian trust land and collecting lease fees. Advertising for bids to lease land is all right even though it tends to set the going price at the established minimum rate.

Competent Indians should be permitted and encouraged to manage their own lease matters. Jeanette chose one of her neighbor farmers to farm her land. He was a good farmer and neighbor and did a good job of farming her land. He conserved the soil and moisture and maintained the fertility of the soil. This farmer farmed her land year after year, for several years, until this particular soil conservationist was sent to this reservation. He started raising hell with everyone he could. He would dig around and find incompetent, unstable "scalper-type" farmers and jam the leasing to them down the Indian's throats.

The arrogant treatment brought this good woman to tears and unhappiness. Some of the good farmers just dropped the Indian land rather than contend with the bully. He soon had no friends among either the Indians or the non-Indians. His superiors were fully aware of the depredations and foolish judgment of this man. He was a formidable problem for them also. Sometimes they would advise him and try to hold him down. But they hung tenaciously onto him to serve their evil purpose. It was a sad reflection upon their judgment and common sense. The reason is plain when we view the overall picture of their activities, which I will disclose more fully as we go along.

The Episode of Steve — Forcing Them to Their Knees

I found that on the Yankton Reservation, Indians who had livestock were always able to pay their bills, whereas those depending upon crops only were at times hard pressed to meet their bills with money.

My program and recommendations when I was an extension

agent were to get them into some livestock. Most of the agriculture operators on the Yankton Reservation had some livestock when a new farm agent took over for three years. He was one of those who could spend money liberally but seemed to have no sense of balance, or how to make money and keep the spending and costs below their intake or income. In three years he had all of them out of livestock—not one single head left on the entire reservation. Only three or four survived to later get back into the business of livestock. They were forced to sell their livestock to pay their debts that he had caused them to acquire. Steve was one of these. He operated on a Rehab. place. He had done an outstanding job for many years but at this time he was struggling to get back on his feet and got behind on some of his rent on the Rehab. land. One day he came to me feeling very low and almost crying. His ulcers were flaring up. He asked me: "What shall I do? They have ordered me to pay up or they will kick me off." This was at the time when rentals were due and the leases renewed. He had already done some farm work for that year's crop, which he would lose—and had no place to move his large family or any other way to support them. The Rehab. Committee made all assignments to Rehab. land and signed the leases as lessor. Only the Rehab. Committee could order him off, and by that time of the year it was too late to legally cause an occupant to move.

The Rehab. land was bought with government appropriated funds for the sole purpose of providing land for landless Indians who wanted to get started farming. This was done with the concurrence of the tribe. The assignments and terms for its use were placed in the management of the Rehab. Committee duly elected by the tribe.

I knew that they (the conspirators) could not make it stick if Steve resisted the ouster. So I told Steve to go back home and carry forward as if nothing had happened and if they said anything more to him, to tell them to go to hell. He went away feeling much better and continued to occupy and operate the project for many years. He has retired from the project and two of his sons incorporated and successfully operated it. They have an irrigation set-up as well as dry-land farming. Steve and his family have responsible jobs, have contributed well to the tribe in its new formative development of self-determination and a higher standard of living. He and his wife, Pearl, raised a family of fourteen children, all received a good education. The Indians took over the Marty Mission including its educational system.

Both Steve and Pearl performed duties at the school. Steve served as a counselor, is a member and has been president of the school board. Steve was the first secretary of the tribal council and continues to be an active member. He was the first chairman of the Housing Project (HUD), and was manager of the tribal farm. After retiring from the farming and livestock job, he engaged in a mercantile business and has continued many official duties for the tribe and for the Marty Community. Fortunately, BIA management's poor judgment and destructive plans backfired. The tribe reorganized under the Indian Reorganization Act and the Self-determination Act and moved forward again.

The conspirators are long gone but much of the damage done by them to the land and soil conservation, noxious weed control, earnings from land, etc. has not fully recovered after twenty years.

I have cited this case for two purposes: (1) to explain the BIA's policy of rehabilitating landless Indians as it operated and progressed under the administration of Superintendent C. R. Whitlock and Extension Agent Carl B. Aamodt and under the direct supervision of the writer, as farm agent; (2) as one case in point where a man who had been put in charge of my job, was rampaging in the "China Shop"—so to speak. The purpose of him and his cohorts was to push the writer out of his job and establish themselves as dictators in charge of the Indians and their lives. They attempted to destroy the existing Indian managed organizations and the progress of same. They needed to destroy the loyalty of the Indians to the writer. This man cursed the Rehab. directors and spoke disparagingly of certain others in his attempt to bring the Indians to submission to his dictatorship.

As can be seen by the reading of these pages they failed dismally but did tremendous damage to the reservation, its people and the BIA in several ways.

I shall describe another case or two to illustrate further.

THE EPISODE OF PERCY—BRINGING HIM TO HIS KNEES

Percy Archambeau was one of the "top" leaders on the reservation. After being brought to his knees, he was helpless before them. He changed in spirit and composure—but came back after the conspirators were ousted from the reservation.

He became chairman of the tribe and chairman of the United Sioux Tribes and made a strong record of accomplishments.

Like all other Indians on the reservation who no longer had any cattle to rely upon for a source of income and credit, he was completely at the mercy of these ruthless BIA employees. His money and fiscal affairs were taken from him by these people to do with as they pleased.

First they threatened him with starvation. His wife became very sick. She was taken to the hospital where the doctor diagnosed her trouble to be anemia and malnutrition and ordered him to buy steaks and red meat for her. She recovered and seemed to enjoy good health thereafter.

Apparently they still could not get his unqualified support, and evidently tried bribery.

One night several of these BIA employees held a meeting with some tribal members at a hall about three miles southeast of Lake Andes. Members of the tribe had asked for a report and accounting of the fiscal matters and the income from the tribal land. I had been informed of the meeting and invited myself to it. One of their number gave a sketchy report on the Indian school land (but no other tracts). This land was rented by Percy. Since I was well acquainted with this land—the total number of acres, the number of acres in crop land and in pasture—I was able to do some mental calculating and could see that the lease department was not charging him the minimum price for rentals. When I began to ask questions, the lease clerk became terribly nervous and frustrated. To me, it appeared that they were granting him unauthorized concessions for some purpose and were keeping it covered up.

After the meeting Percy, driving home, had a head-on collision with another car. The driver of the other car was killed. Percy and Steve were hurt. One other passenger was thrown through the windshield. Too much tension and too much nervousness blends dangerously with driving. No liquor was involved. He might have reacted differently in the situation had he not been under pressure.

To show how inhumane treatment can affect the lives of the victims I will recite more of this man's life. He became stoical and less communicative. He said, you can not fight the bureau, so he went along the best he could. He had a very large family to raise and support.

The most outstanding impression I got of Percy when I came to the Yankton Reservation was his open-faced, frank, candid, childlike truthfulness and honesty. He was a young man living on the White Swan River bottom, active and ambitious. He worked at any available job including a spell at a C.C.C. camp in the Black Hills. He participated in community affairs and programs. This was in the hard times of the thirties. He obtained a small loan and purchased a team and small farming equipment. Eventually he got an assignment to a Rehab. place and several head of replacement cattle. The herd grew and he got a larger Rehab. tract and was off on his career as a farmer. He did a good job of farming and raising livestock. He raised big corn crops during the war years and was able to pay his debts from the sale of corn and livestock.

The BIA wrecking crew put him out of the livestock business and tried to trample him into the dust—to force him to conform to their senseless and evil domination.

After about three years the ignominious BIA gang, themselves, were wrecked as far as this reservation was concerned. Some got transferred, some got fired, some died, and one went to the State Hospital for mental and emotional problems. Percy continued his farming and resumed livestock operations with the help of his sons, some of whom have carried on. Percy had also added irrigation to their projects. His son, Larry, currently is secretary of the Yankton Sioux Tribe.

And eventually Percy became the tribe's greatest leader. He served many years as chairman of the tribe as well as getting elected chairman of the United Sioux Tribes. He obtained many of the federal programs and fundings for his tribe and reservation, often making trips to Washington, D.C. He sought and obtained these programs following the congressional enactment of civil rights and self-determination legislation to help minority groups. In a short time the transformation for our Indian people which occurred was most miraculous. Their housing, sanitation facilities, educational and health improvements, general standard of living, their initiative, planning, and management of their own affairs was the greatest thing that ever happened to them.

Percy Archambeau died suddenly of a heart attack while chairman of the tribe. His funeral, no doubt, was the largest ever seen in this area. People came from all over the United States and Canada. His dream and ideal, ever foremost in his thoughts, was that peace, harmony and unity among all Indians within the United States and Canada would prevail, if the Indian could survive. He was chosen Honorary Parade Marshal of Wagner's big Labor Day celebration in 1973. HIS ENEMIES WERE IGNO-MINIOUS—BUT HE HAS BEEN EXALTED INDEED.

172

The Episode of Poor Terry

Three times while the author was the soil and moisture conservationist on the Yankton Sub-agency we got applicants who were serving their one-year probation period preceding their qualifying for their Civil Service rating. When completed the first two were promoted to an SMC position of their own on other reservations.

The third one who had his Civil Service rating was a nice friendly fellow, but he soon became worthless on the job. He would fail to carry out assignments and wanted to spend his time sitting around in the office gossiping with the office employees. He would do harassing and unauthorized things in the office such as completely rearranging the office furnishings when I was out. He finally got let out. After turning down a transfer to a dead-end station, he came to me crying for help. He confessed what he had done to me and said he did not want to do it, but that he was instructed and pressured to do so. The die was cast and there was nothing that I could do for him. He resigned and moved back to his native state. He wrote to me afterwards and I understand that he went into the ministry. Kinda reminds us of some of the Watergate principals—only he did not commit any crime or too serious sin.

The Episode of an Honest BIA Employee

While I had no inkling of it at the time, I now realize why a certain other person who was transferred here to work with me suddenly resigned, gave up his accumulated Civil Service benefits and hired out to a tribe in the Southwest as a non-Civil Service person.

He was experienced and a good man. I was very happy to have him to work with.

Of course, while he breathed no word about it, it is very evident now to me that he had been instructed to subvert me. Thank God we do still have a few honest and honorable people. We need to know about these people too. I feel certain that God loved him.

The Tragedy of a Career Woman

There came to the Yankton Reservation Agency a steno-typist with a commendable reputation of ability and efficiency. She was assigned to work jointly part-time for my SMC office and the lease office.

When the conspirators entered our agency with definite plans to disrupt our reservation management, they had a pipeline that seemed to arise from someplace up the line and on down to us. I was not propositioned to join the pipeline, but was innocently unaware of its presence until sometime later—when it finally reared its ugly head in our midst and I was the victim.

Those in the pipeline were instructed to work against me and force me out. This lady was induced to join the conspirators and aid them in many ways. She was paid to work half-time for me but often refused. What carrot they proffered her I do not know but can guess. It turned out to be a very bad deal for her. When she submitted a false and devastating written statement as a witness against me, I told her she could be sued for defamation of character and damages. She confidently replied that "the government will protect me."

The statement was fraudulently admitted at a hearing and transcribed therein. When I got a copy of the transcription six months later, I told her it was then public property and provided grounds for a lawsuit. She replied with excuses including, "They made me do it. I did it to save my job," and she lamentingly said, "The government promised to protect me." In fact when I stated she might have to testify under oath, she said that she could not do that because "she would have to tell the truth!" I replied, "What is wrong about telling the truth?"

After they had no more use for her, they arranged grounds to illegally retire her and thereby get her out of their way.

After being replaced and forced out of her job, evidently the traumatic experience emotionally unsettled her. She became alcoholic for which she was admitted to the State Hospital. Here she spent the last eighteen years of her life.

What a tragic ending for an otherwise useful and efficient worker!

Soil and Moisture Conservation Association

The Soil and Moisture Conservation program on the Yankton Reservation is another example of good accomplishment with Indian programming, initiative, industriousness, self-help, and sound fiscal management.

We did not have the personnel and financial aid from the government or the tribe, as did the Rosebud and larger reservations operating under the Wheeler-Howard Act. Money was necessary for certain things needed for a progressive program. We had to earn that and obtain it by our own efforts—which we did. This

174

was a private enterprise fund and did not involve the agency or BIA in any respect, except we had the superintendent's approval and blessing for us to do so. It was organized with a constitution and by-laws.

To initiate and create organizations and enterprises of these types is part of the American Way. They would have solved the Indian problem long ago had they been allowed to do so. To destroy them or avert these free enterprises is a great American sin that blots our history.

This, the SMCO on the Yankton Reservation, is one of the several enterprises that the BIA wreckers (or our Watergate) set about to destroy and get their hands on the bank account (a substantial working fund).

The other two chief organizations were the Credit Committee and the Rehab. Committee. These three organizations were the backbone of the origin and subsequent progress made by the Yankton people. All were well accomplished and managed in a democratic way by honest, dedicated, hard working directors. The Yankton Agency was scheduled for termination in five years as a result of their progress. It could be that the motive behind the conspiracy was to kill such programs, to save their Civil Service jobs by keeping the Indian down.

For the reader to get a true picture of what was being destroyed by them, one needs to realize these facts.

Enter the Bull into the China Shop — The Squeeze is On

The next move made was to send a roughneck (I'll call him, not his real name, Mr. Bull) to my reservation in their cowardly underhanded efforts to freeze me out, since they could not do it honestly or legitimately.

I describe the character of this man and some of his deeds at various places as we go along. The apparent goal of the conspirators was to wreck everything on the reservation and to destroy me. To destroy anything that resisted their destructive purposes; I want to show what it was they were destroying—as a background.

They were out to destroy my influence and the loyalty of the Indians and non-Indians to me and the progress of the Indian organizations and efforts to self-determination and self-sufficiency. They didn't want the Indian to be on his own.

This man, with his coerced cohorts was truly like the fabled bull in the china shop. Mr. Bull began to give me orders to do the routine things that I had always done for years—just to give me orders, then he invariably failed to do the same things himself. This is only one example of many hypocritical deeds that polluted the domain hereabouts.

While on the subject of calling such people hypocrites, do you realize the frequency that Christ called such characters hypocrites, snakes, fools, vipers, and liars? We do not feel that we are being blasphemous here. Quoting the Bible: "Woe unto you, scribes, pharisees, hypocrites! Ye fools. Woe unto you that laugh now! for ye shall mourn and weep (Luke, Chap. 6:25). James 3:5 warns us that sin begins in a small way, but grows and leads to death. "Behold, how great a matter a little fire kindleth!" How true it turned out to be on this reservation!

Yes, our sins will grow if not dealt with appropriately. At the time it was my great concern, and so expressed, that this corruption in the BIA would spread to other departments of our government. The news today bears this out. It raised its ugly head in the highest places—even unto the White House.

We have a problem and an obligation—expose it, fight it, and root it out and correct by replacing it with honesty, justice and constructive action.

The people who are in the best position to spot corruption are those who are working in the system. But during these days they had no sensitivity to do so. Their only reward would be punishment, which only a few could afford—a real prospect of losing their jobs and future security, most of them with families to support. Yes, it took courage and sacrifice! Isn't that a part of life? The decision is ours to make—to yield to or to resist temptation. What is our obligation and duty? I like to quote what President Kennedy said on January 30, 1961 in his inaugural address—"Our Role in the New Frontier":

"Let every public servant, whether his part is high or low, that a man's mark and reputation in this administration will be determined by the size of his job he does and not by the size of his staff, his office or budget. Let it be clear that this administration recognizes the value of daring and dissent—that we greet healthy controversy as a hallmark of healthy change. Let the public service be a proud and lively career. And let every man and woman who works in any area of our National government in any branch at any level be able to say with pride to honor in future years, 'I served the United States Government in that hour of our national need.'"

The President held up an ideal for every government worker and set the stage for good government, by honest decent people. But then he got assassinated! (Strong evidence, eighteen years later, points to a possible conspiracy there.)

Mr. Bull's General Character

To get a better picture of this man's character, whom I will call Mr. Bull, let us listen to him a little bit. These are words uttered in the presence of witnesses, including the writer, some of which he wrote down at the time and entered in his diary.

Mr. M., a prominent farmer and businessman, was in our office talking to Mr. Bull, for his first meeting with him. Mr. Bull said, "I don't give a God damn for you."

He told Steve, referring to the Rehab. (Rehabilitation Committee, duly elected): "The Rehab. group are all bastards."

To Phil, a cripple who walked with a cane, "Phillip, someday someone will pull that cane out from under you and clobber you over the head with it"—following a joking remark by Phillip.

One party said Mr. Bull knows nothing about local conditions and Mr. E. said, "Mr. Bull is crazy."

Mrs. E., who lived a few blocks from the small farm where Mr. Bull and family lived and did some farming and raising livestock on the side from his government job, told people they could hear him yelling at and cussing his kids. Also yelling and cussed his boy when he was helping plant corn by lowering and raising the marker. He was farming her small tract of land, which was contrary to federal regulations—conflict of interest, she being an Indian. Mrs. E. also said that his wife told her that he never tells her anything that goes on at the office. It was well known that he was abusive to his family.

M.J.S. said if Mr. Bull ever comes on his place again he will run him off—won't stand having his dad abused without defending him.

Several farmers complained about how he approached them—an example: drove through an oat field, jumped out of his pickup and without introducing himself started accusing him of some mismanagement. In one case it was a case of mistaken identity (accusing the wrong man) and almost resulted in a fight.

HYPROCRISY

The hyprocrisy was very glaring and hypocritical at the office. He tried to intimidate the writer constantly, at the office by accusing him of wrong practices and not following rules, which he himself so contemptuously did not follow, but which the writer always did—even for years. It led to a conspiracy with others in the office to get them to cooperate with him to subvert me. One lady finally resigned her job rather than get involved in the hyprocrisy and controversies.

And so it went, on and on, until all of the people involved were removed from the agency for one reason or another. More will be recorded of what happened to the culprits before the end of this chapter.

Mr. Bull almost invariably failed to practice what he preached to others.

One day we were riding down the highway together when he looked at a pasture with grazing cattle on it at a date too early in the spring to start grazing. The pasture was one of those grossly over grazed and abused by the owner. The pasture was non-Indian land, and not BIA concern. It was too early in the spring to start grazing properly managed grazing. He made a degrading remark about it. It was true and the remark was not displaced. But it was no BIA concern. It gave me a thought and I decided to investigate and see if I was thinking correctly—sure enough my thinking bore fruit.

He had purchased a small farm near town and also rented some land from an Indian, which was illegal for a BIA employee to do, because of a conflict of interest. But then, he paid no attention to such matters himself but he sure would jump on me or someone else if we did it. He had a pasture and some livestock and sure enough he was grazing his pasture and it was terribly over grazed too and too early for proper grazing.

Another thing, while we are on the subject—he was busting himself all over cramming terracing down the throats of others in a desperate effort to make some kind of a record for himself. He had to make a better record than I had done previous to his assignment to force me out of the service. It was one of the BIA gang's weapons used against me—claiming that I was not making enough progress. It turned out that, after three years, he accomplished about the same number of miles completed as I had done in one year. And besides that the rest of the BIA gang were getting very little if any done on the Rosebud—where complaints came from. That has been twenty years ago and very little, if any, has been done here since then. That was the type of progress made by incompetent conniving BIA employees during those infamous years.

Now, for the rest of the hypocrisy of this human interest episode. Yes, Mr. Bull's land needed terracing but it got none. What a farce!! Or as Mr. Gildersleeve, I believe it was, used to say on his radio program: "What a revolting situation this turned out to be!"

The Assault on Productive Tribal Organizations
Prologue

Humpty Dumpty Sat upon a wall
Humpty Dumpty had a great fall.
All of the Area Director's conspirators and
all of the Area Director's dumb clucks
Could not put Humpty Dumpty back
again.

It was the gang of conspirators who pushed "Humpty Dumpty" off the wall and broke into pieces the established organizations that were working well and serving the Yankton Sioux people. Then for two or three years they tried to re-establish new tribal organizations, built in their own image. Their efforts of rebuilding were a dismal failure.

The Assault Against Tribal Management

The BIA management participants arranged for a tribal meeting at Greenwood for March 19, 1959. Their stated purpose was a step towards their planned wreckage of the Rehab. Committee. As a part of their insidious purpose, I was notified to attend. I had been responsible for the organizing and the successful operation of same. I went there with a financial report. They had selected a tough talking, fault-finding guy to preside. He started out by telling me that they thought I had been there too long.

I stuck to my purpose and gave a comprehensive report, including how the governing body was elected and managed the affairs—how it progressed and produced good and sound services and facilities for the benefit of the tribe. There was no further discussion and the meeting ended amicably, but a failure for them.

However, the BIA group was like the Communists and Facists—persistent, try again and again. Try more brain washing. They called another meeting shortly, and brought in their heavy artillery from the Rosebud and Aberdeen offices. Suddenly these commanders from above took an interest in the home affairs of the Yankton people. They called the meeting and after that they called the shots.

They succeeded in voting the old Rehab. Committee out and

electing a new one. When I asked them to read the minutes of the last meeting, Mr. Holmes, Superintendent of Rosebud, asked "Is it necessary?" After reading the minutes it provoked Bill O'Connor, one of the newly elected directors, to remark: "The old committee had a lot of business and they (the new committee) had strong competition, as based on the minutes and records."

What an insidious thing for the superintendent to say! He is supposed to be honest, an adviser and a leader for the Indians. What a failure as superintendent! Well, he shortly transferred and left us. It has been my observation that people are inclined to be honest when governed by honest leaders and administrators and likely to be corrupt when ruled by crooked leaders. We did not see all this corruption under the John Collier, C. R. Whitlock and Robert's administrations.

Backfire

It was not long (May 29, 1959) when reaction set in and backfired in their faces. The first act of the new committee was to double the pay to the committee and one of them started putting in a claim for a lot of time which he created for himself. The old Rehab. Committee served many years without a cent of pay for expenses. But later, when their funds became sufficient to do so, they granted themselves a very modest stipend for expenses to attend business meetings. The new committee was voted out with only one dissenting vote.

It was more than a year (7-18-60) before they again attempted to organize and to pick up the shattered pieces of their devastation. They called a tribal meeting at Marty with about one hundred in attendance. They had Cornelius from the central office, Bennett from the area office, several from the Rosebud office, and the local office.

The new Superintendent of the Rosebud Reservation, Mr. Harold Schunk, told them that they came here for two things: (1) tribal organization to sign tribal land business (formerly done by the Rehab. Committee) and (2) commodities business.

Stricker said: Indians mistrust the area office and administration.

Clem Smith: We are back where we started from, prior to the Wheeler-Howard Act (1933). A motion was made to elect a five-member committee, but it was filibustered to death. Smith told them the vote would have to be a secret one and include non-residents to organize the tribe.

180

They failed again to form an organization (a puppet organization).

They did approve Bolin's (administrative officer of the Yankton Reservation) recommendation of a budget of $3500 for the commodities and distribution of same on the reservation, which needed tribal approval.

They had failed again, after trying every device they could contrive. My diary asks—What will they do now? Mr. Bolin and his cohorts should resign and the bureau should get decent people back in charge.

(My question in 1979—who was there in the bureau honest enough to take the "bull" by the horns? What is it that was so important that the top level had to "Watergate" it? I am still researching for the answer.)

Yankton Soil and Moisture Conservation Association Loses Its Fight For Survival

The organization of the Yankton Indian Soil and Moisture Conservation Association was accomplished by the writer, the agency soil and moisture conservationist, and interested Indians. The purpose was to aid in conserving soil and moisture on tribal and individual Indian's trust land. It recommended practices to be used and to incorporate specified practices to be included as part of leases on tribal and Indian trust land. This is another example implementing our Indian policy of organizing the Indians to make decisions for themselves, self-implementation and bring about the management of their affairs by themselves—instead of the government employees doing it for them. Then they would cram it down their throats—with the sole purpose of perpetuating themselves in their jobs at the expense of taxpayers and to the detriment of the Indians.

Indians are very capable of handling their own affairs when given a chance and have proven it over and over again.

The organization has its constitution and by-laws—its election of the officers and directors. They had their own finances for operations and maintenance deposited in the local bank. The funds were raised by the association who did a good and commendable job.

The Y.I.S.C.A.'s annual meeting was held on January 29, 1962, as required by the constitution. Several BIA employees from the Rosebud Agency and the area office made it a point to be present for the first time in its existence. Others were three of us from

181

the local office and the interested Indians, including the directors and officers.

Some of the BIA wreckers instituted an effort to amend the constitution.)There was no need for any amendment; it was only a gimmick by the BIA wrecking crew to get in a wedge.)

Some of the comments: Assistant Superintendent Shubert—"Area office thought perhaps it should operate independently of the BIA, excepting for technical assistance. The association should be put to more use." A new constitution and by-laws were discussed by Denzil Martin and Gene Barrett from the area office—to better utilize the enterprise they said.

Myers—"The association can be very useful—it's purpose to serve self-management by the group. Soil conservationist to assist in maintaining equipment. The constitution and by-laws are fairly complete but might make some changes to better serve. The conservationist should be responsible for countersigning the association checks. Adoption and plan of operations to be approved by the superintendent and area office."

All of these things were already in effect and being done, with the exception of having the area office sign its approval, which was deemed unnecessary.

It is very plain that the *real* purpose of these BIA conspirators was sinister. Like the Communists they don't give up—just back up and take another shot at it.

Percy suggested that Myers and Baird meet with the directors and formulate the change, then present it to the association's general meeting to be voted on.

Mr. Shubert further stated that the funds cannot be deposited in the IIM account.

Further results and comments among others—"the designed purpose by the BIA, is to replace the constitution and by-laws instead of amending as they first suggested." No reference was made to the constitution's provision to amend it or dissolve same. It was very obvious that they wanted to evade that process. They did suggest changing the name from Yankton Indian Soil Conservation Association to Yankton Indian Soil Conservation Service. (Not much of a reason for changing the constitution and by-laws!)

They never did get the association going again. But they did get the money out of the bank, and what happened to it after that? God only knows! Whatever it was—it was illegal. To do so they had to use lies, innuendo, tricks, and illegal maneuvering.

The writer can cite and verify examples of their efforts.

I had some correspondence with Congressman Ben Reifel and from that I learned that the Rosebud Superintendent had written the Aberdeen office and said that our Yankton Soil Conservation Association was dissolved and non-existent and therefore, there is no one to act for the association so they wanted to transfer out their account. They asked the Aberdeen office to authorize them to journal voucher it out. This occurred in Feb. 1960, two years prior to the above described meeting.

The Aberdeen office had no jurisdiction over this association. Apparently the superintendent wanted to get the area office involved, to give him more backing for evasion of his responsibility or entangling maneuvers. Besides they could not "journal voucher" out funds in a private deposit in a commercial bank. I tried to stop their raid as I was the one with the legal responsibility and it could only be done with the consent and authority of the association directors and me. The statement that the association was dissolved and non-existent was an outright lie.

In the process of getting control of the Y.I.S.C.A. and its funds, the BIA gang resorted to changing or getting a new constitution and by-laws with their stamp on it. The tribe would take no action on it at the meeting. Percy told them that the tribe was suspicious and that they do not trust the bureau.

Without any voting on the matter or approval by the tribe, someone, no doubt Mr. Bull, made up a copy and submitted it to the Y.I.S.C.A. directors to sign and thereby give it their approval and by-pass the tribe. I am told that they were given a copy of the existing constitution and by-laws to look at which they requested. He retrieved it after only a very short time before they could study it. No one was able to find or get a copy since. Presumably someone destroyed all of the copies. It is obvious who.

Apparently the organization just died a fadeaway death (or probably more correct to say, was murdered) without an obituary. The broken pieces of china could not be put together again.

A Surprising Find — Resurrection

But at this point in time there appeared better days for the tribe waiting in the wings. Two things happened, first practically all of the BIA gang were either fired or transferred.

Secondly, a miracle must have come out of the woodpile. Someone discovered, after a dormancy of thirty years, that the tribe had a constitution and by-laws to a tribal organization under the

Indian Reorganization Act, sometimes called the Wheeler-Howard Act. It had been signed by the secretary of the interior and was fully legal.

For all of these years, we operated under the assumption that the tribe voted to accept reorganization under this act in 1934, but had never accepted a constitution and by-laws. Therefore, the tribe could not operate as an organized tribe and were not so recognized by the federal government. They could not enter into contracts or get certain benefits from the government. They could not get tribal credit loans for tribal aid and development.

The only alternative they had was to organize local community associations and operate with limited funds. Each association elected directors and officers, for a specific purpose only. The elections were made at open tribal meetings. These officers and directors were a committee to manage the project they represented. Thus, there were the Rehab. Committee, the Credit Committee, the Soil and Moisture Conservation Committee, the Surplus Commodity and Relief Committee, Health and Educational Committee, etc., as already indicated above.

Credit was given to Clem Smith for discovering the lost constitution and by-laws in the bureau's central Washington, D.C. office where it apparently had been gathering dust those many years. This should give the tribe grounds to sue the federal government for some more millions in claims.

Could it lay in their office for thirty years and they had forgotten about it? Or did some enemy steal it and after thirty years resurrect it? In any case, it was sloppy business by the BIA to completely forget what happened.

Thirty years lost for the tribe!

The Roy Lempke Episode

Roy Lempke came to the Yankton Reservation as a soil conservationist. He was a civil engineer and in a short time started working on an irrigation project on the Missouri River bottom for Steve Cournoyer. He initiated and completed the project, then the irrigation started. It became the first field irrigation in that area. He designed and installed the project from beginning to end solely by his own efforts. He did the engineering work, contracted the ditch-system, and the pumping unit. He procured the source of credit for financing the project. It thereby became a private enterprise accomplishment, not involving the government and taxpayers in the bureaucratic red tape, confusion, delay, and inefficiency.

184

This meant that an Indian was the first to irrigate in that area, which lead to others setting up irrigation systems, all using water from the Missouri River.

The success of the project attracted the attention of the news media and farm magazines. Feature write-ups appeared in several publications.

Evidently someone in the area office read it and it caused the 'powers-that-be' to sit up and take notice. They called the agency office and wanted to know what was going on down there and how come they did not know anything about it. So they dispatched a group of their bigshots and so-called experts to go there and tramp over the project and make an investigation. They evidently found it successful and working out with a good first-year crop- and without their unnecessary input, which displeased them very much. It resulted in the little bigshots immediately taking steps to fire the young man who dared to get a job done and earn his salary, and help the Indian at the same time. This man was using common sense and helping the Indian to help himself, in the American way of individual enterprise and self-sufficiency. This is supposed to be the aim of the BIA.

It is not easy to fire a Civil Service employee who does his job, excepting by fraud and subversion of the Merit System. The outlet for doing so is by transferring him to some remote, unimportant station where he has little chance to perform constructive and honest work or gain promotions.

If Mr. Lempke had not gone ahead and done the job in the ordinary course of his duties, but depended upon his superiors to direct him what, where, why, how, and when to do, it would have taken several years' time, great expense to the taxpayers and the Indians. It probably would never have been done. He should have been commended! As it turned out the little bigshots could not claim the credit for the job.

For his punishment and to teach him a lesson they transferred him out of the area. This is a typical example of the BIA personnel operation and why the Indian is held down and maintained in submission. Their purpose and concern is mostly to hold a job successfully or gain promotions in the BIA. To do so one needs to be a very mediocre person. If he is too incompetent, he might get fired. If he does a bang-up job he most likely will get fired or demoted. This is not an uncommon practice in the bureau. Informed persons see this happening right along.

The above mentioned irrigation project is still operating many years later and raising abundant yields of crops for the Indian operators. A permanent enterprise not financed by the taxpayers, except for the salary of one employee for a short time.

How ironic it turned out to be for his superiors!

Snubbed

At this point in time I was not conscious of the conspiracy that was developing. As I became aware of a conspiracy I could not focus on the point of infection. I am still trying to locate the source. I am certain that it did not occur locally, and I feel it's not at the Rosebud Agency level. But, for certain, those involved all along the pipeline were whipped into line, promised promotions or threatened with loss of their jobs, to obey orders. I feel sure that at least one of my former friends and fellow employees was involved. He apologized for Terry and his failure to produce, saying he appointed him, and thought he had a previous good record.

But the second thing he did to me really showed him up. This occurred at a Conference at Rapid City, S.D. All BIA employees who could were advised to attend. I did not get a notice or instructions to attend until the very last moment, when they evidently had second thoughts.

Gene Barrett arranged and directed the conference. He divided us into two groups. One group consisted of those in lesser positions, non administrative, etc. There was no program for them only pure entertainment was provided-of no value, only to occupy time. I was relegated to this group. This was too glaring a snub. I got up and went to the other group-and stayed there. I took complete notes on the whole conference, excepting for one long speech, by Robert Bennett, a copy of which I could obtain to complete my notes.

Rendezvous with Civil Service Inspectors

In October, 1959, a Mr. R.W. Miller and Mr. W. Fahey, Civil Service inspectors, made a trip through South Dakota. It was made known through the news media and memorandums from the area office to all agencies. Any employee who wished to do so was invited to meet with them to discuss any problem they might have regarding their employment.

I asked them for an appointment. They made the appointment for Oct. 26, 1959, after dinner in the office of the superintendent of the Flandreau Indian School at Flandreau, South Dakota. I made arrangements for leave for that afternoon and the next day.

All correspondence, leave request and approval went through our administrator's office, so he knew everything about it.

When my wife and I arrived there, the campus was quiet—no lights in the superintendent's office or his home. We inquired about him and was informed that he had gone to some other place for a ball game.

We went on to Pipe Stone, Minnesota, where we got a motel room for the night. The next morning we went back to Flandreau and called on the superintendent and told him of my mission and the appointment and wondered why the appointment wasn't kept. He said they waited around until eleven o'clock a.m. and when I did not show up they went on. Of course I told him that the appointment was for evening and that I was there at the appointed hour. I asked him if he knew where they went. He said they went to the area office at Aberdeen. I called the area office and got in touch with them, and asked why they did not keep the appointment. Their answer was that someone called from the Wagner office and said that the appointment was called off. They made another appointment for me that evening in the Alonzo Hotel in Aberdeen.

After talking to the Civil Service men, they said they would arrange for the bureau office to permit me to have access to my personnel file and to read same.

This was done the next morning. I found devastating material in it of which I had had no knowledge, and of course it was all untrue, and they did not want me to see it. They had pulled out certain other material before giving the file to me, so I would not see that. I found this out later, which I shall relate later under "Hearing."

I am sure that the bureau people had briefed the Civil Service men before I met them to poison their minds about me. Judging by past experience with them, I could expect nothing less from them. Although after talking to them, I don't believe they thought of me as the devil. What else makes me think so? They came to the door of the restaurant, where they knew we were eating a late dinner, and looked us over beforehand. Wonder what they thought of what they saw? When we went up to the lobby on the second floor they had everything arranged for us. They had a nice easy chair for me and they each sat one on either side and just a little back of me. They placed my wife, a lady, on a hard straight chair off to one side. Then they placed a bright light just in front of me so it hit me squarely in the face.

What is this practice called when used interrogating criminals? What was their purpose?

I called Mr. Bolin at the office of the Yankton Agency and told him where I was and that I would not be back at the time planned. I also told him why. I wonder what went through his mind at this news? (Their conspiracy plans failed again!) When I got back to the office I questioned him about telling the Civil Service examiners that my appointment with them had been canceled. He gave no answer, only sulked.

HARASSMENTS

One of the strategies these plotters used against me beside threats, innuendo, etc., was harassment. Mr. Bull was constantly employing these in the office, without truth or facts. Someone evidently asked the IRS to investigate my Income Tax report. I was called to meet them at Armour at a certain time and bring my material with me. They examined my reports for the years of 1958 and 1959. Everything checked out fine. I am sure that my name was not picked at random for a routine because that happened only a year or two before and would not have happened again so soon unless someone suggested that they do so, on complaint or suspicion.

One day Mr. Bull asked me to accompany him out in the country, under the guise of inspecting a field of Indian land for conservation compliance. I knew what the condition was without a visit to it and I am sure that he did also. The land was located out in the middle of a section, with no one nearby. When we arrived at the spot, he showed no interest in the land. He attempted to intimidate and threaten me. I paid no attention to his intimidation but went right ahead and talked about the land and conservation needs. We went back to town and nothing else happened. He is a big and rugged guy but not very smart. He never was able to get anything irregular or wrong on me, and make it hold water. That was also true of all of his cohorts.

In early 1960 the County Weed Board gave me a special letter of commendation because of my work in the control of weeds, and especially noxious weeds. On January eleventh I showed this letter to Mr. Bolin for him to read. I don't think he liked the idea and said nothing about congratulations.

For years, those of us whose duties included both office and field work, made it a practice when going out in the field to leave word in the office when we expected to return. Sometimes it would

188

be left with some office personnel, other times a black board was used to put it on. Mr. Bull would create situations or falsely accuse me so he could falsely claim I did not leave this information when I would be out of the office. I would leave a pad on my desk with this information and I would also inform Ms. Friday. I soon learned that when office callers asked for me she was telling them that she did not know where I was or when I was expected to return. She proved to be one of the conspirators.

After that I left word with another girl. She would not lie for them and was under pressure from Mr. Bull and perhaps Mr. Bolin, administrative officer, also. She soon revolted and notified him to take care of the job himself. She would not be involved. She finally gave up and resigned from her Civil Service job.

Mr. Bull and Mr. Bolin seldom left word when they would return to the office. When I noticed this I started keeping a written record of same and have the detailed record.

A certain member of our employee force was so slow that he took an unreasonable amount of time to get his share of a job done. This incompetence caused many stalemates and much mismanagement in the office. It was his responsibility to issue and arrange for storage and distribution of surplus commodities. He put a considerable quantity of cheese in the vacant old office building in Greenwood. There it remained for several months and until hot weather when it melted and ran out and over the floor. The Indians complained about this but it did no good.

Another bad deal of his was his failure to open official mail. He would throw it into a desk drawer unopened. I noticed that there were three or four letters from one person alone. It was his responsibility to take care of that mail. That went on for months.

It is difficult for a fellow-worker to insist on corrective measures. Although there were a few times when it brought some project of my work to a complete stop—when I had to take things into my own hands to prevent a complete flop. There are places and times when and if you do complain, they brand you as a "troublemaker." Sometimes that can be used against said person.

One day when an official from the area office was in our office and while this person was out of the office, I opened the drawer and showed him the pile of unopened letters. He picked up one of them and put it in his pocket. I never did learn what disposition was finally made of those letters. The answers to those people who wrote the letters no doubt was important to them. *How Things Can Get Bad Because of Incompetency, Mismanagement*

189

And Get Worse When Corruption Takes Over!! All unnecessary!
And Shameful For All Who Were Responsible.

I had arranged in advance, for a few days of annual leave to attend an event in a city some distance from Wagner. A new superintendent was to make his first visit to our agency on one of these days. Those who knew about it were looking forward to it and would put on a good first impression for him. I was not informed of the event. In fact no one was to let me know, but someone smelled the rat and leaked the news. That presented a little problem for me because I wanted to be there too, to make my impression and protect my image that he might form aided by my absence.

I decided to come back for part of that day. I drove most of the night to do so. I drove up to the front of the office just a few minutes before eight o'clock. As I did so, three of the BIA gang from Rosebud and the Aberdeen area office came gaily swinging out of the post office next door to our office. I shall never forget the dumbfounded expressions that suddenly came over them as they saw me there in the flesh. They quickly turned into the office and I followed them in. You never heard such silence that met my ears. It spoiled their "mice's play," because the cat did not stay away. What an atmosphere under which to work!! Such craftiness has its detrimental effects upon the morale of all workers.

A Corrupt Doctor

The area office ordered me to go to a doctor of their choosing for a physical examination. I was instructed to go to the doctor at the Indian Hospital where they have some authority. The doctor was very unhappy about this. Instead of using the official form used for the purpose, they sent him special instructions. When I reported to him he had already returned it to them and thereby averted dishonesty and got himself off the hook. That did not succeed for them, so they ordered me to the Vets' Hospital at Sioux Falls, where I was directed to a psychiatrist. He was very much frustrated—shirt collar unbuttoned, no tie, his hair all ruffled. He said he did not know what was the matter with him that day. Probably his conscience churning within him! My wife, who possesses a keen sense of hearing, remained out in the hall. She heard him talking to someone in his office and said: "They didn't give us much to go on."

He gave me no examination, he did not touch me, in fact, he hardly saw me. He asked a few questions on my background and

190

looked down all of the time for the few minutes we were together. He probably looked at me through the corner of his eye. He asked me what my problem was. I asked him what was his problem, since I thought the problem was his. I said, "I feel fine. How do you feel?"

He got rid of me by sending me to a small room with some type of puzzle on a table. It was a childish 'True or False' thing. Some kid hung around while I monkeyed with it. Then I left and they were rid of me.

I asked the doctor if I would get a copy of his report. His answer was yes. However, I never did get it. When one of my doctors wrote to him about it, he said the area office ordered the examination and paid for it and they had instructed him not to give out a report. I would have to get it from them. When I wrote the area office for it they told me it was confidential and classified—I could not have it.

Talk about Castro and the Russians! We don't need to go further than the BIA to see the same principle in operation in our own government.

I went to four other doctors besides my own two, including a neurologist-psychiatrist for consultation and examination. He advised me to go to work. According to the Civil Service's reason for retiring me, I was totally and permanently disabled. They would not tell me why I was disabled, or how. My doctors tried to find out and they got some hints, by leaks, such as paranoia, imagining that I was being followed, watched, and talked about. My congressman got a letter from the Board of Appeals and he sent me a copy of it. It said a "nervous disability."

My own doctor's report on the claim that I was disabled was "far-fetched!" Having known me for many years, they found the claims false.

While my health was being undermined and damaged by the constant pressure of harassment and false claims, I remarked: I could set a pace for either field or office work or combination of both for employees of the BIA and if they followed me I could outwork ninety percent of them. If I was disabled at this time, it would have been due to the BIA, their fault, and I should be awarded $1,000,000 in damages!

If the statements by all of these other doctors is not enough to raise serious doubts about the claims of disability, then the subsequent years should belie the slanderous claims and their insidious statements and deeds. I performed many jobs successfully, as usual. I set up a feed and seed store and obtained seed salesmen for large companies and supervised them over a several county area. I also sold livestock equipment. I served as fieldman for a dairyherd improvement association covering several counties. I bred and raised registered hogs winning awards at shows and sales and served as a director on both the state association and a national breed association. I also served many years as a director on the South Dakota Water Development association. I was one of only two to receive an Honorary Lifetime Directorship and a T.V. set for award for my work. I remained very active in the Rotary, Community Council, Izaak Walton League, Weed Board, director of a state and national livestock breed associations, county fair, Chamber of Commerce, and several community and area projects. I received an honorary lifetime membership and plaque from the Chamber of Commerce in 1980—probably the only one in its entire seventy-five-year history.

I am now retired from some of these activities and am traveling and doing research work. I have many friends scattered over the entire U.S.—the greatest reward of all.

Dr. Blank in his report to the BIA stated that he examined me on two occasions, January 16, 1962 and January 23, 1962. (I suppose he quoted two dates to make it appear he did a thorough job-to earn his pay, whatever it was.) The first date was the day I met with him for a very short time. The second date was a complete misrepresentation. On that day I attended an all-day Crop Improvement Association meeting and that night an Izaak Walton League Meeting, many miles distance from Sioux Falls where Dr. Blank was. Minutes of both meetings would confirm this fact and belie Dr. Blank's report. My diary also confirms it. This lie would discredit every thing else that he reported and crumble the entire Civil Service's ruling action against me. This arrangement was a predetermined, cut-and dried proposition.

The BIA was firmly in the saddle and they could exercise their authority with very little fear of opposition.

I went to Sioux Falls and spent most of one day tracing the doctor to ask him what he meant by the January 23, 1962 date. I caught up to him at the McKennan Hospital where they told me to wait in the waiting room until he could see me. As I waited I saw him there and he saw me also, I am sure. After waiting until late afternoon, I realized ha had given me the slip by leaving by a back way. Nothing for me to do but return home, where I wrote him a letter. Of course I received no reply. Another victory scored temporarily for the Area Director and his gang.

That the triumphing of the wicked is short, and the joy of the hypocrite but for a moment. *Job 20:5.*

For what is the hope of the hypocrite though he hath gained, when God taketh away his soul? *Job 27:8*

My righteousness I hold fast, and will not let it go: my heart shall not reproach me so long as I live. *Job 27:6*

Those that remain of him shall be buried in death: And his widows shall not weep. *Job 27:15.*

Government officials, who would be so unjust and underhanded, should be condemned and sent to prison. The doctor should be stripped of his license, instead of being allowed to continue to prey upon the public. The same applies to the Civil Service doctors for their rendition of the episode.

Mockery of a Hearing

The area director condescended to grant a hearing where I could present my grievances at Aberdeen on May 10, 1960.

Mr. Balsiger was to preside over and conduct the hearing. Two responsible members of the establishment were selected to judge the hearing.

I started by presenting my case in the forenoon. My presentation so completely floored them that during their get-together for the noon hour they asked, upon reassembling at one o'clock that the hearing be postponed for a later date at Wagner. It was first set for July 19, 1960, but was not consummated until Sept. 26, 1960. They had difficulty getting someone to sit as judges. No one wanted to do it and be the judges. It took them over two months to get someone and to proceed with the hearing. The presiding officer was supportive of the opposition. The other two must have rendered their honest decision, since no indicting charges came out of it or were used against me.

Later, I met Mr. Balsiger face-to-face out on the street. He avoided looking me in the face or speaking to me, but hurried by. Whether it was a case of shame for his conduct or a sense of failure to achieve wanted results for his bosses, I don't know—could be both.

Quite a crew attended the hearing from the Rosebud Agency and the Aberdeen area office and two others from our local office. The Rosebud superintendent who was lined up on the opposition side later told a very close friend of mine when they evidently brought up the question of the hearing, "It was all hogwash."

I had notified several persons to appear for the hearing as witnesses.

I am not going into many of the things brought out and put on record in this hearing—it could fill two large books.

Suffice one or two more:

Coker to the superintendent—"he (the writer) has never in all his twenty-two years in Civil Service accepted supervision himself." He also said that I could not supervise men.

When I said that I had always received top rating on my annual efficiency reports, (over twenty years) both he and Richard Ohmeke denied this fact. Finally Mr. Coker said something about all of those who gave me the efficiency reports didn't know what they were doing. I can quote some typical examples: 1944,1945,1946,1947,1948 and 1949 all very good; 1952—Satisfactory in all categories.

Narrative Report 1953 (which is representative of all years):

August Nylander does a volume quality of work that is above the average required. Often he works a 10 to 12 hour day and does not hesitate to work the extra hours in order to complete a job.

He knows how to deal with both Indians and white farmers and ranchers in getting conservation applied to the land. He is thorough in dealing with special problems. He organizes his work well.

He gets along well with other employees. Is cheerful in his work attitudes. Is free to offer suggestions to employees under his supervision that help to improve their work.

He easily accepts responsibility and is very conscientious about his work.

Arlo Nielson
Conservation Supervisor

Affidavit

This is to certify that I served in the capacity of Agriculture Extension Agent on the Rosebud Jurisdiction of South Dakota from 1935 to 1950.

That during this time August L. Nylander was a Farm Agent on the Yankton for about ten years.

During the time that Mr. Nylander served under me, I found him efficient and at all times cooperative. He always accepted my supervision and did a very good job.

(Signed) Sincerely, Carl B. Aamodt

Mr. Balsiger, the chairman, instructed—"The committee will disregard the testimony of Mr. Aamodt." Why?

I will cite another testimonial letter. But I don't believe I offered it at the hearing. It also belies Mr. Coker's blind statement above.

Resettlement Administration
Cheyenne, Who.
Nov. 13, 1935

To Whom it May Concern:

Regarding Mr. August Nylander:

Mr. Nylander came to Cheyenne early in the Spring of 1934 at my request to act as my assistant in the Emergency Relief Garden Program. Mr. Nylander acted as co-author in several of the instructoral bulletins sent out regarding the soil problems connected with the garden program. As the season advanced, Mr. Nylander was transferred from the state office to the Laramie County Relief Garden Project as supervisor. Mr. Nylander had direct charge of 120 acres of dry land garden. In spite of the worst drought in history, this garden came within a few pennies of breaking even. The ground was rented, machinery had to be bought, trucking charges had to be paid and only relief labor at 45¢ per hour was used on this project. Mr. Nylander proved to be a very hard worker and a good handler of labor on this project.

Signed
Carl Bingemer
State Director of Subsistence
Gardens, 1934
Cheyenne, Wyoming

I have in my possession my efficiency reports for every year of my service in the BIA and all of them are rated "tops"—very good and the narrative part is similar in extolling my performance, as the ones just quoted—over twenty years of them.

One of the cases Mr. Coker was trying to build against me was his claim that I was not pushing terraces fast enough. Let's compare results with what Mr. "Bull" got done when he took over. I had to start from zero, with no assistance, no equipment or operating funds (until we got a fund established, through our own resources and initiative). There was no contractor to build terraces in the entire area, until I induced a party to buy the necessary equipment and we promised him our business.

The following three years Mr. Bull had considerable help. After two years he had not equalled my one-year record. I did ten miles the first year. Mr. Bull after two years got eleven miles completed and approved. An average of five and a half miles per year. There was no improvement in the kind of terraces made. Some of them needed it badly. One valuable field was left in such shape that no crop was raised on it for over twenty years. The condition was corrected only last fall and it is now in good shape. The loss of the crops over those years was considerable for the tribe.

Notes taken from my diary:

> In the desperate attempt to make a record building ter-races you have put on extra help and equipment and have forced through any kind of structure which you call a terrace. Structures not up to specification can do much harm to the land instead of helping. According to A.S.C. office 5 terrace projects have been completed this Spring for a total of 19,275 feet or 3.65 miles. If we count the incompleted terraces it would be another 2/3 miles. And one of these was only a diversion ditch. Count these too, if you please, and you still are running behind-14.70 miles- and average of under 5 miles per year. Another irony and hypocrisy of this episode is that no terraces have been required built since then. And even the Rosebud Agency was not getting terracing done on a comparable basis on their own reservation while making this great ado about us.

What a bunch of bums they turned out to be!

On June 11, 1962 a Civil Service investigator said to me: "It is brain washing, harassment and inhumane treatment of an employee." He advised to try a senator, try an employee orga-nization such as the N.F.E. (National Federal Employees).

A letter by the Secretary of Interior, Mr. Udall, May 15, 1961, said: "The B.I.A. acted in an unbusiness like and inhumane way."

More Hypocrisy

An example of what was constantly being practiced in our office: A performance report given me belatedly charged that I was not properly writing up grazing limitations on our Plans of Conser-vation Operations. He told me it had to be worded differently to make it enforceable. It would mean the same thing, only with a different arrangement of a few words. When I asked him when and where was the authorization to make such a change, he could not give a satisfactory answer, only saying, "I am telling you (orally) and that is good enough." I asked him if that was the official decree—why does not the area office replace our forms being used with new ones to comply with his dictum? No answer! (The only purpose was for background for false claims against me.)

I checked and made a list of grazing leases, with said plans of operations which he had prepared, covering a period of a year. My list included the allotment number, allottee name, number of acres of grazing land, and the dates he prepared them.

Not on a single one of them did he himself follow his instructions which he used as a foundation to record a false accusation against me. Every lease, even months afterwards, was prepared as of old. In fact, some of them even lacked any entry in a certain section which was required.

I cite this as a typical example of many ruses that were being perpetrated over a three or four year period.

The philosopher Socrates said: "It is better to suffer evil than to inflict it."

James 1:15 warns us that sin begins in a small way, but it grows and leads to death. "Then when lust hath conceived it bringeth forth; and sin, when it is finished bringeth forth death."

Now, we can look upon what has happened to these sinners and realize how true were the prophecies of James and Job and the Bible.

Christ's trial was a mockery also.

What Finally Happened to the Conspirators

What has happened since, to those who participated in the conspiracy? All of them that I have knowledge of, either got fired, transferred or retired—some soon died. One got caught in another fraud and had to retire, under fraudulent conditions, to save his hide. Another had murder occur in his family. One superintendent who had no enthusiasm for the conspiracy, and involved himself only in a little nit-picking got himself transferred to another place. The other superintendent retired, sometime later, under a heavy cloud. Another, who was chiefly a soft-soaper and had very little push, made it through to retirement. I recall when a new superintendent, who was dynamic and aggressive, was coming to be our superintendent, and for some reason or other knew he would not fit in and began looking for another job. It so happened that the job to head his department at the area office became availale and he applied for it at our advice and urging. Several of us boosted him for the position and he got it. Later, when I needed support, he did not return the favor. In fact he did the opposite. Of course, he had a good personal reason. It is a pretty bitter pill to take to save one's job. But it is lack of character as well as courage not to stand for decency and justice. Someday the price may catch up and become pretty high—when it is too late to reverse it.

I understand that Mr. Balsiger, the chairman of the hearing, soon resigned. Mr. Bolin, administrative officer, had a moving truck backed up to his door and loaded with his possessions the very next morning after the hearing. He left for a new job. He had already obtained a transfer and sneaked away from the scandalous mess he helped make. Ms. Friday met with tragedy.

Zona Worthy of Her Noble Race

Zona, a Rosebud Sioux employed in the Yankton Agency Office, proved to be a true noblewoman and proud member of her race. She resisted the temptations of the evil persons at the agency, and sacrificed her job to retain the honor of her noble and proud race. She would have nothing to do with the coercion and conspiracy. GOD BLESS HER HEART.

Mr. "C" very shortly got fired from the Rosebud Agency via a transfer to the Southwest. He evidently got in trouble there, and to get off the hook, retired from the service under claims of disability. He was not old enough to qualify for retirement, neither did he have the minimum years of service to qualify. The way out—to claim disability—then he could retire at full retirement pay. All it takes is a doctor who will certify that he is disabled. This method is illegal and fraudulent for all, the employees, his supervisor and the doctor who fraudulently cooperated. We know that this practice is quite commonly used.

The official report is that this man got bucked off a horse and injured his neck. I have been reliably informed that there is nothing to the story—that he is still as able as always.

I have not heard what happened to some of the others.

Oh yes, what happened to me? I am fine and comfortably retired and doing research work and writing. I have so many fine friends everywhere I go and it is a joy to visit with them. I owe much to some of them. I enjoy the wonderful friendship of my many loyal Indian friends and I rejoice in the greatly improved conditions that are coming to them.

I owe much to my country and its government for what it has done for me. Now, as President Kennedy said—"What can I do for my government?"

The answer is "plenty." To accept it as a privilege and a responsibility, I will never cease in my efforts to support and promote honest and efficient administration of government—to my dying day if necessary.

Our inner-enemies are the worst ones. The choice for each and every one of us lies between supporting, with courage, our moral standards and ideals or falling prey to the forces of darkness and evil dominance. God save America—It was created by Godly men.

After my arbitrary retirement from the Bureau of Indian Affairs, some anonymous friend at the area office sent me a note informing me that I was entitled to unemployment insurance, which had accumulated to about $800. I was not aware of that fact before and I may never have learned about it otherwise.

I applied for it but got only a payment or two when I was suddenly cut off. Certain procedures of appeal were available. I appealed first to the one rendering the adverse decision. Of course he upheld his decision. I appealed it to the next level above him. This level said they had to uphold their subordinates (If that is the case what purpose does it serve to have the other appeals?). The top level also upheld the decisions.

I then took it to the court, who ruled in my favor. It cost me over half of my compensation for attorney and court fees.

The young man in the Unemployment Service who instigated the deed, very soon thereafter, was fired and had to get another job.

We had no personal disagreement between us that I ever was aware of. Why did he he do it? Others far better off than I were not cut off. There surely was some promise or compensation involved. People do not do such things without a motive, or reward. Why were the conspirators activated to continue their harassment after I was no longer connected with the BIA? I think I know—I did not leave the area, I would continue to live here. This no doubt bothered them no end.

Truth Out of the Past

The truth catches up—you can not keep it down.

The Congress a few years ago passed a law requiring the Civil Service and governmental agencies to make personnel files available to any employee on whom they had a file. The employee

199

could make answer to anything he found therein that he wished answered. It could be added to and filed in his Civil Service personnel file.

Recently, I obtained the material in my file for the period of eighteen months, 1936-1938, when I served at the United Pueblos in New Mexico. I was shocked by some of the material that had been admitted therein—unknown and unsuspected by me for over forty years.

It was then that I discovered who were some of my false friends, and what others were my real friends. Those in the bureau's top position in Washington, D.C. proved to be honest and the real friends. They were not swallowing the false charges directed at me by some of my fellow workers who wanted me out of their way in the interest of their ambitions.

It is shocking to suddenly realize a trusted and respected friend had knifed you in the back and then covered it up. Oh, how they can corrupt their own character and soul to further their sinful interests!!

The extension agent was no surprise because I was aware what a false witness he was. It soon caught up with him and trapped him in the web of his own doing. He got fired after twenty years of extension related work. A foul way to end a career!

In those days there were honest people running the Bureau of Indian Affairs in Washington, D.C. They could see through the evil designs of the superintendent, extension agent and project manager of the Soil Conservation Service and their incredibly underhanded written testimony about my qualifications.

But, after reading their secret statements about me, I can understand why it was done. Dewey was employed by the SCS. The BIA had a contract with the SCS to set up a range improvement program with cooperating Indian Pueblos. Surveys and inventories or resources and their productive capabilities had to be made and a short-term schedule made to reduce the number of livestock to the carrying capacity of the ranges. It would give the forage plants a chance to come back to maximum production and the right number of livestock maintained to balance the range carrying capacity. To attain and maintain this status the Indian livestock owners would be required to dispose of a predetermined number of their livestock. This livestock was greatly needed in their economy and it required a sacrifice for them to dispose of any number.

The writer, as the BIA representative, worked under Dewey

who was in charge of the program. I became familiar with all aspects of the program.

The contract was a short-term deal. No doubt, the BIA would then take it over and manage the program in the future with its own men.

It can be seen that Dewey would want to continue with the program. He was capable of performing the job, and would deserve to have it. But his problem would be that he was not an employee of the BIA and feared difficulty might confront him for a transfer to the BIA. Someone already in the BIA might be available for the job. He feared that might be me. I don't believe he had a college degree and that might raise a problem for him. He tried to show that a college degree was not practical, judging by the tone of his statements, belittling my qualifications. His scheme was to get me removed from the area. I quote some of his statements. The following is an exact copy of a letter the superintendent of the United Pueblo Agency sent to the BIA Washington office:

United Pueblos Agency
Albuquerque, New Mexico
September 8, 1937
Air Mail

Re: August L. Nylander, Farm Agent, Gr. 8, $1800, No. 370
Commissioner of Indian Affairs
Washington, D.C.

Attention: Mr. Crostwait

Dear Sir:

Enclosed is the report on the services of Mr. August L. Nylander whose probationary period expires October 2, 1937.

Mr. Nylander is not familiar with local range vegetation nor is he able to recognize factors which influence ranges. He is unable to determine proper relations between range and livestock as grazed under local conditions. He is untrained in the practical management of both sheep and cattle as they are grazed locally. Mr. Nylander does not possess knowledge required of a range administrator and is therefore not able to suggest methods for management in a practical way. He has not resided in this region sufficient time to enable him to become familiar with local conditions. A large number of his ideas are theoretical and would likely work out in a laboratory test, i.e., with a very limited number of livestock. But he does not seem to be able to apply his technical knowledge in a practical manner. Often times years of close contact with the livestock situation as it is in this part of the country are necessary to be able to properly demonstrate to the Indians the best methods in animal husbandry and range management.

Mr. Nylander's method of approach and degree to which he seems to be able to interest the Indians is poor. His lack of success in this direction seems to spring in large measure from his lack of knowledge of the problem at hand, which makes him unable to explain thoroughly the exact manner in which the desired program is to be carried out. An intimate knowledge of animal husbandry, characteristics and habits of different animals is absolutely essential, and Mr. Nylander does not possess this knowledge.

It is possible that Mr. Nylander might successfully carry on farm demonstration work on a small scale and under the constant direction and close supervision of an administrator, but for work of the kind required in this jurisdiction he seems to be unfitted.

Respectfully yours,
General Superintendent

Along with this letter the superintendent attached a copy of an Efficiency Report, at the conclusion of my first year's service and my probation period, which is required of all employees entering Civil Service.

Here are the ratings she gave me: Quality of Performance—8 Fair; Productiveness—9 Unsatisfactory; Qualifications Shown On Job—10; Unsatisfactory; Sum of Ratings—27, Unsatisfactory. Rated and signed by S.D. Aberle, Gen'l. Supt.

I may remark, that after my transfer to the Rosebud and Yankton Reservations in South Dakota, all of my annual Effeciency Reports (over twenty years of them) were in the top rating category.

The difference here was that the administration officials in South Dakota were dedicated, unselfish, honest, loyal, and decent people.

An office note was attached to the above letter which said: Mr. Dismuke states Mr. Nylander cannot be trusted with handling anything of much importance.

The subsequent truth has proven that my education, experience and record of performance, both before and since that time, completely belie such statements. I cite the many cases of my record throughout this book. Speaking of not being trusted Mr. Dewey—a liar cannot be trusted with anything of much importance.

At the end of my one-year probation required of all Civil Service applicants this superintendent gave me an unsatisfactory rating which stands as an act of shame for her. This is another example when the Washington office disregarded these two persons reports. Notations made on documents by the Washinton office plainly indicated that they were not in agreement with misrepresentations contained therein. (Too bad that the management in the Washington Office has not remained as capable and honest in these later years to the shame of the BIA and the Civil Service).

The records I referred to above and many otherpertinent documents are in my possession now.

I wish to comment further on the unsatisfactory probation rating: Civil Service regulations require that when an applicant for Civil Service status is failing to perform satisfactorily in any element of his job, his supervisor should point them out to him and suggest ways for him to correct his problem. He is then given an extended period of time to comply. And at the end of the period of time if he still is lacking in some element he is given a second period of time. It is his supervisor's responsibility and duty to give him the necessary instruction and help to overcome his deficiency.

As further proof of dereliction of responsibility I did not, at any time, as much as have a hint of any shortcomings on my part. Nor was I provided the necessary other measures to meet them. It provided no opportunity for me to defend myself. There was no discussion between us about such matters. They were completely secretive and underhanded because they knew their charges were without merit and that they could not justify their actions.

All of those contentions are so far-fetched that if they were serious, one would have to conclude that they were made by someone who was unable to determine the difference between darkness and light or possess any rational judgment, even on matters pertaining to his own profession, at that time.

All of my experiences and training prior to this time and my subsequent experiences completely belie these statements. I had programs, including Range Management, similar to this one on the Yankton and Rosebud Reservations, where I took over, upon a transfer, shortly after this incident. The results and progress on the Yankton obtained under my supervision can be stacked against the best on any reservation under comparable conditions. I offer here briefly a few of my experiences and qualifications to counter these outlandish claims: I have a BS degree in agriculture. The sometimes practice used by those lacking a college education was to imply that those who do have are impractical and sometimes lacking in good sense.

I was raised on a Wyoming ranch. I also worked for the world's largest and most famous (at that time) breeder of breeding sheep (The King Bros. of Laramie, Wyoming). I was experienced in all phases of sheep husbandry-range management, feedlot feeding, both breeding stock and mutton and wool production. I fed sheep for them on my own farm, when I was farming for myself. I also fed some in a feed lot at Torrington, Wyoming for them. I had complete charge of the feeding, without any immediate supervision. The results were always good. I also fed registered Hereford bulls for Dean Prosser. Since the time of this epidsode I have managed Indian cooperative associations including livestock. I also have engaged in the livestock business for myself, including registered stock and meat production animals. I have experience fitting and showing livestock at fairs and livestock shows in various parts of the U.S. I have taken my share of awards, including grand championships.

I understand forage plants and their nutrition usage. I have my own personal herbarium, which I collected in my studies of them over the years.

Suffice it here to tell this story of their unscrupulous and devious evil deeds. Little did they dream that the time would come when the sanctuary for their dirty tricks (the federal personnel file) would someday reveal its secrets. All is now recorded history, and cannot be taken back or reversed.

I have in my possession the copies, and some of them the original copies, of these letters and related material.

I quote here a few verses of scripture which vividly exemplify that similar situations existed thousands of years ago. One wonders if man has grown or progressed in moral character. For sure, the evil forces are still extant. But the word of God is as good as ever and we do have so many wonderful people.

Yea, mine own familiar friend, in whom I trusted, which did eat of my bread, hath lifted up his head against me. Ps. 42:9.

For it was not an enemy that reproached me; then I could have borne it: neither was it he that hated me that did magnify himself against me; then I would havè hid myself from him. Ps 55:12.

He hath delivered my soul in peace from the battle that was against me: for there were many with me. Ps 55:18.

Another Example of Evil Design

The following is a copy of an original letter which I sent through regular office channels. It got waylaid and never reached its destination.

The superintendent in all decency and in a businesslike administration should have forwarded the letter to the addressee, or if she thought it incorrect or objectionable for any reason, referred it back to the writer.

It was over forty years before I realized that my good friend Jim Mirabal of Toas Pueblo never received this letter. I transferred out of the area at that time and never saw Jim again.

Some office personnel pinned a note to the letter for the superintendent which asked: Shall we mail this letter to Jim Mirabal? The handwritten instruction on the slip read: File with Nylander's other "stuff."

I believe that this letter explains what the problem was all about.

> United Pueblos Agency
> Albuquerque, New Mexico
> March 21, 1938

Mr. Jim Mirabal
Taos Pueblo
Taos, New Mexico
Through Superintendent, S.D. Aberle
Dear Mr. Mirabal:

A copy of a statement made and signed by you regarding the calf lost out of your corral about December 3 or 4th has been placed on my desk.

You state in this statement that "you did not sleep at the corral as has been stated." I am not aware of any statement being made by any one that you did, but judging from circumstances involved, I might be lead to believe that the source of the statement has been attributed to me.

Please accept my statement, here and now, that I have never stated nor implied in any way that you or any one else did so, at that time nor at any other time. Perhaps, the story was instigated for the purpose of inciting your indignation in order to get a statement from you, with a certain slant, bearing on the loss of the calf.

The only thing that I have ever said in any way concerning the case was said in a letter, over my signature, to the Commissioner of Indian Affairs. A copy of the letter is in this office. No such statement was made in it. This letter must represent what I have said and my position on the matter.

I appreciate to the fullest extent your kindness in permitting us to use your corral on this and all previous occasions and would not for a moment have you involved in any slanderous attempts. I was fully conscious of the danger involved by the escape of the fifty head of hungry calves into the outer corral, where you had your alfalfa hay stored, and eating and destroying much of it. I was concerned, as you were, that it should not happen. The fact that you permitted us to use your corral under such circumstances makes me doubly appreciative of your kindness and cooperation.

I also appreciate having the circulation of the story brought to my attention and will say for the benefit of any other stories that might be rousting-about that I am able to speak for myself and that I can not be responsible for just any thing that might be said.

With kindest regards, I remain,

Respectfully yours,
August Nylander, Farm Agent
CC: Commissioner of Indian Affairs
Through the Superintendent
L.F. Jones, Ext. Agent

Area Director Strikes Back With Threats
In a letter from the Area director, received December 2, 1960, he evaded answering points I made and my request for a vital and necessary document containing false and libelous charges against me. It was admitted to the hearing without a copy being furnished to me, as regulations required and a letter of instructions by the acting director. I had no chance to answer the statements contained therein or cross-examine the author of same. In other words I was denied my civil rights.

This letter was an answer to my letter to him dated Nov. 18, 1960. He was contributing and continuing the violation of the chairman's instruction to the hearing and the acting area director's letter of April 26, 1960. "All written material which is to be used as evidence should be prepared in duplicate in order that a copy may be furnished to the opposing side."

The area director was still reacting, as in desperation and still evading his legal responsibilities and denying me my rights and acting in violation of regulations.

For the threat, I quote—"You are warned, therefore, that continued violations of conduct and procedures on your part may result in drastic administrative action by this office. A copy of this letter is being filed in your official personnel folder." (I wonder if my letter will also be filed along with it.) And at this time we can not find the Personnel File itself.

The main answer to my request was a direct evasion and a false premise. Note what he said: "Since you now have an official grievance pending, and to assure adjudication of that grievance without fear of interference, coercion, or reprisal, no action is being taken at this time in connection with the points previously raised in this letter."

What did he mean, "an official grievance hearing pending?" The hearing was concluded over two months before these letters were written. My right to defend myself against specific charges was still being denied. I was attempting to get the necessary documented charges, or to forestall a false charge by attempting to answer it without the document, before it was too late.

It was nearly six months after the hearing—or four months after these letters—before I got a copy of the charges. It was when the transcription of the hearing came out. The document was transcribed therein.

So, my answers to the charges never got consideration by the judges of the hearing, nor into the transcription. It was denied as a part of the recorded hearing.

One wonders why the area director acted as he did. Was he incoherent? Brainwashed? Or was he one in the pipeline, taking orders from the central office? He *was* desperate!

Whatever it was, coming from the Washington headquarters, it had to be a cover-up of some serious consequence! The cover-up is still being maintained twenty years later. I am still being denied access to much of my Civil Service personnel folder after twenty years time and my efforts for four years to obtain it. The law by Congress requires that they give me access to it upon my request.

I believe a quotation from Samual Taylor Coleridge is appropriate here.

"Few men are so reprobate as not to have some lucid moments, and in such moments few can stand up unshaken against the appeal of their own experience. What has been the wages of sin? What has the devil done for you?"

It was very evident that the area director was very much shaken up. The tenacious cover-up or the subsequent destruction of my government personnel file speaks loud and clear. *The truth is not dead and buried; it shall rise and assert itself.*

Episode of "X" Area Director

(Not the same Area Director mentioned above, but his successor)

Quoting from News Media. May 23, 1979

B.I.A. director's wife hospitalized.—46.

Was rushed by ambulance to an Aberdeen hospital after suffering from chest pains. Says she has a history of heart problems.

"We've been going through an extensive amount of stress," said 'X' Director, who is contesting his transfer to the Washington, D. C., B.I.A. office. "I am sure this has contributed to her condition right now."

The "X" Director said the transfer move took him by surprise. "I had no idea at all relative to any decision being made," he said. "No one had ever discussed anything with me relative to a transfer to Washington."

(Once again, review Psalm 35: verse 11, 12, 15)

The news had reported that some people from the west river reservations had been complaining about him, and then asked the Washington office to remove him. There was no evidence that any investigations were made or hearings held.

We need only to read between the lines, put two and two together, and consider what the Bureau has done in numerous similar cases in the last twenty years, to come up with some answers.

We have the record of the many cases of scandals occuring, right and left, on these reservations, and almost nothing being done to correct the corrupt practices. They are costing the tax payers millions and millions of dollars and corrupting the moral standards, as well.

It is highly suspicious that those people managing the several programs and their funds were the ones making the complaints against the 'X' Director. Very likely he wasn't going along with their scandalous and corruptive management of their programs and its funds.

This case follows the general pattern used by the B.I.A. the past twenty years in dealing with injustices and corruptions.

We explained Civil Service regulations required for "down rating" employees (page 203).

In retrospect, supported by collaboration of personal experiences, records, reports of various sources including reports of interested organizations, the period of time centering in the late 1950s and early 1960s, probably will go down in history as the 'Black Regime' of the Bureau of Indian Affairs' management. Personnel cover-up is still being maintained. Corruptions by the millions of dollars still abound on the reservations uncontrolled. Corrective action is being avoided by default.

It used to be more congressmen, senators and others would investigate suspected thievery and corruption and thereby become famous, win recognition and eventual promotion. Some of them got their start on the way to the highest office in the land. Calvin Coolidge, Harry Truman and Richard Nixon were among them. Much proof of guilt has already been done by a task force. Guilt sticks out over most of the Great Plains Indian reservations.

We have high hopes the new Reagan administration will usher in a new era that will turn the country around and kick out the crooks and corrupt bureaucrats and once again decency and justice can prevail.

So far (to date) for the writer, a certain truth and anti-truth are still elusive. The disclosure of devastating material therein is being resisted by all devious means by the keepers of the personnel files. If the records with the evidence has not been destroyed it has been successfully kept well guarded and covered up. However, copies of most of the records and evidence is still in my possession and a new personnel file could be reconstructed. Only certain of the sneaky, devastating falsehoods are missing, those which have never been exposed to my attention. We have been working four years trying to pry this material from the Office of Personnel Management (OPM) of the Civil Service Commission. They have been evading and evading releasing it to us. We, Senator Abdnor and I, have kept chiseling away at it. Reluctantly they have been releasing bits of it, at times, piece by piece. As of this date, the real culprits are still covered up. They and their cohorts are skillful and well educated in the art of evasion.

Someday the guardians of the cover-up will either die or otherwise abandon their posts. Then, what will be their legacy? What profited their life and gifts to posterity?

When they do die or retire from their jobs, do they think that they will be free, safe, and no longer fearful of exposure? Who, besides the original Indians, would say that their spirit or ghosts will be sticking around?

Even the guilty have lucid moments and realize that they are wrong and committing crimes. They hide from exposure and are afraid of the truth. They compound their sins and guilty conscience and will eventually find their escape-antics collapsing on them. (Such is the price of sin.) They sometimes get desperate and resort to desperate deeds. Justice will eventually track them down and when they are overtaken, personal tragedy may strike them too. Their attempt to escape may, and often does, lead them to alcoholism, insanity or suicide.

It may never dawn upon their befuddled and distorted minds to seek mental relief and peace through prayer, repentance, and forgiveness. They have failed to find 'The Way.' Crime never pays but always costs.

"Fret not thyself because of evil doers. Neither be thou envious against the workers of iniquity. For they shall soon be cut down like grass, and wither as the green herb. Trust in the Lord, and do good; so shall thou dwell in the land, and verily thou shall be fed. Delight thyself also in the Lord; and he shall give thee the desires of thine heart. Rest in the Lord and wait patiently for him: fret not thyself because of him who prospereth in his way, because of the man who bringeth wicked devices to pass."Psalm 37; 1-4, 7.

CHAPTER 8: THE NEW INDIAN—FINDING THEMSELVES

Where is the life we have lost in living?
Where is the wisdom we have lost in knowledge?
Where is the knowledge we have lost in information?
T. S. Ellot
We shall gain knowledge from discovered information.
We shall use knowledge to gain wisdom.
In wise living we shall find life.

What is a new Indian? What is the old Indian? How do they differ from each other? Is the change inherent in the progression of constant and inevitable evolution? There is no question about the fact of evolution. Her law is a supreme law of the Great Spirit: Any species, in the long history of the earth, which refuses or fails for any reason to change and conform to the changed conditions becomes extinct, as have hundreds of species already.

The so-called new Indians—we read books about them; we listen to their speeches and diatribes at conferences and in personal conversations. We note some of their slogans, such as Red Power and self-determination. We take note of their several organizations, such as Youth Organizations, American Indian Movement (AIM), Warrior Societies, and many others.

Emerging since the enactment of the Civil Liberty Act and self-determination policy are young Indians and a few of the older ones are activated too. Some of them take it to mean the signal to erupt, emerge, rile their emotions, and gird themselves for battle—and loudly, and sometimes violently proclaim the emergence and dominence of their rebirth—to bring back the slumbering memories of their so-called glorious days. All of this in the face of the universe's renowned, never failing evolutionary process and the demand that all creation must move along with it or perish.

These backward looking people are a small minority group. Mostly youth with some education who have read books and history, which reveals the injustices and suppression of their fathers and forefathers by the whites for so long.

They have invented slogans, proclaiming, prophesying and dancing to the changing events for them, which they think will reverse the past history and they will become the dominant race, and rule over the white man. This gives them great hope and courage. It is almost as if there still is some spark in the dead. If they were looking forward to and working for the emergence of a God-ordained advanced way of life, they could, once again, find peace, hope and harmony with the Great Spirit—a greater approach to the time when they could live closer to Him, in this earthly life as well as when they reach the Happy Hunting Grounds.

We must at least give these (the new Indians) people credit for emerging and trying to do something to project themselves into the Space Age—to provide leadership and education.

I can agree with much that has been said and written on the subject of the new Indian. Good books have been written, well written, informative and interesting to read—portraying much truth and history that serves a valuable purpose and needed to be told.

Authors are inclined to focus only on the good side of their subject and only on the bad side of the opposite subject. In other words they lack a balance that must prevail.

I must disagree, in part, with what some authors say on the subject of the new Indian. I do not think that the Indian they describe is the real new Indian. I think they are portraying an attempted revival of the old Indian, even if done by young educated Indians. They are misguided, and as I have said, looking backward. Like a snake you must shed your old skin, so a new one can replace it. The old Indian can save himself but he'll have

212

to shed some of his useless ideas and methods first or perish with them.

A medicine man recently said: "I saw this in my mind not long ago—In my vision the electric light will stop sometime. The day is coming when nature will stop the electricity." The Ghost Dancers had their visions too (note what happened to them).

The Ghost Dancers sang and danced until they dropped from exhaustion, swooning, fainting, seeing visions. They danced in this way to bring back the dead, to bring back the buffalo. A prophet had told them that through the power of the Ghost Dance they would roll up like a carpet all the white man's work—the fences and the mining towns with their brothel houses, the factories, the farms with their stinking unnatural animals, the railroads, the telephone poles, the whole works. And underneath this rolled-up white man's world we would find again the flowering prairie, unspoiled, with its herds of buffalo and antelope, its clouds of birds, belonging to everyone, enjoyed by all.

Note how disastrously their visions failed them. This shows how their so-called visions were just illusions brought about, no doubt, by harshly abusing their God-given brain. All of their power, symbolic prayers and prophecies failed miserably. Did it teach them anything?

It is well to be knowledgable of the past—and try to see history in its true perspective; and to acquire wisdom therefrom and invest that wisdom in the present and the future. In that, we can have faith that God, the Great Spirit will guide us.

Who Owns the Land?

Let us review for our knowledge and perspective, some of the tenets embraced in the philosophy of both the white man, his Bible and the Indians.

What does the Indian hold about land and the natural resources? Study the following quotation.

"The land and all that goes with it belongs to The Great Creator. For millions of years—man is here for only a second of time. He can not take it with him nor continue to occupy it himself, or send it with some one else. He can only use it for his convenience and for only an infinitely short period of time. These resources are used over and over by different people—they have no further claim, when they have passed on.

"The Great Creator, the Great Spirit, the great Father of all Creation and all mankind, has provided very greatly and very

213

generously for all of his earthly Creatures. He provided abundantly for their preservation, propagation, promise of eternity, and the way to attain it. The alternative is extinction. The system operates by evolution and progression (governed by nature's immutable laws). To get out of tune, to fail or refuse for any reason to adjust and adapt to the necessary change is to become, like the dinosaur, the dodo bird and hundreds of other species—extinct."

Man makes his decisions, only God judges. He punishes and rewards according to right or wrong doing. He does not hesitate to cause removal of any segment of people for their refusal to obey His laws or misuse of the natural or human resources that He has placed at their disposal. Even his chosen people he has sent out of their homeland and into slavery—up to 2000 years at a time. He had no qualms about doing that to them. *He had a purpose in America too.*

Is God going to stand by for ever and let 2 million people monopolize a continent when it can support hundreds of millions with a higher standard of life, a greater, more abundant and progressive life?

The Indian had stalled for many centuries towards progress, and sitting on the great God-given resources when the progressive and growing world of life needed them for God's growing number of creatures whom he made after His own image.

Can you imagine hearing God saying—"Move over Mr. Indian and share and cooperate with your new found brothers. Do you get my communication? The time has come for you to learn a higher standard of communication with the Great Spirit. Do not fail it and go down the drain. I love you, as one of my very own, and I command your new brothers to love you too.

Use it or lose it. That is what God says too. You have used these lands and natural resources insufficiently over the many hundreds of years of occupancy. I have sent in a strong nation of people to do the job you are failing to do, or to prepare yourself to be able to do. I have asked these people to share their love and the fruits from this land with you and the world beyond. I require that you prepare yourself to share the responsibilities that are a part of the deal.

These people brought Christ to America and the way of salvation for you. *This is the greatest gift of all.*

The time is here for you to put away your outgrown, outmoded ways of life and the worship of your Holy Father, the Great Spirit. Learn, and follow the example and teaching as given to the world by Christ.

214

I commanded those good and dedicated servants of nearly 2000 years ago, to go forth and carry the gospel, as given to them by Christ, to all parts of the world, that all of my people should hear the Good News—of salvation through Christ Jesus.

In the middle nineteenth century Black Hawk is credited as having said—"The Great Spirit created this country for the use and benefit of his red children, and placed them in full possession of it, and we were happy and contented. Why did he send the pale-faces across the great ocean to take it from us?"

Perhaps the answer to Black Hawk's probing question can be found in the story I have told. (My apologies to God for my paraphrasing Him—putting words in His mouth so to speak—or did He put the words in my mouth?)

Chief Joseph, that great Nez Perse leader, said at the closing days of the Indian's dominance over this country: "It is the order of Nature and regret is useless" (wisely said by a great and understanding man).

All Indians held that land belongs to God. We are stewards. We must use it for the benefit of the most humans and animals. It is like the biblical story of the talents—when the boss left for a period of time on an extended trip—and the accounting, upon his return, of the use made of the talents. Each was rewarded according to the increase returned. One guarded his well, but made no increase. That which he had was taken from him and given to the one who had made the greatest return: To neglect using and developing one's God-given talents is a sin and finds no place in Heaven or God's scheme.

This great country of ours received people and is made up of all nationalities and races and became the "Melting Pot." Your native country contributed great natural wealth. Together with the newcomers the world's greatest wealth and standard of living was produced into usable form and shared with people of the entire earth. These great gifts of God occurred in your ancient homeland. It was God's purpose and will. The Great Spirit has not forsaken you in your many troubles any more than He forsakes the Mother in her travail. Likewise do not forsake him. You must retain your "Proud and Noble" status.

The Real New Indian

There is a real new Indian emerging. He is the the one I am going to tell you about.

The American Indian race has been brainwashed, cheated,

robbed, beaten, betrayed, intimidated, degraded, pushed around, driven out, and treated as a child and incompetent for over two-hundred years—until a sterotyped image had been forced upon him.

Some tribes in the East and the Southwest adjusted themselves firmly with the white man's culture and way of life. Many of them achieved a life of self-sufficiency. Nearly all of them could have, had not the white man robbed them and driven them from their homes and carried on two-hundred years of costly wars.

Following the enactment of the Indian Reorganization Act in 1934 things began to improve for many tribes, but it was in the early 1960s when the real progress set in for the new Indian.

Since then, in many areas, the results have been astonishing to behold. Even many of the older Indian people started to get more education and training and take over responsible tribal and governmental jobs. And the jobs they are doing in many instances is highly commendable. It is a living demonstration of the fact that people have to solve their own problems and take the responsibility—from planning to execution. They faced their problems with determination.

As an example of how they grasped their problems—at conferences and other places, at different points in the nation as of that time—I would ask what they considered their most important problem. Invariably the answer was "education." Nowadays they are likely to say alcoholism, drugs, child abuse, and suicide.

Previously, Indians were not zealous for education. Now, thousands of them are enrolled in colleges and other schools, including vocational schools. They are creating some of their own schools and colleges.

They have set up programs, facilities, educational institutions to help combat alcoholism and drug use. An important thing for many of them is counseling and setting up halfway houses for those that need it. Our national suicide rate is the highest among the Indians.

Greatly improved housing, nutrition, sanitation, and water supply are taking place everywhere. Many new jobs are being provided. Hospitals and health facilities are greatly improved and homes for the elderly.

These are some samples of what is being done for and by the the new Indians.

I quote here a letter by one of the new Indians, which expresses much so well, appearing in the *Sioux Messenger*, and written by Steve Cournoyer:

Although I am not a full blooded Indian due to circumstances beyond my control, I too take pride in the fact that I am immediately recognizable as a person of Indian descent without reverting to the attire of my ancestors. I cannot condemn my great great Grandmother because of her tolerance for another human in need or her ability and sensitivity to love and cherish and to produce offspring. I am here as I am and I love and respect all of those in my family background who gave me my life as it is. I am an Indian, a fact I cannot or would not want changed.

We live in a period of history that allows a person to grow in stature, as an individual as his personal aspirations dictate and as he establishes his priorities, the same principles of the great Indian society persists in us and we pattern our lives on them. We have pride, courtesy, courage to face what we meet-sharing of our personal possessions and compassion for our own kind. We respect our elders and treat them with human dignity.

The term breed is distasteful to us. Especially when used by persons too ignorant to understand that we are flesh and blood, that we bleed when cut, that we can cry, that we experience discrimination, double in fact because we get it from both sides. We are the injured party, not fully acceptable in either society.

Programs are mentioned also. True, they do not reach out to all members. The diversity of needs is why we have many programs. Sometimes I am frightened by the creation of another program because I see people becoming dependent on existing ones and incapable of existence if they are dropped.

The Superintendent has been severely criticized for calling a special election to fill an abandonment of position by the former Chairman. The Superintendent carries a very heavy burden of trust responsibility for all of the members of the Yankton Sioux Tribe and at his discretion must act in the best interests of the whole tribe. We bear no malice towards the former Chairman and we hope that his choice of endeavor will be more satisfying and rewarding.

The new homes on the reservation have given many of our families their first opportunity of a lifetime to provide safe and sanitary shelters for their children, in which they can develop a new sense of pride and worth in comfortable and attractive surroundings. Great personal sacrifices were made by individuals, (breeds and whites) who could accept feeling of accomplishment by filling a portion of the void that caused much suffering. I see many persons sharing the benefits, whose only contribution has been adverse criticism. That's the sad point.

I suppose that somewhere in the treaties there is a clause that obligates the government to feed and clothe us because we are Indians. I truly hope and pray that this is not the objective of the majority and I do not see it that way. The infirm and the needy are the realistic concern.

We are embarking on a crusade to control and administer the educational program that can be geared to the special and diverse needs of all our youth. The needs are great, the frustrations are many, the participation is minimal. We will however, persist in the endeavor to create for them a legacy of understanding, adequate educational opportunity, and a value system that is realistic and meaningful to them.

We too, are a proud and agressive (breed). We believe in the future of the race. It is inevitable that we shall reach the capability to self determine. Anyone can critize but only those who act can be criticized.

Steve Cournoyer Sr.
P.S.C. Counselor
Yankton Sioux Tribe

We have seen almost miraculous performances of the reservation Indians in their jobs with the BIA and tribal offices, following the early 1960s when they assumed the determination and management of their own affairs. After being held down for so many years, or we should say generations, they demonstrated what they were able and capable of doing. We are happy for them and hope this will be a permanent emergence. *We hope it will be built on honesty and justice*, and that any and all corruption that will attempt to take over will be severely dealt with. May it reestablish the qualities of a noble and proud race.

We know that some of these Indians worked hard and hoped to improve the image of their race about town and among other people. We also know that they had contempt and hatred for the renegades who were out to spoil their every effort. It was a heartbreaking experience for them. And the worst part of it all was the misguided and "blind" white people who make it impossible for them to achieve their goals. Yes ministers, bishops, church councils, the media, and the corrupt and inept BIA officials were the guilty ones!

No doubt their indignation and ire raised against injustices were acquired from reading books exposing and portraying the crimes and injustices practiced against the Indians by many whites and the federal government down through the generations. An aroused public should have occurred long ago. Does it take terrorism, destruction and murder to arouse citizens? The writer's position about it is that it occurred simultaneously, because of an opportunity created from confusion and ignorance, by changing conditions. It is the devil's chance to get in his licks. He blinds and misleads the unsuspecting and well meaning people.

We explained to one bishop how they were breaking the hearts and dashing the hopes of these truly good and worthy souls, by their aid and support of their enemies. He offered no defense or dialogue.

We see the emergence of many good Indians taking their places in the American society today, and their examples are improving the Indian's image—very much worthwhile. But the evil doers have hurt the cause—and the loafers and drunks are not helping the cause any. However, good programs, well managed, are helping many of these to overcome their drinking and are working at useful jobs. The old image of these is extant, and work for them still remains to be done. The renegade's time seems to be running out, but we hear so much these days of corruption among several of the Sioux tribal officers and council members. The corruptions in the government programs on the reservations is reported to run into the thousands and millions of dollars and no one seems to control it. The BIA is unfit to straighten them out because of their guilt. This is an important job for the new Indian to do, or he will never again be a noble race. We are confident that he can meet the challenge! He needs only to make a firm decision.

The new Indians have schools and colleges at various places. They hold conferences, workshops and meetings, including Christian religious schools and conferences. They do not get the attention and publicity that goes to renegades and outlaws, but they are accomplishing something worthwhile instead of destruction.

Everything in creation, it seems, has its opposite: high-low hot-cold, hard-soft, good-bad or evil, love-hate, light-darkness, life-death, and so on and on. God, the Creator also has His opposite. It is Satan, composed of evil and with the power to do mischief and lead people into sin and death.

We are going to say a few words about the AIM leaders and their Russian Communist collaborators. They were a handful of renegades bent on overthrowing the established Indian government and their duly elected officials and council members. They aimed to reestablish the old)centuries old) Indian type of chiefton government and, of course, they would be the chiefs. It could never be done by the consent of the people, so their aim was to take over by terrorism and sheer force. They traveled to other countries, including Russia, where they preached traitorous doctrines about our country. Back in this country they carried Soviet AK-47 assault rifles. They had a Soviet official as a guest at Wounded Knee.

Their revolution was a phony. It disrupted or paralyzed tribal governments; they disrupted schools, churches and homes. They intimidated any Indian who spoke against AIM.

A chairman of the Yankton Reservation suddenly up and deserted his office and left the state—no doubt to escape threats. Leo Wilcox, a Pine Ridge tribal councilman, spoke out against them. Shortly thereafter he was found burned to death in his car out on a county road. Many terrorist deeds were committed against individuals. They burned down the store, church and homes at Wounded Knee. They butchered many of the neighbors' cattle while they occupied Wounded Knee. They destroyed or damaged a courthouse, a federal justice building in Sioux Falls, S.D., and other government buildings including the Federal Bureau of Indian Affairs in Washington, D.C.

Reports had it that only Russel Means of the AIM leaders was a member of the Oglala Sioux of the Pine Ridge Reservation and he had not lived there. Only about twenty of the Indians holding Wounded Knee were Oglala Sioux. Most of them were outside invaders, like the Russian Communists invading countries—they probably were copying the Soviet Communists which they learned when in Russia—and probably got suggestions from a Russian official when he was their guest at Wounded Knee.

The duly elected Tribal Council repeatedly, by a vote of fourteen to two, asked the federal government to evict the AIM invaders from its reservation. It even offered to do the job itself. They were sold out by the federal government. They were harassed and threatened with death in Pine Ridge, by someone driving through the streets at night shooting into houses.

How about the character of the AIM leaders? Russell Means, Dennis Banks, Carter Camp and Clyde Bellcourt: These men share a total of forty-two criminal convictions. Means has a long string of arrests dating back to 1957, including theft and mugging. Those not loyal to him at Wounded Knee (spies, he called them) would be "shot before a firing squad." Banks is a paroled burglar with fifteen criminal convictions. Camp has a record similar to Means. Bellecourt is a much-convicted burglar and armed robber. Banks is a fugitive from justice, harbored in California because he claims he would be killed if returned to the state penitentiary at Sioux Falls, S.D. (killed by other inmates).

At Wounded Knee they were charged with larceny, civil disorder, obstructing federal officers, burglary, assault, arson, unlawful possession of firearms, conspiracy, and possible murder. They tried to take over the Pine Ridge Reservation, abolish the elected officers and tribal council and set themselves up as self designated chiefs, with monarchical powers.

The outlaws took over, and held illegally, small industrial establishments, provided by government loans and assistance to provide jobs for Indians on reservations. These acts were outright outlawry. These acts were tolerated by the federal government, but not by the Indians. Some tribes drove them off their reservations and forbade them to enter their reservation, and in at least one case, severely punsihed them for so doing.

If the BIA had left the Wounded Knee affair to Dick Wilson, chairman of the tribe, there would not have been that infamous insurrection on the Pine Ridge Reservation, or at least it would have been less violent, with less loss of life, including an FBI family man. It, no doubt, would have saved property from so much damage and saved the taxpayers a million dollars in cost. The BIA beat down the tribal chairman and told him to keep still, while the government sent in several hundred law officers and kept them there for perhaps a month. About all they did was to protect the invading outlaws and prolong the murderous ordeal. The legal approach, as well as the practical and sensible one, was to have left the job to the tribe under the leadership of Dick Wilson.

Another case was the takeover of the tribal pork plant on the Yankton Reservation. The first takeover lasted some time with damage done to the plant and shooting at cars. When it was over what happened to the outlaws? Not much!

A short time later some young punks took it over. They surrendered the same day and were sentenced to the penitentiary. The federal government "processed" the first takeover, resulting in a long, drawn-out costly affair and the culprits were let go free.

The second time the local bureau superintendent took matters into his own hands. He enlisted the help and cooperation of the Wagner mayor, city and tribal police, the sheriffs, highway patrolmen, the state's attorney general, and the national guard. The mayor placed the town of Wagner under martial law and ordered everyone off the streets and to stay indoors, which lasted only a short time. The attorney general looped teargas into the plant, which brought them out to surrender. These poor boys were sent to the penitentiary, unlike the big wheels before them who went free (most of them).

The agency superintendent, Mr. Lorin Farmer, an Indian, notified the area office about the takeover, but he did not wait for them to get delayed action—he went ahead and got the job done before nightfall—a peaceful, lawful, and permanent settlement was achieved—a good sensible job well done. And, we might say also, a brave job done, because the superintendent was risking almost certain loss of his job with the BIA. He should be awarded an eagle feather to wear in his headgear for his bravery. And the responsible bureau officials would have their "right hand cut off," if the Islamics had been in charge.

It began to look for awhile that he (the superintendent) would escape punishment. I told him that it was a good thing for him that he was an Indian. At this time Indians were gaining preference for the Indian Service jobs, and gaining power in the administration of their affairs. But, shortly, it did not turn out that way. They removed him from his job and assigned him to a less desirable job, out of the area. They no doubt told him "to teach you a lesson." Eventually he did get back into a superintendency job, thank God! We commend him. He still has some of the nobleness inherent in his race.

What has been the cost in support of all this terrorism to the taxpayers and certain religious organizations?

AIM is only one of the smaller terrorist outfits which our federal government has been pleased to subsidize over the years.

The Federal Building in Washington, D.C., suffered $3,000,000 damage by AIM. They were finally arrested and then handed $66,000 in cash of OEO tax money, just to go away. They were given at least $400,000 in grants from federal offices and $300,000 by Churches of U.S. and World Council of Churches.

Leader Dennis Banks said he had been offered almost a million dollars for film rights to the story of AIM's terrorism at Wounded Knee.

222

The following letter appeared in the *Oglala News*, June 4, 1973:

To: Bishop James S. Thomas
United Methodist Church of Iowa
1019 Chestnut, Des Moines, Ia.
Al Parrish, Atty at Law
Social Division
Catholic Church, 1301 21st. Des Moines, Iowa
United Presbyterian Church 525-6th Ave. Des Moines, Ia.

We understand your church has donated substantial sums of money to AIM. I would hope that your organization will see its moral obligation to provide funds for the relief of the victims of AIM's criminal activities at Wounded Knee, S.D., many of whom lost homes and all worldly belongings at AIM's hands—at least in amount equivalent to those you have so judiciously offered that violence-oriented anti-Christian organization.

Dick Wilson,
President

Note! We have never learned if Oglala Sioux Tribe got any favorable response from them.

Advice from Roger C.B. Morton, Sec. of the Interior, in a foreword. "If looking backwards means that Indians are filled with regrets over land and culture lost, it serves no useful purpose. But if a backward look means that mistakes of the past are not repeated, looking backwards can help both Indians and the non-Indian."

Another source of good advice from *The Gift is Rich*:

No river can return to its source, yet all rivers must have a beginning. "So it is with life," which is the sum total of the contributions of varied cultures. Many trails lead to the main road; many tributaries lead to the main stream and mingle with the other waters, so that the river flows ever wider, richer and deeper. As Americans we will grow spiritually stronger and richer, not by shutting off some of the contributing currents but rather by accepting their flow into the life-stream of our society, where they can be glorified and used.

VISTA

For more collaborative support for the ideas we are expounding in this book we present a news article by Ms. Shenk which appeared from Fort Collins, Colo., in July, 1979:

The headline reads—"Reservation Worker Finds History Is Misleading:

"American education has been misleading in telling the story of our country's history and the American Indians."

Speaking was Barbara A. Shenk, Secretary to the Coordinator of Graduate Studies in the Department of Education at Colorado State University; Ms. Shenk once lived and worked for six years on Indian reservations in South Dakota.

She joined the CSU staff in 1979, one year after receiving her BS degree in Sociology from Black Hills State College (BHSC), Spearfish, S.D.

From 1968-1970 she was a VISTA (Volunteers In Service To America) worker on the Cheyenne River Sioux Reservation in South Dakota. From 1970-71 she was employed as a secretary and counselor at an Episcopal boarding home for Indian boys on the Rosebud Sioux Reservation in South Dakota.

Ms. Shenk also served as secretary to the Indian Special Services program at BHSC from 1972-73.

Her main objective while working as a VISTA volunteer, she said, was to encourage the Indians to take advantage of programs and opportunities available to them on the reservation.

To "completely understand" the problems faced by Native Americans, she said, the VISTA staff lived in the same housing area as the Indians.

"Working with people so culturally different from my own became a unique learning experience for me," she said, adding: "I quickly felt a love that they (the Sioux) had for one another and shared with us that I had never experienced among non-Indians."

She said she also "felt a much deeper awareness of the relationship (the Indians had) between God and man." Also the Sioux displayed "a sense of humor that was to fill many late hours over coffee."

Ms. Shenk's initial exposure to the misleading direction that American education took on topics related to Native Americans and their impact on the country's history came during her VISTA experience.

"Our supervisor, a member of the tribe, had asked us from the day we arrived to encourage the young people to get an education," she said, explaining that education was regarded as the Indians' way of surviving in the world.

"But I quickly discovered that the system in which the young people were being educated was not meeting their needs and from a non-Indian value system point of view," she said.

If the basic purpose of education is to "turn out happy, adjusted individuals" who will be contributing members to society, Ms. Shenk observed, "this purpose was not being realized from the school situation there."

At that time, she said, "history books still viewed American Indians as aggressors in disrupting westward expansion instead of viewing them as a people trying to defend their land, culture and heritage."

Said Ms. Shenk: "We could have learned so much from the early Native Americans regarding nature, land use and ecology and, consequently, not be in the situation we are today with our energy problems."

Textbooks now used in reservation classrooms, she said, are written, illustrated and the subjects taught by Indians. In addition, she said, there are at least twelve community colleges in that region that are owned, administered and instructed by native American educators.

"We still have a lot to learn about the American Indians," Ms. Shenk said. "One thing I would like to see happen now is for an agency or institution to offer workshops that would bring in Indian people from many different tribes and from some of the Indian programs in Denver to teach the non-Indian public school teachers so that they can teach our children about the Native Americans," she added.

Ms. Shenk said her idea for the workshops grew from a suggestion her former VISTA supervisor gave when she asked how she could further help the Indians.

The supervisor told her, she recalled, to "tell them (non-Indians) about the Native American, talk to people, and tell them the truth about our way of life, our culture and our history as it really happened."

We want to reemphasize the important points in Ms. Shenk's attributive discourse, especially as they relate to the non-Indian's attitude towards our Indian people and for helpful suggestions for the new Indians. We have expounded upon these ideas and facts throughout this book.

The writer's comments on Ms. Shenk's discourse:

Quote: (Q) "American education has been misleading in telling the story of our country's history and the American Indian."

Comment: (C) The greatest factor, in the misleading has been the almost complete absence of any mention of the Indian's part and contributions in the recorded history of this nation, used in our schools' textbooks. The new Indian as well as the rest of us should work to correct this gross error. You educators are specially guilty of this overt neglect.

Q—"Her main object while working as a VISTA volunteer, was to encourage the Indians to take advantage of programs and opportunities available to them on the reservations."

C—There are still a few Indians who resist these programs on the basis that they think they would lose some of their liberties and self-sufficiency by getting involved with a paternalistic government. They have an admirable point, but they should not neglect to promote and advance education.

Q—"To completely understand the problem faced by Native Americans the VISTA staff lived in the same housing area as the Indians."

C—A true grass roots approach.

Q—She "quickly felt a love that they (the Sioux) had for one another and shared with us that we had never experienced among non-Indians."

She said she also "felt a much deeper awareness of the relationship (the Sioux had) between God and man." Also a display of a sense of humor.

C—We have discoursed on this subject in our chapters "A Noble Race" and "Religion," and agree with her in full.

Q—Ms. Shenk's initial exposure to the misleading direction that American education took on topics related to Native Americans and their impact on the country's history came during her VISTA experience."

C—VISTA must have been doing a good job—on the right track.

Q—Her supervisor, a member of the tribe, had asked them from their first day, to encourage the young people to get an education—explaining that education was regarded as the Indian's way of surviving in the world.

C—Good advice and from the best source.

Q—She quickly discovered, she said, that the system in which the youth were being educated was not meeting their needs and was from a non-Indian value system point of view. The purpose of an education to meet their needs was not being realized there.

C—The basics and fundamentals of an education to survive in the present day world, is the same for all ethnics, races, and cultures. The specialities may vary from one to another, but should be available for choice of skills and talents—and a correct and competent history of our country needs to be taught.

Q—At that time, Ms. Shenk said—"history books still view American Indians as aggressors in disrupting westward expansion instead of viewing them as a people trying to defend their land, culture and heritage."

Some Choice Advice by Ella Deloria:

... Unfortunately these many decades of paternalism and protection and gratuity have left their mark.

... An appeal to their pride, their manhood, their tribehood, would bring a response. But they must be approached with dignity and sincerity, and told earnestly by their friends that there is a profoundly critically essential task for them all to unite on for the good of their children.

... Only a people motivated by spiritual power and committed to the teachings of the Master can help bring the right thing to pass.

... For Ella, spiritual concerns, Christian and non-Christian alike, are the most important aspect of being human.

Ella is both an Indian and a white. She understands fully and equally well both races, and assesses equally the values of both—better than anyone else that I know of. She is a new Indian that can be a superb teacher and counselor for both the new Indian and the non-Indian.

The new Indian, Vine Deloria, Jr. is the son of Vine Deloria, Sr., a Christian minister and the nephew of Ella Deloria. I have briefly featured both of them in this book.

I quote a few pertinent remarks on assimilations attributed to this young man:

There is a gradual dissolution of the differences. . . . There can be adaptations all the way along.

What I would like to refer to in terms of assimilations is what we find in the Old Testament—

Hebrews in Egypt for 400 years, . . . they continue their religion, continued to be one people, is the reason we have the great religions stemming out of these people.

. . . the Vietnamese were conquered and ruled by the Chinese for 1182 years.

The Incas of Peru; the obstinate Basques of Spain; the resurgent French-Canadians of Quebec; the tribes throughout Africa; the Icelanders, ruled by the Danes 638 years; the Irish 740 years. Stovcks were assimilated by Hungary 1010 years, Iranians by Arab and Ottoman empires 1138 years; Uzbeks, Yakuts, Kazakls and Tadzhiks of Soviet Union, survived centuries of Russification.

Some Isleta Pueblo Indians of New Mexico were taken as prisoners to El Paso in the seventeenth century. Thirty young men sprung to one thousand Indians among a booming city of 300,000. They are called Tiguas.

The Mohicans—their land is gone, their religion desecrated and way of life vanquished—"The Last of the Mohicans" assimilated for two-hundred years, have worked in factories for generations. They still are identified as Indians.

The Indians of Quebec and northern New York State long ago demonstrated their superb skills as steel workers in the construction of skyscrapers in New York City. They then spread out to jobs across the nation, to the Golden Gate Bridge at San Francisco. They took contracts and did the work faster and cheaper then the white workers. Few people in other parts of the nation realize this fact.

The Navahos, among many other tribes and groups, including the Cherokees, have demonstrated the Indian's ability to integrate into a foreign culture and at the same time retain their nobleness and culture. They can live comfortably with both cultures and sustain their economic self-sufficiency in the modern day civilization.

WEBSTER TWO HAWK—former minister of the Christian gospel, ex-chairman of the Rosebud Sioux Tribe, worker and leader in many other worthy enterprises benefiting Indians, is a good example of the new Indian. Quoting Two Hawk, he said, "Indians believe that people belong to the land and are sojourners on earth." "We can't" he said, "go back to the blanket and buffalo." "We can't practice the Indian religion as we used to: But we can still retain the principle on which it was based—that the Great Spirit is part of everyday life. Indian people know the Great Spirit will never forsake us," he said.

CHARLES A EASTMAN (Ohiyesa), who lived from 1858 to 1939, was a Santee Sioux. He is an outstanding example of the new Indian, exemplified many years ago. He was raised completely in the Native Indian environment and way of life. He was fatherless until he was fifteen years of age. His father had been captured and imprisoned and his whereabouts were unknown to his family until at that time he returned to them. While in prison his father was converted to Christ and brought the religion to his family.

Charles started his schooling at a missionary boarding school at Santee, Nebraska. He went on to get college degrees, including one from Dartmouth College. He graduated from Boston University with a doctor's medical degree and soon went to the Pine Ridge Reservation as a government doctor in 1890 at age thirty-two. He engaged in several pursuits including being a lobbyist and author of several books. He worked for the International YMCA for a period of years doing field religious work. It was while he was engaged promoting Christian doctrine that he organized Boy Scouts and Campfire Girls clubs among both Indian and non-Indian youth. He has become the acknowledged hero of both groups. He held other responsible jobs of trust, including working for the Bureau of Indian Affairs and practiced medicine at different times.

We would like to quote some words from his wisdom: My good grandmother, who had brought me up as a motherless child, bestowed upon me her blessing. "Always remember," said she, "that the Great Mystery is good; evil can come only from ourselves!"

Advice from his father—"Remember, my boy, it is the same as if I sent you on your first warpath. I shall expect you to conquer. It was my father's farewell."

I had been taught that the Supreme Being is only concerned with spirits, and that when one wishes to commune with Him in nature he must be in a spiritual attitude, and must retire from human sound or influence, alone in the wilderness.

I learned that scarcely one of our treaties with the United States had been carried out in good faith in all of its provisions.

Conflicts between the two races have been due as much to mutual misunderstandings as to the selfish greed of the white man. These children of nature once had faith in man as well as in God. Today, they would suspect even their best friend. A "century of dishonor" and abuse of their trust has brought them to this.

Eastman commenting on his lecture tour:
My chief object has been, not to entertain, but to present the

229

American Indian in his true character before Americans. The barbarous and atrocious character commonly attributed to him has dated from the transition period, when the strong drink, powerful temptations, and the commerialism of the white man led to deep demoralization. Really it was a campaign of education on the Indian and his true place in American history.

Those are realistic words of wisdom nobly said by a man of education and experience—right from the heart of his race.

We have cited these outstanding Indians as examples of what their race can do, and has done. There, no doubt, are those who will say that they are exceptions only. However, they are teachers, heroes, and leaders, and can do much to encourage others of their race to do better and fit more successfully into the civilization dominated by the white race. These are good examples for all of us to emulate. The white man is fully as ignorant about the character and nature of the Indian and his gifts and contributions to the whole world and its civilization as the Indian is hesitant about his transition into the new world. It can probably be truthfully said that the white people are more responsible than are the Indians for their plighted state.

Dr. Frederic F. Flack wrote:

The process of growing up and growing older involves a series of changes. Every transitional phase of life from childhood to marriage, to old age requires some degree of giving up or letting go.

Trying to hang on when the time has come to move on can trip you up. Letting go can free you—and others—for the process of living full.

The process known as recapitulation is where the fetus, the babe, and young animals repeat ancestral evolutionary stages in their development and growth. The same processes happen to mankind and to races of men in their history over the stages of time. This is a fundamental and scientific fact. To ignore it will keep one out of harmony with Creation.

The Bible says, "Brethren, I count not myself to have apprehended: but this one thing I do, forgetting those things which are behind, and reaching forth unto those things which are before" (Philippians 3:13).

We can do better and the Indian people can do better. Let us keep that in mind and quit wasting time and lives by the destruction by radicals so prevalent in recent years. It is the real new Indian who will survive. Emulation of the great is far better than weeping and raving over broken treaties of another period.

Indians Gaining Rights for Self-Responsibility

The successful achievements by some of the tribes is convincing the government administration that Indians are ready to assume more responsibility for tribal affairs without supervision from the bureaucrats at the Bureau of Indian Affairs in Washington.

BEWARE—Watch that those BIA bureaucrats do not yet foil the policy and good intentions that the administration hopes for they are well known for doing that.

Indians already enjoy unprecedented economic and political freedom after more than a century of strict federal supervision of virtually every aspect of tribal life. The tribes of the Southwest are producing good and honest results, while the Great Plains tribes have allowed far too much corruption and mismanagement to creep in.

The administration promises to put more power into the hands of local Indian leaders. To support legislation that will establish tax-free "enterprise zones" on reservations and permit tribes to issue tax-free bonds to raise capital, and provide greater tribal flexibility in developing Indian mineral deposits. (Indian reservation land is rich in timber, fishing, mineral, and energy resources. It includes 5% of the nation's oil and gas reserves, nearly 500 billion tons of high-quality coal and half the nation's uranium supply, valued at 400 billion dollars.)

The Navaho Indians, by their skillful negotiating, succeeded in converting an Atlantic Richfield Company's offer of $300,000 for an oil pipeline right-of-way into a contract that will bring the tribe 78 million dollars over a period of twenty years. The Navahos also are preparing to supervise commercial coal-mining operations on their vast southwestern reservation. This is an improvement for negotiating contracts involving their property and natural resources. It promises to greatly increase their economic income and to eliminate the inefficient and sometimes crooked BIA bureaucrats in Washington, regional areas and local agencies.

The Jicarilla Apaches of northwestern New Mexico are the first tribe to acquire 100% ownership of oil and gas wells on their land and in a Supreme Court ruling they won the right to impose severance taxes on oil, gas and minerals extracted from their lands.

The Colville Tribes in Washington State used their own tribal members, instead of the usual federal negotiators, to work out a multi-million-dollar molybdenum mining contract.

Indian tribes throughout the West are renegotiating existing coal leases to get a larger share of the $22-a-ton selling price for coal. Indians now get as little as fifteen cents a ton. Most important, these tribes are beginning to get more income from development of their abundant natural resources. They are capitalizing on their resource wealth and have shown that they can be shrewd negotiators.

The government has funded numerous job-training programs for both Indian and non-Indian peoples. Some industrial and mining firms are providing funds to train Indians for technical and managing skills. Atlantic Richfield is spending $40,000 a year to train as engineers four Navahos at the University of Oklahoma.

There are those who are convinced that the end to Washington's domination of Indian affairs will produce resourceful self-rule.

Mescalero Apaches

"Apaches are still tough and independent. We are determined to make progress on our own." Thus spoke Wendell Chino, president of the Mescalero Tribe in New Mexico for nearly thirty years.

A century ago, the deserts and mountains of the Southwest were ablaze. Fierce Apache warriors including the famous Geronimo (Goyathlay), Cochise and Chato killed many white settlers on lands the Indians claimed. Geronimo with sixty or so warriors terrorized the white settlers and would whip a U.S. Army by means of the famous Indian strategy of surprise, attack, strike, disperse, scatter, and fade away in all directions. The stunned army could not follow, round-up and corral them. Their escape always worked for them. Geromino and his small group of warriors, in their final efforts to stave off the white invaders ranged over New Mexico, Arizona, part of Texas and into Old Mexico, striking terror wherever they went.

In the long-run, they could not win. They nobly accepted this fact and resigned themselves to build a new kind of life for themselves on a reservation sprawling over nearly a half million acres of the Sacramento Mountains in New Mexico. They point out the progress they are making in the white man's world. Their land is without oil that has enriched some Indians elsewhere. The Apaches have pulled themselves up by their bootstraps, so to speak, to a prosperity and self-esteem that is the envy of Indian and non-Indian neighbors alike.

"Times have changed," observes Wendell Chino, president of the tribe. Today Geronimo's granddaughter runs the Head Start Program. Cochise's great granddaughter is helping compile an Apache dictionary. Chato's great grandson heads tribal housing programs.

The tribe owns and operates two long-established multi-million-dollar businesses—a cattle ranch and a logging company. A more recent investment is a 22-million-dollar luxury resort, with accommodations and facilities for sports, from skiing to horseback riding. It is being expanded to include a convention center. The Ruidoso Downs race track is nearby.

President Chino said virtually every resident who wants a job has one. Thirty years ago there was 73% unemployment. Most of them earn about $5000 to $8000 a year. This goes a long ways with Indian families whose housing, medical care and education often are subsidized by the tribe or federal government, which allocated more than 5 million dollars a year to the reservation. Typical rent for a new two-bedroom house is $150 a month.

Most families have at least one car and conveniences such as freezers and TV sets. They pay federal income taxes. The average tribal member has completed eleven years of schooling. Forty-seven young people are in college, taking courses in subjects ranging from mechanics to medicine. Chato's great-grandson, thirty-two-year-old Fred Kaydahzinne, is college educated and heads the reservation's housing programs. Many receive substantial aid from a 2-million-dollar tribal scholarship fund.

Three-fourths of the reservation's population of over 2200 live in handsome new two-story houses built by the tribe on spacious lots under ponderosa pines. A pleasant striking sight which we remember well, as we drove along the highway road, were the houses along the valley and hillsides. The houses were similar in appearance and all were painted white.

The buildings in and out of the village were neat and orderly. As on many reservations the Head Start building plays a very important part in their educational system and community affairs. The village of Mescalero is neat and flourishing, with a new general store, garage, museum, hospital, five churches, and tribal headquarters containing offices, swimming pool and gymnasium.

In a community of this size and kind everybody knows everybody else and there is very little serious crime.

Life was not always so well ordered. Many families are descended from tribesmen held or born in federal stockades in Oklahoma, Florida and Alabama. Apaches who survived battles with the white man were sent to these places after Geronimo surrendered his entire band of 340 people to the U.S. Army in 1886—among the last Indians to succumb to federal authority. Geronimo's supporters paid a heavy price for their independence, including near starvation and loss of the right to practice old tribal customs. For twenty-seven years they languished as federal prisoners until allowed to settle on this reservation and elsewhere.

Many years transpired between the Geronimo days and the present time. They spent twenty-seven years as prisoners in stockades and the greater part of the next sixty years battling the hardships and surviving on the reservation. Kaydahzinne said: "My generation spent all of our time learning the white man's ways. We mastered them, but we lost a lot of Indian heritage. Now we are trying to make up for that."

The heart of the effort to learn about old ways is a program that was started in 1975 to teach Apache children some of the language, legends, songs, and religion of their ancestors. Few of the present generation of children speak the Apache language. The teaching is conducted by a few of the elder men and women in the tradition of old-time medicine men. They guided the children, for example, in the almost lost art of making food and medicine from local plants, such as prickly pears and sumac berries.

All such efforts are part of the tribe's careful plan to balance what President Chino calls "the best of both worlds— the white man's and the Indians. From the white man, we have picked up the work ethic, while we have retained the Apache's independence."

It took a lot of patience, persuasion and hard work to convince many residents that improvements were possible on the reservation. Too many thought: there is no use in my trying to get anywhere. "We've tried to change that attitude," said Chino, "and I think we've succeeded very well.

"So it was hard to adjust to new ideas of how to make a living. Now we have our own big companies, and our people are working at all sorts of jobs, from cowboys to administrators, advancing all the time."

Plans for the future include building a sawmill and some small manufacturing plants. Also a recently completed study offers the possibility of mining for coal, gold and silver.

The tribe is aiming for eventual takeover of the management of all their projects. At the present time, white managers help run some of the operations, such as the inn, ski areas and cattle-production facilities.

The Apaches' "quiet revolution" seems to be working out well for them. More young people are going to college, and more important they are coming home to apply their skills in fields such as business administration, mechanics, education, and medical doctors. Some of the young people enjoy the bright lights and excitement of larger communities, such as Albuquerque, and wish there was some way to import a little of it to Mescalero.

Oregon's Warm Springs Reservation

Warm Springs Reservation comes near to paying its own way with tribal businesses, such as a first-class resort and a forest products company and the construction of one of the few Indian-owned, hydroelectric projects.

Nationwide, self-determination has meant steadily increasing tribal control of federal programs like schools, health clinics and jails formerly operated on reservations by federal employees. This year (1981) tribes contracted to run $229 million in programs of the BIA alone, up from $77 million in 1976. All these steps are aimed at assuring the survival of Indians whose population has grown a startling 72% in the last decade to 1.36 million.

Crow Indians recently blocked non-Indian access to the Bighorn River on their Montana reservation to dramatize their claim of ownership to the bed of the river.

Nine-hundred miles away from Warm Springs, Oregon, weeds crowd the entrance to the Oglala Sioux Plastics Inc. a closed factory with equipment that could mold almost any plastic product.

Warm Springs received $4 million in 1981 for loss of traditional fishing sites. Tribal leaders banked most of the money and hired Oregon State University (OSU) staff to prepare a comprehensive blueprint for development of the reservation.

"We need something to guarantee us an income," Olney Patt, Sr., a long time tribal council member, told the OSU staff. "I told them we don't want anything fancy. No fancy horns, just a tune up."

The OSU came up with a plan of development that led to the

Kah-Nee-Ta Resort, a wood products plant that processes timber from the tribes 365,000 acres of forests, and the building of a $30 million hydroelectric generating plant on a reservation river.

In each instance the tribal council hired the best managers possible.

(This reminds the writer, when he was taking a course in rural sociology at the University of Wyoming, of one distinct thing Professor Dadisman said when on the subject of farm cooperatives. He said, "Hire the highest price manager you can get.")

The tribal council stayed out of the daily operation of the enterprises. This strategy has allowed the tribe to provide almost 1200 jobs in a range of activities, and 90% of its own annual budget from gross tribal revenues of $45 million in 1979. Altogether unemployment is 20%, far below the average of 40% for Indian reservations nationwide.

For the 2500 Warm Springs Indians, this success means monthly individual payments of $75, annual dividends that reached $2400 in 1979.

"All of this has come to pass," Patt said. "It is no longer a dream."

It is apparent that Mr. Patt was aware how "somewhat" similiar projects were faring on the Pine Ridge Reservation hundreds of miles away in South Dakota.

On the 1.78-million-acre Pine Ridge Reservation success is still a dream at best. The 20,000 Ogalas are heavily dependent on the federal government and able to generate only $1.1 million of their own revenue.

Now the federal connection is turning sour. Federal officials have eliminated more than five-hundred job-training positions on the reservation in recent months (1981) and are demanding repayment of $1.75 million in unaccounted-for housing funds.

Despite an unemployment rate here estimated at more than 80%, the reservation is dotted with closed or anemic business enterprises that could provide additional jobs in making plastic products, fishing lures and electronic components as well as in agriculture.

In the next episode we are going to relate some of the results on the Pine Ridge Reservation in South Dakota as an example of what has happened on the Great Plains. We will tell the latest judgment pronounced upon their management (more correctly mismanagement). Then let us compare the management, supervision and results of the South Dakota tribes with those of New

Mexico, Arizona, Cherokees, and tribes of the Northwest. There are others not mentioned. Why the differences? The writer will present his version of some of them at the end of these citations. These living active examples should provide some lessons for the new Indians. Yes, and likewise for non-Indians and the Bureau of Indian Affairs.

Dollars Have Little Effect on Reservation
Reported by newspapers over the state—

Millions of federal dollars spent for economic development on the Pine Ridge Reservation have had little effect, according to a federal report.

An audit of $3.3 million in economic development programs shows the money was spent to set up an industrial park, a plastics factory, a saw mill and several other enterprises. But only one enterprise of significance is operating today, and it is in jeopardy, said Interior Department Inspector General Richard Mulberry.

In another review, Oglala Sioux Community College was found to have purchased "items of questionable necessity because it had too much money."

Outgoing Tribal Chairman Stanley Looking Elk said the tribe is answering allegations made in both audits. But he said many of the cases go back before his administration and it is difficult to find some of the necessary information.

Despite the heavy investment of federal money, the reservation's economy is, at best, only marginally better than it was 20 years ago, Mulberry's report said, "unemployment on the reservation is severe. And, if not the number one problem, it is certainly close to being that," the report said.

"Creating private-sector jobs through economic development is the obvious remedy, and millions of dollars have been spent pursuing that remedy," the auditors said.

"Unfortunately, positive results are difficult to find. Except for the moccasin manufacturing concern (which employees 200), we could not find a single private-sector employer of over 25 people in business at the time of our review."

The review of contracts issued between 1977 and 1980 included the defunct Oglala Sioux Agriculture Enterprise, which sought to establish irrigation farming as a tribal enterprise. Launched in 1976 the farming operation received nearly $2 million.

"The money is gone and the remaining equipment either has been sold to pay off portions to defaulted loans or will be sold," the report said.

"Nothing is left to show for the enterprise, and a case can be made that the reservation is in worse condition because previously existing (canal) irrigation facilities were destroyed in the process of attempting to change the irrigation system."

The tribe also bought a Pennsylvania fish bait firm, although that company already was in financial trouble, the audit said. The company was moved to Porcupine and lasted about two years before it defaulted, costing the government and others about $400,000.

Equipment valued at $1,817 was listed as stolen or missing and another $28,485 in equipment was scattered in three states.

The report also said:

—In 1973, the Bureau of Indian Affairs and Small Business Administration spent $410,000 for a building to house Oglala Sioux Plastics Co. The building remains, but the company has failed.

—From 1975 through 1977, the B.I.A. gave 20 individuals $470,000 in economic development grants. The B.I.A. staff estimated 60 percent of the enterprises failed.

—Auditors found rusted remnants of a sawmill at four locations on the reservation, but were unable to learn details of its two-year operation in the early 1970's.

—From 1975 through 1981, the tribes small business development program received $825,000, most of which went for salaries and expenses. "We could not identify any viable enterprises or any permanent jobs that were created as a direct result." the report said.

—A motor home purchased for $14,450 in 1976 to distribute federal program literature around the reservation "was never used for its intended purpose and it more or less disappeared for about a year." It was reclaimed by the B.I.A. in 1978.

—Two airplanes were bought for nearly $37,000 in 1976 and 1977 with which to teach tribal members to fly, qualifying them for careers in aviation. Two students were licensed in the program. After the program died, the airplanes were stored off the reservation and seldom used.

This type of mismanagement and corruption has been going on, on Indian reservations in the Aberdeen Area office's jurisdiction for two decades and more and has been in the news and the public eye all the time. People and the news media editorials are now expressing shock and indignation over these happenings. In this book the writer has detailed the extensive and wide range of corruption that was persistently taking place, and our refusal to participate and cover up. The BIA, Interior Department, and congressmen have had plenty of warnings.

Pine Ridge Seeks New Start

Joe American Horse, who just took office (4-17-82) as newly elected chairman of the Pine Ridge Indian Reservation, says his top priority will be getting more federal aid and tax breaks to create jobs for the tribal members. The tribe is plagued by high unemployment, widespread poverty, and a $1,000,000 debt.

"The federal government is neglecting some of their responsibilities to the tribe," said American Horse. "The Sioux are justified in demanding more aid because their poverty was brought on by white seizure of their lands," he said. The official estimation of unemployment on the reservation is about 80%.

"Our people want work, they're tired of handouts. The Indians on the reservation would be willing to work for low wages if new industry came in.

"Federal budget cuts in the Comprehensive Employment Training Act programs forced the tribe to wipe out the jobs of about 1200 tribal employees last year. Operating schools, the hospital, ambulance service and the police force on the reservation without CETA employees that filled their ranks is difficult," American Horse said.

In addition to private jobs, he wants the tribe to get more money to invest in its own industries and to build a tourist industry.

Although other tribal chiarmen have tried and failed to get more federal aid, he hopes to succeed by ending problems of management. "The federal government will be more willing to give a well run tribal government money," he said.

American Horse repeated the fact that only the moccasin factory has survived. The factory which also makes boots and Indian dolls, employs two-hundred people and could be a model for other reservation industries.

The chairman said that one of his major challenges is to unite members of Oglala Sioux, after the heated battle of the election.

"Once you have Indians fighting among themselves, there's no progress at all," he said.

Since American Horse, the new tribal chairman, is virtually proposing the same measures to correct their poverty situation that was used the last decade or two, and resulted in such colossal failures, how can he now reverse the process of management and expect success?

He has offered to try uniting a divided people and to replace gross mismanagement with good management. Well and good but how is this to be accomplished? The writer would advise getting help from a university as a priority step. Their staff could make a survey and study of possibilities and draw up a comprehensive blueprint for development of the reservation. The tribe could get the funds for this purpose and hire qualified and honest managers for each project. And for God's sake hammer away against dishonesty and corruption. *This no doubt has been the greatest cause of failures on the South Dakota reservations.*

You must purge the thievery and corruption out of the system of management and supervision. It has a stranglehold on Indian affairs on the South Dakota reservations.

Honesty is hard to keep down. If cut down it will raise its head again, sooner or later. The feds want to see and keep the failures for the preservation of their jobs and many times for their thievery, as well.

Stamp out stealing, corruption and mismanagement. Punish the guilty and offer incentives and reward for good. Teach *nobleness* in the schools, churches and homes.

Man can not live by subsidies alone.

Private Enterprise — The American Way

We would like to suggest as an example of ingenuity and industry the case of Tim Giago, a tribal member of the Pine Ridge Reservation. Mr. Giago established a newspaper last July which he calls *The Lakota Times.* It carries local news items and covers the entire Pine Ridge Reservation. He claims a circulation of about 2000 with a potential of 3,000.

The forty-seven-year-old editor said he is proud that his paper, which serves the second largest Indian reservation in the United States, is not subsidized or controlled by the tribal government or whites, as other Indian newspapers are.

However, he is concerned that he may face competition from a tribal paper which may be launched by the tribal chairman.

The independence of *The Lakota Times* gives it the ability to be fair to all sides in coverage of Indian affairs, Giago claims.

The tribal paper can't be critical of the tribal administration because its employees know where their paychecks are coming from, Giago said.

Everyone get behind this worthy private enterprise and support it. It can serve a very useful purpose. Turn on your *noble* spirit. It needs exercise.

Good News and Hope From the Lower Brule Reservation — Grass Rope Irrigation Project

After going over the disastrous results of the three irrigation projects and the other costly programs for irrigation and industries on the Rosebud, Pine Ridge and Fort Thompson Reservations, we can hopefully expect that the corruption and mismanagement of these affairs on reservations in the Aberdeen area office jurisdiction may be facing their Waterloo at last.

One could hardly expect to find a more favorable prospect for developing irrigation than that which exists on the Lower Brule. It has river bottom land along the Missouri River of excellent quality soil, water, topography, and climate. It is excellent for corn, hay and other valuable crops. With the feed production potential and adjoining grazing land the location offers excellent prospects for cattle raising and perhaps feed lot fattening.

What is important is that the Indians and the controlling officials realize the potential here and are eager to pull the stops and get it going. Construction is already under way and financing appears to be assured. The irrigation may be ready for the 1983 crop.

They already have 2000 acres under irrigation as part of a gravity system called the LaRoche unit. The Grass Rope 5000 acres will give them 7000 acres of good irrigation. The site is located in a loup of the river surrounding it on three sides with water. The lift is only 240 feet and does not have to be transported any distance. What could be more favorable? A chance of a lifetime.

Furthermore, the Pick-Sloan Act offers low rates for electricity produced at the dams on the river. This is partially in lieu of the valuable land lost to the reservoirs. This rate applies for irrigation purposes.

The 1500 acres under irrigation reached a yield of 150 bushels of corn in 1981. With more experience they should reach two-hundred bushels. We have seen some beautiful fields of irrigated corn fields in the area. Earlier this season they already had eleven pivitols installed and twenty-six more to go. In 1983 they should be ready for complete irrigation and turn their efforts to their proposed subsidiary programs. They have a 50% unemployment rate and need to create more jobs.

One of the interesting features regarding the financing of the project is that some of the funds used for the construction were funds reallocated by the BIA from other approved projects. This will enable them to expedite the completion of this project ahead of some others. It is most important to get it completed and operating as soon as possible. It would make a good and much needed success story. Such a story is sadly needed.

The tribe hopes and plans to develop and expand with subsidiary enterprises which can provide good jobs for their people. Some of their thinking includes a cattle feed lot of 5000 head. They hope to get a slaughter plant. They could use the hides for leather craft. They say the hides and beef by-products could be used for a pet food plant. For a long-term plan they are considering utilizing crops for a 500,000-gallon ethanol plant.

Some of these projects should turn out successes, some may not. It will depend on the Indian operators and managers. They should exercise complete control of all phases, ask for outside help when and where needed, both technical and managerial, hire experts (only those you can trust), permit no corruption, and make everyone involved accountable to the tribe.

They can not succeed if corruption, poor judgment and mismanagement are tolerated, as has been too often the case on the reservations in recent decades.

Can the imagination construct what this country and our civilization would be like today if we erased everything contributed by the Indians of the North and South American continents that was unknown to the rest of the world prior to 1492?

We must abandon our legendary sins and crimes (both whites and Indians) and try for a truly Christian way of life. It appears possible to destroy the survival of all races. God forbid.

How far has the Indian come in the last fifty or one-hundred years? Many of them have made much progress and can stand straight and tall. Others do not yet clear the hurdles. The mismanagement and lack of accountability of their tribal affairs is far too prevalent on the reservations of the Great Plains.

However, hopeful signs are beginning to break through. Tribal members in certain instances are asserting themselves by rising up in general tribal meetings and voting out members of the governing council for alleged mismanagement and graft.

Restoring nobleness to the race by exalting moral character of excellence should be a constant goal. Strive for unity, peace and harmony to build a united and stronger nation. These are legendary principles and characteristics of the Indian race. They *can* do it. To do so would not be retrogression. On the contrary, it would be lost character regained.

CHAPTER 9: A CHRONOLOGY AND SUMMARY OF INDIAN AFFAIRS

Perhaps, the best way to grasp an overall view and understanding of events and to evaluate their rightness and wrongness is to bring the highlights and landmarks of the most significant facts into focus, together in their sequence. This is the objective of the writer in this, the last chapter.

There are proclamations, official orders and decrees, policy declarations, legislative acts, court rulings, etc., to declare and define these things. Then others will follow, conflicting with or reversing them. Besides that, there will be outright subversions, contradictions, ignoring and by-passing compliance and enforcing the rules and laws by many of those charged with the duties or conditions of same. Public opinion is really the final dominating influence determining what happens. In a democracy, politicians, judges and administrators are influenced by desires of the people. However, at times, they defy the will of the people and sometimes the law of the land and get by with it for a time. There were other times when the government did its best to enforce the terms of its treaties with the Indians but were foiled by thieving and conniving citizens.

Dates as well as ideas and thinking are significant in the development of Indian policy. We can see progress as well as many reversals over the long period of time.

1000 to 1006 AD: Contacts between Native Americans and the Vikings.

1492: Contact between Native Americans and the Spanish resulting in first permanent settlement by Europeans.

1537: Pope Paul by the Bull *Sublimis Deus* supports the doctrine promoted by Bartolome de las Casas and Francisco de Victoria that Indians are "truly men" with the right to enjoy liberty and possess property.

1539: Lectures of Francisco de Victoria at University of Sola-

244

manca, Spain, advocating that Indians were free men and were exempt from slavery. They were to be dealt with through treaties and fair trade.

(Here we have the Pope, universities and the early explorers and colonists supporting the idea that the Native Americans were truly men and possessing praiseworthy integrity, character and nobleness. Three-hundred years later we find our people supported by our government claiming that they were not a person and denying them protection and justice under the Constitution of the government of the country, and any recourse to the courts. It is very evident that these travesties of justice were sinister in purpose, concocted by evil persons who are guilty of crime and slander against humanity.)

1598: Establishment of Spanish settlement in New Mexico.

1602 to 1612: Contacts between Native Americans and the Dutch.

1607: First permanent English colony established at Jamestown.

1608: First permanent French colony established at Quebec.

1609: Sovereign rights were reaffirmed by the English courts in the judgment of "Calvin's Case."

1619: Virginia Company started the first mission schools which were abandoned in 1622.

1621: The Dutch West India Company was formed on the principles of opening trade routes by means of treaties.

1626: Dutch purchase Manhattan Island from the Indians and found New Amsterdam.

1643: First known Indian treaty signed between the Mohawks and Dutch in the state of New York.

1643 to 1684: New England Confederation attempts to provide mutual defense against Indians, Dutch, French, etc.

1663: The French occupied the "Northwest Territory."

1675 to 1676: King Philip's War results in an end to organized resistance to the colonies by tribes of southern New England.

1680: In a revolt led by the Pueblo Indians the Spanish were driven from New Mexico until the reconquest began in 1692.

(After their reconquest the white man treated the Indians with greater respect and thereafter the two races resided side by side in comparative peace.)

1680s: In precedents set by men such as William Penn the idea is presented that Indian land should be acquired by purchase.

1680s: The French under LaSalle open the Mississippi region, expand their trade with Indians, and gradually settle this heartland of America.

1689 to 1763: In a series of wars stemming from English, French, and Spanish rivalry in both Europe and America, Indian tribes are allied with each of the three powers and against one another in the American theater.

It is the impression of this writer that always more Indians fought against the colonists and the United States than were fighting with them. This includes all wars and battles on the continent including the Civil War and the War of 1812 and Indian wars. They always were more friendly with the French, English, Canadians, and Dutch. The exception may have been the Spanish. The Canadians took much of their land but never went to war with them.

1694: The English court held that sovereign nations cannot change the customs and laws beyond their treaty agreements.

1750s: French establish a string of forts in the Ohio country to consolidate their holdings and strengthen their ties with Indian allies. The English retaliate by establishing their own forts and improving relations with Indian friends.

1753: The French and Indian War started as the result of sovereign interference between the English, French and Iroquois Confederacy

1754: At the Albany Congress the English discuss ways of pacifying Indian leaders, and of achieving a united Indian policy.

1763: The French and Indian War ended making it illegal to issue patents on Indian land, and establishing the principle that Indian land title cannot be altered without a treaty. This was the first appearance of the provision "The utmost good faith shall always be observed towards the Indian, their land and property shall never be taken from them without their consent, and their property rights and liberty shall never be invaded or disturbed."

1763: The English inherit French territory in Canada and east of the Mississippi River, as well as their contacts with Indian tribes in that area.

1763: Pontiac's Rebellion—An attempt by former Indian allies of the French to reclaim frontier posts held by the English.

1763: Proclamation of King George III attempting to keep settlers east of the Appalacian Divide, and establishing an "Indian country" or "reserved lands" not available for purchase west thereof, from the Indians.

1775: Continental Congress assumes control of Indian affairs and names commissioners for the northern, middle, and southern departments.

1777: The Articles of Confederation assumed the job of "regulating commerce between the several Indian tribes."

1783: Congress issues a proclamation warning against purchasing of or squatting on Indian land.

1786: Secretary of War made responsible for Indian Affairs by an Ordinance of August 7th.

1786 to 1789: A series of treaties by an Ordinance of August 7th.

1786 to 1789: A series of treaties establishes a policy of acquiring Indian lands by purchase rather than by right of conquest.

1787: The Northwest Territory Ordinance of July 13, 1787, adopted the provision of the English Royal Proclamation of 1763 as the policy of the U.S.A.

1789: The Northwest Territory Ordinance was enacted into U.S. status on Aug. 7th.

1793: Congress appropriated $20,000 to treaty with Indians.

1803: As a result of the Louisiana Purchase from France a vast new territory with a large Indian population is added to the United States, and Thomas Jefferson proposed the removal of eastern Indians to the area west of the Mississippi.

1803: $3,000 appropriated to civilize and educate the heathens.

1812 to 1819: West Florida, then East Florida acquired from Spain and the United States is involved in the Seminole War.

1812: Andrew Jackson saved by an enemy Indian.

1814: President Jackson stripped the Creeks of their land, property and money. When the administration removed the Cherokees they stripped them of everything including livestock, sawmills, grist mills, bank accounts, and all property.

1819: Fund created by the Congress for the civilization of the Indians—$10,000 annually.

1824: Bureau of Indian Affairs established within War Department.

1830: Indian Removal Act—to Indian Territory—$500,000 appropriated for the purpose.

1831: Landmark decision in *Worcester vs. Georgia.*

1832: Portion of "Five Civilized Tribes" removed to Indian Territory.

1832: Office of Commissioner of Indian Affairs created within the War Department.

1834: The Indian Trade and Intercourse Act—known as the Reorganization Act of 1834.

1835: Cherokee treaty for removal.

1835: The Seminole War started, costing 1500 men and $50,000,000.

1836: Creek Indians removal—about half (1000) arrived at Fort Gibson.

1838: Cherokee "Trail of Tears," 4000 lost their lives.

1840: Winnebagos removed, cost fifty percent of members. Most of these returned to their Wisconsin River by 1845.

1843: The BIA issued a solution to Indian affairs by promoting "less pay for less population"—reduce the population and the land will be cheaper to buy.

1846: Winnebagos removed again, this time to Blue Earth River. They migrated back to Wisconsin and to Iowa.

1846: The Oregon Country with its Indian tribes becomes part of the United States as a result of a settlement with England.

1848: Treaty of Guadalupe Hidalgo—U.S. and Mexico ceding Southwest areas to U.S.

1849: By congressional action the Bureau of Indian Affairs is transferred from the War Department to the new Department of the Interior.

1849: Gold seekers brought and spread infectious diseases and wiped out large portions of Indian groups. Mandans, totally; Mission Indians in California survived with one-tenth.

1850: With the opening of Indian Territory west of the Mississippi to settlement it became government policy to set aside reservations for Indian tribes.

1853: By the Gadsden Purchase the United States acquires additional territory and Indian lands from Mexico.

1854: Indian lands taken in trust by the government after tribes ceded other land to the United States.

1862: Winnebago Indians removed again, this time to Crow Creed, South Dakota—a few of them still remain there but most of them left for Nebraska and some returned to Wisconsin.

1864: The Navajos and Apaches took "The Long Walk" to the Pecos country to be "quarantined for civilization." Cheyenne and Arapahoes were burned out at Sand Creek, Arkansas.

1866: As punishment for their support of the Confederacy, the Five Civilized Tribes were compelled to accept new treaties by which they relinquished the western half of Indian Territory where some twenty tribes from Kansas and Nebraska were settled in thirteen new reservations.

1869: The completion of the transcontinental railroad and the beginning of the end of the buffalo herds bring great change in the lives of the Plains Indians.

1870s: Beginnings of a federal program to provide schools for the education of Indians.

1871: Treaty making with Indian tribes is ended by congressional action. Some 370 treaties had been made.

1876: Custer wiped out. It was published that each Indian killed cost the government $1,000,000. The Indian population was down to 44,000 souls. Geronimo and his thirty-six men kept 5000 troops busy.

1879: The Ponco chief, Standing Bear, vs General Crook—hearing for his refusal to give up his tribe's home and remove to Indian Territory in Oklahoma. The judge ruled in his favor and Standing Bear also won historical fame and a place in the Nebraska Hall of Fame.

1887: The General Allotment or Dawes Severalty Act makes the allotment of land to individual Indians and the breaking up of tribal landholdings the official policy of the United States.

1889: Two million acres of Oklahoma Territory was bought from the Indians and thrown open for settlement.

1891: Provision is made for the leasing of allotted Indian land.

1898: The Curtis Act extended the effect of the Allotment Policy to the Five Civilized Tribes in Indian Territory.

1901: The Congress conferred citizenship on all Indians in the Indian Territory.

1902: The Secretary of the Interior made the first oil and gas leases on Indian lands within present boundaries of Oklahoma.

1907: Oklahoma, including Indian Territory, is admitted as a State of the Union, and citizens begin agitation to have Indian land made available on the market and to increase the state's taxpaying lands.

1910: A Division of Medical Assistance established after communicable diseases reduced Indian population to under 250,000 persons.

1924: The Congress grants citizenship to all Indians. A majority were already citizens as a result of treaties or earlier blanket grants to particular groups. (Indians did not gain the right to vote in all states, however, until 1948.)

1924: A Division of Indian Health is established within the Bureau of Indian Affairs.

1928: The Meriam Report on the problems of Indian administration is published, after a two-year study, recommending various reforms and changes of policy in Indian affairs.

1928 to 1943: The Senate Committee on Indian Affairs conducts a survey of Indian programs and policies that has far-reaching repercussions. (The John Collier Days as Commissioner of Indian Affairs).

1931: $50,000 is appropriated to secure remunerative employment through the BIA's new Guidance and Placement Division.

1931: A new Division of Agricultural Extension and Industry is established with the Bureau of Indian Affairs.

1932: The Leavitt Act frees the Indians of liens on allotted lands totaling millions of dollars. The Preston-Eagle Report had recommended such action along with a complete reorganization of Indian Irrigation services and the abandonment of useless projects.

1933: Steps are taken to emphasize the right of Indians to practice their own customs and religion and to stress the fact that interference with such practices would no longer be tolerated.

1934: New Indian legislation such as the Wheeler-Howard or Indian Reorganization Act officially reverses the trend to break up tribal governments and landholdings typical of the allotment period (1887 to 1933), provides for tribal self-government, and launches an Indian Credit program; and the John O'Malley Act allows the Secretary of the Interior to contract with states, territories, and other agencies to provide services to Indians, especially education.

1935: An act to estabish an Indian Arts and Crafts Board (Accomplished in 1936).

1937: The Bureau of Indian Affairs reports that total Indian landholdings have increased 2,100,000 acres since 1935.

1940: Naturalization for Indians to become citizens.

1943 to 1944: The "Partial Report" and "Supplemental Report" of the Senate Indian Affairs Committee calls for changes in Indian Policy and the "Liquidation of the Indian Bureau."

1943 to 1944: The Bureau of Indian Affairs calls for the preparation of basic development programs by each tribe, band or group to "facilitate the Federal Government in dispatching its obligation to the Indian . . ."

1944: The National Congress of American Indians is organized at Denver, Colorado.

1944 to 1947: The House Indian Affairs Committee conducts its own investigation of government Indian policies.

1945: By the close of World War II it is apparent that experience gained by thousands of Indians on the work relief programs of the 1930s, and by some 65,000 who left reservations to join the armed services or for war work in cities, has wrought considerable change that will strongly affect future Indian action throughout the United States.

1946: Act to create an Indian Claims Commission to hear claims of Indian tribes against the United States. All of these acts point to officially prepare the Indians to be ready for the termination of the Bureau of Indian Affairs. Someday it will be attained.

1947: The Senate Committee on the Post Office and Civil Service calls for testimony from the Bureau of Indian Affairs on the readiness of particular tribes to have the services of the Indian Bureau withdrawn.

1948: The Hoover Commission recommends the transfer of the Bureau of Indian Affairs to the Federal Security Agency and states that "assimilation must be the dominant goal of public policy" for Indians. Results show that thirty years later the Indians are not yet ready. Only one small reservation was actually withdrawn. It still has troubles and some strings attached, according to reports. However, the Zuni Pueblo Indians of New Mexico began their "home rule" experiment in 1970, and the Miccosukee Indians of Florida assumed control over their own affairs in 1971.

Most of the tribes in these recent years have assumed much of the responsibilities of planning and managing some of the programs and projects on their reservations. Some are making more progress than others, but they are getting needed experience to eventually take over completely.

1948 to 1953: The BIA job replacement program evolves into the "Relocation" program for Indians. Although this program resulted in failure for many Indians, the overall results were valuable and an important success.

1949: Representatives of the BIA ask Indian tribes to assist with development of programs that will help the Indian bureau "to work itself out of a job." (This is one of the most sensible things the bureau ever did in these later years. However, the venture was not without its problems. Many of the bureau employees and certain departments sought to destroy the scheme, with the idea of preserving their jobs.)

1951: The Bureau of Indian Affairs states as program objectives "a standard of living for Indians comparable with that enjoyed by other elements of our society," and the "Step by step transfer of Bureau functions to the Indians themselves or to appropriate agencies of local, State or Federal Government," (a worthy project well done and largely with the Indian's funds, claims against the federal government which they won in the courts).

1952: A Division of Program is established by the BIA to work with individual tribes to achieve the goals stated in 1951.

1953: House adopts policy for termination of special services of the Bureau of Indian Affairs to specified tribes and in particular states "at the earliest possible time."

1953 to 1964: The Navajo emergency educational program more than doubled Navajo school enrollments.

1954: Act to transfer the Division of Indian Health from the Bureau of Indian Affairs to the U.S. Public Health Service (PHS) (accomplished in 1955). Appropriations for Indian health rose from over $12 million in 1950 to over $61 million in 1965.

1954: Legislation to secure transfer of Bureau of Indian Affairs Agricultural Extension to the Department of Agriculture failed enactment, but was later accomplished by administrative action (agriculture engaged in by Indians took a slump).

1955: Indian Hospitals and medical services transferred to Federal Department of Health, Education and Welfare (HEW).

1957: Legislation authorized PHS to assist communities with the construction of health facilities that would benefit both Indians and non-Indians.

1958: Legislation allowed Indian tribes to benefit from federally impacted area bills (PL 81-815 and PL 81-874) by securing financial assistance for the construction and operations of schools that would benefit Indians.

1959: Legislation authoirzed PHS to contract sanitary facilities for Indians.

1961: Interior Department and Bureau of Indian Affairs changed their land sales policy to allow Indian tribes or other Indians the first opportunity to acquire individually owned lands offered for sale by Indians—this was a great assistance in tribal land consolidation programs.

(C.R. Whitlock, superintendent of the Rosebud Reservation developed a land consolidating plan a number of years prior to this called TLE (Tribal Land Enterprise). This organization did a good job of solving the problem of fractionated heirship land which had become almost impossible of management.

1961: Authorization for Indian revolving loan fund increased from $10 million to $20 million; and benefits from the Area Redevelopment Act and Housing Act are extended to Indian reservations.

1961: Commissioner of Indian Affairs Philleo Nash names a task force to study Indian affairs and make longe-range recommendations; the Commission on the Rights, Liberties, and Responsibilities of the American Indian publish their program for Indian citizens; and Indians gather at Chicago to make their Declaration of Indian Purpose.

1962: Benefits of Manpower Development and Training Act made available to Indians; and the Congress authorized nearly $135 million for the Navajo Irrigation Project.

1964: The Economic Opportunity Act through the Office of Economic Opportunity (OEO) Indian Desk extends its benefits to Indian reservations.

1966: The appointment of a new commissioner, Robert Bennett, a highly qualified full blood Indian brings a flurry of congressional interest in termination that eventually results in further stress on Indian economic development.

1966: Special programs for Indian children are provided under the Elementary and Secondary Education Act.

1968: Special message to the congress on "The Forgotten American," March 6, 1968, by President Lyndon B. Johnson, in which he calls for the establishment of a National Council on Indian Opportunity to be chaired by the vice-president and to include a "a cross section of Indian leaders" and the secretaries or directors of those departments or agencies that are significantly involved with Indian programs (NCIO) are to encourage all government agencies to make their services available to Indians, and to coordinate their efforts to achieve particular purposes. *President Johnson also suggested that the idea of "termination" should be replaced by Indian "self-determination."*

1968: As a presidential candidate Richard M. Nixon also speaks out against the termination philosophy and suggests that "American society can allow many different cultures to flourish in harmony."

Tribal termination was an item for discussion during the April, 1966, congressional hearings on the "Nomination of Robert L. Bennett to be Commissioner of Indian Affairs" as successor to Commissioner Philleo Nash:

House Report 2680 of the 83rd Congress set forth a list of tribes who were found by the bureau itself to be qualified for full management of their own affairs. The House committee expressed its opinion that steps should be taken to effect discontinuánce of further operation of the bureau on those reservations. In the intervening twelve or thirteen years almost nothing has been done. *If these tribes were prepared to go their own way more than a decade ago, the committee can only conclude that the bureau is more interested in perpetuating its hold on Indians and their property than in bringing them into the mainstream of American life.*

Even when this committee in three specific instances requested legislation from the bureau during the 88th Congress that would give these tribes the opportunity to be released from the web of paternalistic control and regulation.

"Even when this committee in three specific instances requested legislation from the bureau during the 88th Congress that would give these tribes the opportunity to be released from the web of paternalistic control and regulation, it was not furnished." (from the USDI's "A History of Indian Policy")

The Senate committee asked the newly appointed commissioner of Indian affairs to respond to their questions in a report to be submitted within ninety days. The response follows:

"Objectives of Federal Indian Programs"

In my talks to Indian people, I find that the Indian leadership accepts the fact that at some time the Congress will change their special relationship with the Federal government. Until the Congress reaches that decision, hopefully with their consent, it is their wish that the Congress meet its responsibilities to them, the same as its national commitments to others, of maximum social and economic development; that the basis for determining readiness be prescribed, that the Congress further direct the States and other Federal agencies to provide them with the services to which they are entitled and guarantee to them the rights and privileges on an equal basis with other citizens. They respectfully request that in the development of criteria they be assured the right, if it is their decision to own, hold and manage their property and the opportunity to maintain their Indian identity and culture.

James Jackson speaking for the Quinault Tribal Council at a conference of Indian leaders held at Spokane, Washington, October, 1966, expressed the Indians' concern that the federal relationship be continued until the tribe decides it is ready for change.

Some day we will speak to you of termination . . . To us, termination means independence from bureauratic control. That day wil come when the Quinault Tribe has assumed active control of the land it now controls on paper. It will come when we are harvesting the economic benefits of the great resources we hold; when our governing body has an educated and competent leadership, and when our tribal civil and criminal jurisdiction is properly implemented through contractual relationships with federal and county governments. It will come when we are ready, and at our request.

We have learned to put outboard motors on our dugout canoes and travel a distance up our river in two hours that formerly took three days. In the same manner we are now trying to put modern governmental procedure behind our great human and natural resources. When we succeed we will travel fast; if we don't succeed, we will be lost.

In his special message on "The Forgotten American" delivered to the Congress, March 6, 1968, President Lyndon B. Johnson called for an end to discussion of tribal termination and proposed a "new goal" for the government's Indian programs:

A goal that ends the old debate about "termination" of Indian programs and stresses self-determination; a goal, that erases old attitudes of paternalism and promotes a partnership of self-help. Our goal must be:

A standard of living for the Indian equal to that of the country as a whole.

Freedom of choice: An opportunity to remain in their homelands, if they choose, without surrendering their dignity; an opportunity to move to the towns and cities of America, if they choose, equipped with the skills to live in equality and dignity.

Full participation in the life of modern America, with a full share of economic opportunity and social justice.

I propose, in short, a policy expressed in programs of self-help; self-development, self-determination.

Senator George McGovern's extended effort to replace House Concurrent Resolution 108, the 1953 tribal termination policy statement, with language more representative of current congressional Indian policy, met with success on September 11, 1968, when Senate Concurrent Resolution 11 was reported by Senator McGovern, without amendment.

1970: In a special message to Congress on Indian affairs, July 8, 1970, President Nixon stated: "The time has come to create conditions for a new era in which the Indian future is determined by Indian acts and Indian decisions." The President also asked for a new concurrent resolution that would "renounce, repudiate, and repeal the termination policy outlined in HCR 108 of the 83rd Congress, (1953).

1970 to 1971: There is a considerable increase in the number of Indians in leadership positions in federal Indian programs.

1970 to 1971: Zuni Pueblo Indians of New Mexico began their "home rule" experiment in 1970; and the Miccosukee Indians of Florida assumed control over their own affairs in 1971.

ESTIMATED INDIAN POPULATION

1492	800,000	1910	266,000	1950	343,410
1870	25,000	1920	244,000	1960	551,169
1880	66,407	1930	332,000	1970	827,091
1890	248,253	1940	334,000	1980	1,400,000
1900	237,000				

1970: New Census records approximately a fifty percent increase in the population of Native Americans from 1960 to 1970. 1960 count 551,169, compared to a 1970 count of 827,091. The count of 1980 comes up with an approximate sixty-nine percent increase over 1970 and a 155 percent or a tripling of the Indian population over the 1960 to 1980 twenty-year period.

This and other disparities over the last hundred years reflects the inefficiency of the Census enumeration of Indians.

The count of the Indian population has never been thorough nor accurate for one reason or another. It was arrived at largely by guesses, estimates, inefficient and careless enumerators. It is very likely that some tribes had an accurate count of their members.

Beginning in the early 1960s some reservations and tribes brought their allotment rolls up-to-date. This was to prepare them to receive the payments of their claims money. They had to determine each and every person who would be eligible to receive a share of the money. They thereby got a good record of their membership.

In 1970 the BIA recognized 220,000 as legal Indians in Oklahoma but that there were 6,000,000 Oklahomans of Indian decent. Many people of Indian decent do not bother about claiming to be Indian.

It is worthy of note, that as many as 600,000 present day (1980) Oklahomans identify themselves as legal Indians. The figure went up by more than fifty percent between the 1960 and 1970 U.S. Census. Very likely this large increase was due to a more intensive enumeration brought out by some monetary incentive that was being proposed at that time.

These cases are examples which show that, as so often happened in the past, the enumerations of Indians has been very unreliable.

To My Readers:

Thank you for reading this book. I thoroughly enjoyed writing it, also the travels, contacts and added knowledge about my subject—the American Indian. I hope that you have too and that it will truly bring about a better understanding and appreciation of these, our brothers and sisters.

INDEX

Others were Turkey, Fine Wool, Fine Cotton and Preserved Grains Found Near Phoenix, Arizona, 1982

CHAPTER 3: RELIGION